Programming the Display PostScript® System with NeXTstep™

Adobe Systems Incorporated

▲▲
▲▲▲

Addison-Wesley Publishing Company, Inc.

Reading, Massachusetts • Menlo Park, California • New York

Don Mills, Ontario • Wokingham, England • Amsterdam

Bonn • Sydney • Singapore • Tokyo • Madrid • San Juan

Paris • Seoul • Milan • Mexico City • Taipei

Library of Congress Cataloging-in-Publication Data

Programming the Display PostScript System with NeXTstep / Adobe
  Systems.
     p. cm.
  Includes index.
  ISBN 0-201-58135-3
   1. PostScript (Computer program language) 2. NeXTstep. I. Adobe
Systems.
QA76.73.P67P76 1992
005.26'2—dc20   91-31035
                                                CIP

Printed in the United States of America.
Published simultaneously in Canada.

The information in this book is furnished for informational use only, is subject to change without notice, and should not be construed as a commitment by Adobe Systems Incorporated. Adobe Systems Incorporated assumes no responsibility or liability for any errors or inaccuracies that may appear in this book. The software described in this book is furnished under license and may only be used or copied in accordance with the terms of such license.

PostScript is a registered trademark of Adobe Systems Incorporated. All instances of the name PostScript in the text are references to the PostScript language as defined by Adobe Systems Incorporated unless otherwise stated. The name PostScript also is used as a product trademark for Adobe Systems' implementation of the PostScript language interpreter.

Any references to a "PostScript printer," a "PostScript file," or a "PostScript driver" refer to printers, files, and driver programs (respectively) which are written in or support the PostScript language. The sentences in this book that use "PostScript language" as an adjective phrase are so constructed to reinforce that the name refers to the standard language definition as set forth by Adobe Systems Incorporated.

Information regarding Client Library functions and operator calls specific to the NeXTstep operating system listed in Appendix C are reprinted with permission of NeXT Computer, Inc. Application Kit, Interface Builder, MegaPixel Display, NeXT, NeXTcube, NeXTstep, and Workspace Manager are trademarks of NeXT Computer, Inc.

PostScript, the PostScript logo, Display PostScript, Adobe, the Adobe logo, Adobe Garamond, Adobe Illustrator, Carta, Charlemagne, Lithos, Sonata, and Trajan are trademarks of Adobe Systems Incorporated registered in the U.S.A. and other countries. Blackoak and Tekton are trademarks of Adobe Systems Incorporated. Apple, Macintosh, and LaserWriter are registered trademarks of Apple Computer, Inc. FrameMaker is a registered trademark of Frame Technology Corporation. ITC Stone is a registered trademark of International Typeface Corporation. Fette Fraktur, Industria, Künstler Script, and Univers are trademarks of Linotype-Hell AG and/or its subsidiaries. Parisian is a trademark of Kingsley/ATF Type Corporation. Post Antiqua is a registered trademark of H. Berthold AG. Futura is a registered trademark of Fundicion Tipografica Neufville S.A. Objective-C is a registered trademark of Stepstone Corporation. Sun-3 is a trademark of Sun Microsystems, Inc. UNIX is a registered trademark of AT&T Information Systems. X Window System is a registered trademark of the Massachusetts Institute of Technology. Other brand or product names are the trademarks or registered trademarks of their respective holders.

 2 3 4 5 6 7 8 9-MW-95949392
Second printing, April 1992

Contents

Chapter 3: The Coordinate System 31

Chapter 4: Single Operator Calls and Wraps 41

Chapter 5: Path Construction and Rendering 61

Chapter 6: User Objects and Graphics State Objects 77

List of Figures

List of Tables

Preface

The PostScript® language was first implemented in interpreters driving printers, but the concept of using a device-independent computer language to drive displays predates the printer implementation. Two early incarnations of the PostScript language were used to create graphics on minicomputers at Evans & Sutherland Computer Corporation and Xerox PARC.

Adobe® and NeXT™ began joint development on PostScript software for displays—the Display PostScript® system—in 1985, soon after NeXT Computer, Inc. was founded. It was also in 1985 that the first printers incorporating PostScript language interpreters appeared. Introduced in 1988 as part of the NeXT computer's systems software, the Display PostScript system images text and graphics on computer displays. It incorporates the same imaging model and language used in printers with PostScript interpreters.

The Display PostScript system was originally developed for the NeXT platform because Adobe and NeXT share a similar vision of the future of computing. Both see the advantages of having the same imaging model driving the display and the printer. Those advantages include the closest possible WYSIWYG correspondence between display and printer and the device independence provided by the PostScript language.

This book is a direct result of the experimentation Adobe began in 1989, during the development of the NeXT version of our Adobe Illustrator® application program. We experimented to find ways to optimize such functions in the program as drawing, scrolling, and the handling of text, graphics and images. We developed prototype PostScript language programs in NeXTstep™ that represented different ways to accomplish a task. We then tested them to find out which was fastest and most efficient. At the end of that process, we had code samples and a series of technical papers documenting our research. Those papers have been collected into this book, and the code samples are available from the Adobe Developers' Association.

Many people at Adobe and elsewhere made valuable contributions to this book. Among them are Ken Anderson, who had the idea for the book and was a key technical contributor in designing and evaluating the programs. Bob Welles, a member of the Adobe Illustrator programming team, brought up many of the right questions and problems. Ken Fromm is the principal author of all the programs and text in the book.

We believe that *Programming the Display PostScript System with NeXTstep*, which represents more than two person-years of programming time, will be of great benefit to anyone developing a NeXTstep application. We hope it saves you time, makes your application more efficient, and helps your application contribute to the success of the NeXT platform.

John Warnock
November 1991

Introduction

The Display PostScript system provides a device-independent imaging model for displaying information on a screen. This imaging model uses the PostScript language to bring powerful graphics capabilities to the display and is fully compatible with the model found in PostScript printers. Drawing can be done in a high-level manner, freeing the developer from display-specific details such as screen resolution and color issues.

Basing an application on the Display PostScript system makes it easy to provide PostScript oriented services to the end user. Incorporating advantages of the PostScript imaging model such as outline fonts, halftoning, arbitrary scaling and rotating, and Bézier curve representation gives users more creative control over the output.

As the PostScript language continues to grow as an industry standard, Display PostScript applications will have the technology needed to meet the requirements of users demanding high-quality printing and display capabilities.

Display PostScript system components include the PostScript interpreter, the Client Library, and the pswrap translator, which are independent of the windowing environment and operating system. The windowing environment manages windows and events. The Display PostScript system handles the imaging of text and graphics in the windows.

The Display PostScript system uses a client-server architecture. Applications are the clients that make use of the PostScript interpreter in the server. Applications communicate with the server through the data structures and procedures in the Client Library. The Client Library is consistent across all Display PostScript systems, so you can send PostScript language calls in the same way across a variety of platforms.

With the pswrap translator, you can create custom PostScript language programs with C-callable interfaces. These programs can be called within applications by using the C interfaces.

How Applications Use the Display PostScript System

An application takes advantage of the Display PostScript system in a three-phase process.

1. An application creates a PostScript execution context and establishes a communication channel to the server. A context can be thought of as a virtual printer. It has its own set of PostScript language stacks, input and output facilities, and memory space. A single PostScript interpreter switches between contexts giving multiple applications access to a single interpreter.

2. The application sends and receives PostScript language operations to and from the server. Typically, these operations perform some form of imaging, but PostScript language is a full programming language, so they are not restricted to imaging operations. The operations are sent and received through single-operator calls in the Client Library or through custom wraps created with the pswrap translator.

3. When the application terminates, it destroys the context and closes the communications channel, freeing resources used during the session.

The Display PostScript system is integrated into the system software by the computer manufacturer. A manufacturer might create tool kits to handle some of the interaction with the Display PostScript system. In the NeXTstep environment, the Application object in the Application Kit™ manages the context for the application as one of its operations. The application programmer is concerned primarily with display issues and not with context or graphics state management issues.

Extensions of the PostScript Language

The Display PostScript system introduces a number of extensions to the PostScript language. Their usefulness, however, is not limited to the display, so most of the extensions are incorporated in PostScript Level 2.

These extensions fall into the following major categories:

- Path construction and imaging operations have been expanded to provide a more convenient generation and optimized execution. User paths, **xyshow**, and **rectfill** are examples.

- Operators have been created specifically for the demands of an interactive display environment. These include user objects and graphics state and hit detection operators.

- Memory management has been extended and multiple processing capabilities have been added to accommodate more dynamic and unpredictable use of resources.

This book does not cover every extension to the language because many are significant only in the context of the system integration. This book approaches the issue with the relatively focused viewpoint of an application developer. The *PostScript Language Reference Manual, Second Edition* contains a complete description of the extensions.

Note   *There is no Display PostScript language. There is only one version of the PostScript language, and it is evolving to encompass a wider variety of device technologies, environments, and applications. A considerable amount of effort has gone into making extensions that are upwardly compatible and integrating them seamlessly into the PostScript language.*

Graphics Capabilities of the Display PostScript System

The Display PostScript system provides a single model for both printing and display. This eliminates the need to develop separate code for the display and the printer. In addition, the Display PostScript system significantly speeds the development of high-quality applications by taking over many of the graphics responsibilities of an application. The following sections list some of the other advantages of the Display PostScript system.

Outline Fonts

PostScript fonts are in outline format, which means they can be scaled and rotated without requiring individual bitmaps for each point size and rotation. In addition, the Type 1 font format uses a set of hints embedded in each font to provide high-quality character rendering at small point sizes and resolutions.

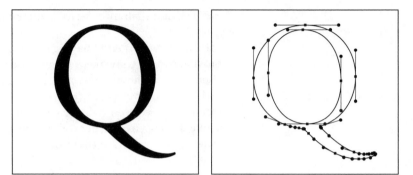

Example of outline font

Type 1 Font Library

There are thousands of typefaces available in the Type 1 font format. This large library of fonts provides a wide range of typographic styles including light, normal, semibold, bold, heavy, condensed, compressed, and more.

There are also many faces that include additional characters such as small caps and ligatures. Display faces for headlines and special fonts for music, math, and maps are also available. Some Display PostScript systems also support the Kanji character set through the PostScript Composite Font mechanism.

Examples of Type 1 fonts

Flexible, Device-Independent Coordinate System

All PostScript language graphics are specified relative to a coordinate system that is independent of the resolution of the display. The PostScript interpreter handles the device-specific code for mapping the graphics to device resolution. All text, graphics, and scanned images are drawn through the coordinate system, which can be scaled, rotated, and translated. Zooming is accomplished by executing the **scale** and **translate** operators, then redrawing the same text and graphics through the adjusted coordinate system.

Examples of flexible, device-independent coordinate systems

Halftoning

The appearance of text, graphics, and images is improved on monochrome, gray-scale, and 8-bit color displays because of PostScript halftoning technology. Colors are described in high-level color models such as RGB, HSB, or CMYK, and the PostScript interpreter determines how to color pixels on a given device. End users see more colors or shades of gray on their monitors. PostScript color models also shield the developer from device-dependent color capabilities.

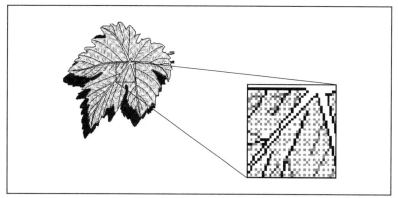

Halftoning

Bézier Representation of Curves

The Bézier representation of curves allows complex curves to be specified in a device- and resolution-independent manner that is compact and efficient. A single Bézier curve requires only four pairs of numbers: the coordinates for two endpoints and two control points. This representation is easily scaled for zooming effects because the interpreter flattens the curve to device resolution. In addition, Bézier curves can be joined to form smooth and continuous sets or groupings.

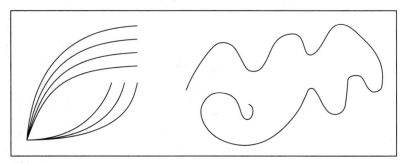

Bézier curves

Encapsulated PostScript Files

The Encapsulated PostScript file format (EPS) is a standard format describing single-page images containing text, graphics, and images. This allows you to import and export PostScript language files into different applications across all computer system environments and has become a standard in the desktop publishing industry.

Display PostScript applications have an advantage over other platforms because EPS files can be interpreted and shown on the display at the highest quality of the monitor. On other platforms, device-dependent bitmaps, frequently monochrome, appear on the screen. The quality of images degrades significantly when bitmaps are resized or rotated. In Display PostScript, EPS files can be scaled and rotated without any loss in quality.

Example of an imported EPS graphic

About This Manual

A complete description of the PostScript language, including the Display PostScript and Level 2 extensions, can be found in the *PostScript Language Reference Manual, Second Edition.* The intent of this book is to provide guidance for developing applications within the Display PostScript system. Because application development is tightly woven into the windowing environment, operating system, and imaging model, any practical instruction is difficult to provide without touching on all three areas. As a result, the examples and applications mentioned in this book have been developed in the NeXTstep environment.

The components of this environment that figure heavily in the examples are Objective-C®, the Application Kit, and Interface Builder™. Objective-C is an extension to the C language that provides object-oriented programming capabilities. The Application Kit is a set of basic objects written in Objective-C and offered to developers by NeXT to assist in developing applications. The objects include items such as Application, Window, Button, and View. Interface Builder is an application that allows you to graphically manipulate Application Kit objects to quickly create a user interface for an application.

Performance is a critical aspect in developing an interactive application. Many of the examples in this book look at the fastest and most efficient ways to handle specific drawing issues. Drawing hash marks around a dial, displaying text, or filling regions with patterns are three examples in which several approaches are tried and the results of each provided to the reader.

In this manual, we provide every approach instead of only the best solution for two reasons:

- The slower approaches might give you a better understanding of how the PostScript language and the Display PostScript system work.

- The best solution for one type of drawing might not be the best solution for other types of drawing. Other approaches might be faster under different conditions or easier to implement for less intensive drawing.

Being able to easily use the techniques mentioned in this manual is as important as performance. Approaches that are complex and difficult to follow are not helpful if you can't use them in your application. The goal of this book is to provide enough information to help you find an approach that balances performance with ease of use.

The remaining examples in the book focus less on the performance issues and more on explanation. Some chapters describe PostScript language issues such as the coordinate system or the client-server model, while others deal with application issues such as offscreen buffering, scrolling, and zooming. The intent is to introduce the subject, provide an example, and expect that the information carries over into other areas and uses.

The sample applications used in this book are available from the Adobe Developers' Association. Portions of the source code are included as examples where they are relevant to the text. Not all chapters contain source code examples nor do the ones that do show every aspect of the application. For the complete listings for the applications, call the Adobe Developer Support Line at (415) 961-4111.

Developer Resources

The following is a list of resources maintained by Adobe for developers:

- Adobe Developers' Association. This is a membership program for active developers. The membership fee provides technical support, monthly mailings, discounts on Adobe Systems application products, and technical literature. To receive a membership application, call the Adobe Developer Support Line at (415) 961-4111.

- Manuals. The following manuals are useful for developers programming with the PostScript language or developing in a Display PostScript environment. The manuals are available from Adobe by calling 1-800-344-8335 or by contacting your technical bookstore.

PostScript Language Reference Manual, Second Edition is the official reference to the PostScript language. It describes the imaging model, the interpreter, and the operators in detail. This book is the definitive resource for all PostScript language programmers.

PostScript Language Tutorial and Cookbook is an introduction to the PostScript language in an informal, interactive style. It contains a collection of example programs that illustrate the PostScript imaging model. (Level 1)

PostScript Language Program Design is a guide for advanced developers to use in designing and debugging PostScript language programs. It is oriented toward printers, but much of the information is relevant to the Display PostScript system. (Level 1)

X Window System® Programmer's Supplement to the Client Library Reference Manual is a reference to the Client Library interface with specific information concerning the X Window System, such as context creation and additional error codes. (This manual is not directly applicable to the NeXT system.) It is available from Adobe Systems in the *Display PostScript System Reference Binder.*

Adobe Type 1 Font Format is a description of the Adobe Type 1 font format and an explanation on how to create a Type 1 font program. The Type 1 font format gives font developers the ability to create a single font program that can be rendered on a wide variety of devices and resolutions.

- Classes. The following classes on PostScript language issues are regularly held on the East and West Coasts and in Europe. To receive a schedule, call the Training Support Line at (415) 961-4949.

  Programming in the PostScript Language is an introductory course that explains the PostScript language imaging model, interpreter, and operators.

  The Display PostScript System is a more advanced course that covers aspects unique to the Display PostScript system.

- Public Access File Server. Users with access to Internet or UUCP electronic mail can use Adobe's public access file server to obtain the following information:

  Code examples
  AFM files
  Documentation updates
  Conventions and standards documents

  The public access file server is a mail-response program. That is, you send it a request by electronic mail and it mails back a response. (The "Subject:" line is treated as part of the message by the file server.)

  To send mail to the file server, use one of the following addresses:

  Internet   ps-file-server@adobe.com
  UUCP   ...!decwrl!adobe!ps-file-server

  To receive a quick summary of file server commands, send the following message:

  help

  To receive detailed information on how to use the file server, send the following message:

  send Documents long.help

- The *PostScript Software Developer Kit* is a collection of code samples and technical papers, many of which deal with issues about supporting Level 2 printers. Call the Adobe Developer Support Line at (415) 961-4111 for more information.

- The *Display PostScript System for NeXTstep Software Development Kit* includes *Programming the Display PostScript System with NeXTstep*; code samples from the book on diskettes; the *PostScript Language Reference Manual, Second Edition*; *Adobe Type 1 Font Format*; and Displaytalk Programming Environment.

- The *Display PostScript System for X Software Development Kit* includes *The Display Postscript System Reference Binder*; *Programming the Display PostScript System with the X Window System*; code samples from the book on diskettes, the *PostScript Language Reference Manual, Second Edition*; *Adobe Type 1 Font Format*; and Displaytalk Programming Environment.

- Adobe Developer Support Line. Call the Support Line at (415) 961-4111 for the following kinds of support:

  - To order the code samples from *Programming the Display PostScript System with NeXTstep* on disk

  - To receive a free Technical Literature Catalog

  - To order technical literature

  - To receive a membership application for the Adobe Developers' Association

  - To request technical assistance (for members of the Adobe Developers' Association only)

About the Timings

The timings in this book were performed on a NeXTcube™ with a Motorola 68040 microprocessor containing 16 MB of RAM and running System Release 2.0 and PostScript Version 2.0.45.8. The timings were taken using the PostScript **realtime** operator. Chapter 4, "Single Operator Calls and Wraps," contains the wraps used in the measurements.

CHAPTER 1

NeXT Overview

This chapter provides an overview of the NeXT programming environment and describes programming issues that concern the Display PostScript system. The examples given in this book were developed on a NeXTcube and are dependent on that programming environment.

The NeXT programming environment is built around an object-oriented approach to software development. Objective-C, an extension to the C language, is used as the main programming language. The Application Kit is a set of predefined classes that can be incorporated within an application. These classes provide a basis for the development of most applications.

Interface Builder is an application provided with NeXT computers to graphically construct a user interface for an application. Using Interface Builder, windows can be created and buttons and text fields added to quickly develop most of the interface to an application.

Other sources of information are available in the NeXT and Objective-C documentation. This chapter provides a foundation for the examples and programs that appear in subsequent chapters of this book.

1.1 Object-Oriented Programming

The prescribed way to develop applications on the NeXT computer is to use object-oriented programming, which is based on organizing an application into distinct objects.

An object is a structure containing data and functions that operate on the data. The difference between this approach and conventional programming is that the structure and the operations are wholly owned by the object, and no other object can access the data. You can send a message from one object to another, instructing the receiver to perform an operation in the receiver's repertoire. Data necessary for the operation can be passed along with the message.

Data within an object can be accessed, in most cases, through the use of an operator within the object. This kind of organization allows data to be hidden from other parts of the application that don't need to access it and simplifies the management of data and operations on the data.

A unit of data within an object is called an *instance variable*. An operation is called a *method*. Objects with the same instance variable descriptions and methods are members of the same *class*. Each class has a *class object*. This object is created by the compiler and serves as the template for *instances* of the class.

An instance is created at run time by the class object. (A structure is allocated for holding the instance variables.) Each instance can have different values for the same data types, but they share and use the same methods on the data. For example, if *phone* is a class, then two instances of the class would be *John's* phone and *Jane's* phone.

Figure 1.1 shows two classes: Object A, an instance of one class, and Object B, an instance of another class.

Figure 1.1 *Sample classes*

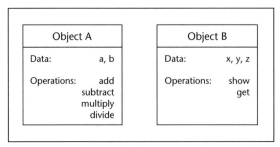

A key feature of an object-oriented approach is inheritance. Objects are grouped in a hierarchy with descendants retaining data types and methods of the ancestor. As a result, a method defined several steps up in the hierarchy chain can be used to operate in a similar yet distinct object. This approach saves code space and allows specific objects to be made from a chain of general and abstract objects. In Objective-C, a class can have only one *superclass* or, in other words, one immediate ancestor, but the number of classes in the chain from the root is unlimited.

The methods of an ancestor can be added to or modified by a descendant, making it easy to use an object as a model and to add or change a small number of characteristics. Creating a descendant is called *subclassing*, and modifying a method is called *overriding* a method. An example of subclassing in order to modify a class is to create a subclass of a ButtonCell in the NeXT interface to turn it into a LightSwitch. The general on/off nature of the button is retained, but the visual display and interaction is overridden so it can be modified.

Figure 1.2 shows the hierarchy within an abbreviated set of NeXT Application Kit classes. The diagram outlines only a portion of the Application Kit classes and capabilities. NeXT documentation and other chapters in this book provide more details.

Figure 1.2 *Hierarchy within a set of NeXT Application Kit objects*

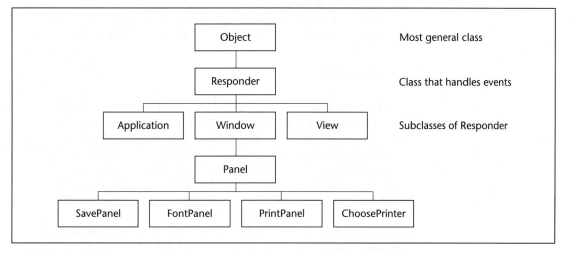

The tree is arranged with more general classes nearer the top. Each subclass adds more specific characteristics to the tree. Classes can be added to the tree to perform more specific operations with very little reworking and no reordering.

For example, you can add a ChooseModem class as a branch under Panel and next to ChoosePrinter. Additionally, you must include the elements of a ChooseModem panel that make it unique when compared to ChoosePrinter or any other type of panel.

Another example is adding a DrawingView under View. View is a class designed for drawing on the screen with PostScript language code. A DrawingView, which is not part of the NeXT hierarchy, is an object created for many of the examples in this book and is designed to handle specific types of drawings. All the characteristics of a View hold true for a DrawingView. The only addition is the subclass DrawingView and its special elements.

Note   *Objects can contain or hold references to other objects without being related to the contained objects. For example, a Window object and a View object are not directly related, although they share the same parent class. Nonetheless, a Window can hold references to many Views and can control their display. A View cannot exist on its own; it must be assigned to a Window.*

1.2   Objective-C

Objective-C is an object-oriented programming language used on the NeXT computer. It is an extension of the C programming language and does not change or affect any standard C language capabilities. Objective-C syntax can be mixed with standard C constructs.

1.2.1   Defining a Class

Creating a class is the first step in developing applications with Objective-C. Each class is defined using two types of files, an *interface* file (*.h*) and an *implementation* file (*.m*). The interface file contains the syntactical definition of the instance variables and the methods, and the implementation file contains the code that implements these methods. Although multiple classes can be declared in the same interface and implementation files, you usually declare only one class per set.

The WorldView class code in Example 1.1 is the only class created for the HelloWorld application, which shows you how to use Interface Builder. (See Chapter 2, "NeXT Interface Builder.") The rest of the functionality is provided by the NeXT Application Kit.

The interface file, *WorldView.h*, defines the new class as a subclass of View. View is a class provided by NeXT in the Application Kit. Since WorldView is a subclass of View, it inherits all the instance variables and methods defined for View and for View's ancestors. Only one additional instance variable is needed, *drawHello*, and it is defined as a Boolean type.

Note   *A Boolean (BOOL) data type can be assigned the values YES or NO. The BOOL type, as well as YES and NO, are defined in the Application Kit and Objective-C libraries.*

The methods are listed next: **drawHello:**, **clearHello:**, and **drawSelf::**. The colons indicate the arguments for the methods; each colon signifies one argument. The argument type is included except when it is the default type, which is an object identifier of type **id**.

The **@interface** and the **@end** are Objective-C directives that enclose the definition of the class. *Class methods* are implemented by class objects and are preceded by a plus sign. *Instance methods* are implemented by instance objects and are preceded by a minus sign. In Example 1.1, the methods referenced by instances of the class are marked with a minus sign. (The import statement includes the header file for the superclass View.)

Example 1.1 *WorldView interface file*

```
/* WorldView.h
 *
 * The instance variable, drawHello, is toggled between YES and NO
 * and indicates whether the "Hello World" message should be
 * displayed in the view.
 */

#import <appkit/View.h>

/*
 * WorldView is a subclass of View. It inherits all View's instance variables
 * and methods.
 */

@interface WorldView:View
{
    BOOL drawHello;
}

- drawHello:sender;
- clearHello:sender;
- drawSelf:(NXRect *)r :(int) count;

@end
```

The implementation file, *WorldView.m*, imports header files that contain methods and references specified in other files. Note that the syntax of the method definitions matches the syntax in the interface file. A warning is generated at compile time if this is not the case. At this time, don't be concerned with the operations of the methods.

Example 1.2 *WorldView implementation file*

```
/*
 * WorldView.m
 *
 * WorldView is a subclass of View. It simply displays and clears a message in
 * the view. The [self display]; message calls a method that is defined in the
 * superclass, View. The display method calls the "drawSelf::" method after
 * performing some view overhead. The "drawSelf::" method should not be
 * called directly in order to conform to Application Kit programming rules.
 */

#import "WorldView.h"
#import <dpsclient/wraps.h>

@implementation WorldView

- drawHello:sender
{
  drawHello = YES;
  [self display];

  return self;
}

- clearHello:sender
{
  drawHello = NO;
  [self display];

  return self;
}

/*
 *The first two lines clear the view. The remainder display the
 * message in the view.
 */
- drawSelf:(NXRect *) r: (int) count
{
  PSsetgray(NX_LTGRAY);
  PSrectfill(bounds.origin.x, bounds.origin.y,
      bounds.size.width, bounds.size.height);
```

```
    if (drawHello)
    {
      PSsetgray (NX_BLACK);
      PSmoveto (100.0, 100.0);
      PSselectfont ("Times-Roman", 40.0);
      PSshow ("Hello World");
    }

    return self;
  }
  @end
```

1.2.2   Messages

Objective-C still uses conventional C functions, but it augments them with *messages*. A message is a call to an object telling it to perform a particular method. Arguments the method needs can also be passed in the message. The message syntax appears in Example 1.3.

Example 1.3 *Objective-C message protocol*

```
[<object id> <method>]

[<object id> <method>:<argument>]

[<object id> <method>:<argument> <methodcont>:<argument>...]
```

Methods can return values. In most cases, the return value is the default type **id**. Square brackets, [ ], identify an expression as an Objective-C message. All statements in C must terminate with a semicolon, but not all messages are statements. A message within an **if** statement is not followed by a semicolon. For example, the following method returns a Boolean value. (This works for integers and other values.)

```
  if ([<object id> <method>])
    { <statement> }
```

object id

Each message is sent to a specific object. Objects are identified by a distinct data type, *id*. This data type is defined as a pointer to an object (in fact, it is a pointer to an object's data structure). An id is assigned to an object at the time the object is created by the system at run time. The first argument in a message is the id of the receiving object. If an object knows another object's id, it can send the second object messages, as long as it knows which messages the object can receive.

method

The *method* is the name of an operation defined in the interface file.
The name of the method is case sensitive. A run-time error occurs if the
method name invoked is different from the one defined, as long as no
other method name in the class hierarchy matches the name invoked.
A method name is also referred to as a *selector.*

argument

A colon signifies that the method takes an argument. The same type
of agreement between sender and receiver regarding the number and
type of arguments must occur in a message call as it does in a regular C
function call or similar errors result. The method name can be separated
by colon-argument pairs, as the following line of code illustrates. The
method name is **replaceSubview:with:**. The argument *viewId1* is inserted
after the first colon, spaces separate *viewId1* and **with**, and then the
argument *viewId2* is inserted after the second colon.

```
[objectId replaceSubview:viewId1 with:viewId2];
```

The following are the key points to messaging:

• Know the id of the object to which to send the message

• Know the name of the correct method or selector

• Know which arguments are passed to the method

A mix-up in ids can send the message to an object of another class.
In this case, a run-time error occurs if the selector can't be found.
Spelling errors in selectors produces similar errors.

1.2.3 Return Arguments

Any message can return a value. The most common return type is
the default type, which is an object id. All the methods in WorldView
return an object id indicated by the return of *self* in each method in
WorldView.m. The *self* identifier is the same as the object's own id.
Since the default is returned, no type definition is required in the
method declaration defined in *WorldView.h*. The return argument can
be used by the sender to nest messages. (This is similar to the orthog-
onality of function calls in regular C.) In other cases, the return argument
is ignored.

If you want a method to return a type other than the default, include a return type definition for the method in the interface and implementation files. In the *if* statement previously described, the method specified returns a Boolean value. The following line of code shows a method definition in an interface file that returns an integer:

```
- (int) intValue; /* This method returns an integer value. */
```

1.2.4 Nesting

Messages can be nested inside one another. The inner messages are resolved first. The following example shows a nesting arrangement. An object, identified by the variable *matrixId*, is sent a message to return the selected cell. The cell id returned is then sent a message to return the cell's state. The state is assigned to the Boolean value, *boolValue*. (Matrix and Cell are Application Kit objects.)

```
BOOL boolValue;

boolValue = [[matrixId selectedCell] state];
```

1.2.5 Sending Messages to self and super

You can use two special object identifiers when sending messages. The first is *self* and refers to the object's own id. In *WorldView.m*, the line **[self display];** appears twice. The method, **display**, is defined in the View class, of which WorldView is a subclass. Sending a message to *self* is one way to invoke one of an object's methods within that same object.

The second special identifier is *super*. It refers to the object's superclass. In the WorldView class, the superclass is View. The *super* identifier is useful for invoking a method in the superclass when it has been overridden in the subclass. Sending a message to the method with *self* invokes the method in the subclass. Sending a message with *super* invokes the method in the superclass. This identifier is helpful when the subclass wants to add a characteristic to a method but still perform the functions of the method in the superclass, as Example 1.4 illustrates.

In Example 1.4, the free method of a nonspecific class has been overridden to include a message to **freeMemory**. Since you also want to perform the free operations that appear in the superclasses, send a message to the free method of the superclass with **[super free]**. If **[super free]** is not used, none of the free operations of the superclasses are performed.

Example 1.4 *Subclassing a method*

```
- free
{
  [self freeMemory];

  return [super free];
}
```

1.3 NeXT Application Kit Classes

The NeXT Application Kit provides a set of classes you can use within
an application. Figure 1.2 shows the class hierarchy for the panels in
the Application Kit. NeXT documentation contains a complete list of
the classes including instance variables and method descriptions. This
section provides an overview of the classes commonly used in examples
throughout this manual.

1.3.1 Object

The top class in the Application Kit hierarchy is *Object*. It is the root
of all Objective-C inheritance hierarchies, so all other classes inherit
from it. The Object class provides its subclasses with a framework for
operations such as creating, freeing, copying, and archiving objects.

1.3.2 Responder

Responder is an abstract class that forms the basis for command and
event processing in the Application Kit. Many of the major classes in
the Application Kit inherit from the Responder class, which links in a
one-way chain. An event passes through the chain, and each responder
in the chain looks at the event in turn. If the class cannot handle the
event, it passes to the next responder in the chain. Application, View,
Window, and Control are subclasses of Responder.

1.3.3 Application

The *Application* class contains some of the methods necessary for a
NeXTstep application. It provides the framework for program execution.
Each program has only one instance of this class. Creating this instance
connects the program to the Window Server and initializes the PostScript
environment. The Application object is usually the first object to receive

events from the Window Server. It often passes the events to windows, which pass them to views. The events then proceed through the responder chain.

1.3.4 View

The *View* class provides the structure for drawing on the screen. Any graphical object that draws on the screen inherits from View. The HelloWorld example subclasses View with WorldView in order to draw "Hello World" on the screen. The View class can respond to events, so interactive tasks like mouse-tracking loops are often placed in View subclasses.

1.3.5 Window

The *Window* class manages a window within an application including interaction with the Window Server. Methods are available to display, hide, resize, and close windows along with other types of operations. A Window object can hold references to a number of Views and can control their display. Events passed to the window can also be passed to one of these Views.

1.3.6 Control

The *Control* class is the superclass for classes needed for the graphical interface of an application. Sliders, Fields, and Buttons (classes defined in the Application Kit) inherit from Control. A Control is an abstract entity concerned with handling an event. A different and unrelated class, Cell, provides the visual aspect to the Control.

1.3.7 Cell

The *Cell* class provides the mechanism to display buttons, icons, and text without the overhead of a full View subclass. Cells are used by the Control class and its subclasses to handle the visual aspects of the control.

Note   *Cells are not subclasses of Control; they are a subclass of Object. A Control object uses a Cell or a number of Cells to control the visual interaction of displaying, editing, formatting, highlighting, and tracking.*

1.4 Interface Builder

Interface Builder is an application provided with the NeXT computer to graphically construct the user interface of an application. Windows can be created and buttons and text fields inserted to quickly develop a large portion of the look of the application. See Chapter 2, "NeXT Interface Builder," for more information.

1.5 Conclusions

- An object is a programming unit that groups a data structure (instance variables) and operations (methods) that can use or modify the data.

- Objects with the same instance variable descriptions and methods are members of the same class. Each object within a class is called an instance of the class.

- Objects communicate with each other by sending messages. An object id is used to identify the receiver. Arguments can be passed from the sender as part of the message protocol.

CHAPTER 2

NeXT Interface Builder

HelloWorld is a simple Display PostScript application that has two purposes: It shows you how to use Interface Builder to create an application and introduces you to drawing in a view.

HelloWorld has the menu and window that appear in Figure 2.1. The menu has four buttons: Hello World, Clear, Hide, and Quit. When you select Hello World, the text, "Hello World," appears in the window. When you select Clear, the window is cleared. Hide hides the application, and Quit quits the application.

Figure 2.1 *HelloWorld application*

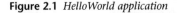

2.1 Interface Builder

Interface Builder is an application supplied with the NeXT computer that helps application developers quickly create a user interface for an application. Windows, buttons, sliders, and similar Application Kit objects can be graphically placed on the screen and incorporated into an application.

In the HelloWorld application, only one class, a subclass of View, was created. The other classes are Application Kit classes brought in through Interface Builder.

Interface Builder allows you to create a variety of objects and to connect one object to another (for example, have one object send a message to another object in response to a certain event). The objects that can be created and connected are a subset of the classes in the Application Kit.

For example, a slider can be connected to a text field so that it sends a message to the text field when the slider is moved. As a result, the text field can display the value of the slider. Another example is selecting a menu item, which causes a window to appear.

Interface Builder creates and stores the interface instructions in a NeXT Interface Builder (*.nib*) file. This file is then linked into the application.

2.2   HelloWorld Application

The sections that follow form a tutorial on how to use Interface Builder to create the user interface for HelloWorld. Begin by launching Interface Builder and selecting the New Application menu option, which appears under the File option in the main menu. A menu, a window, and several panels appear.

2.2.1   .nib File

Save this newly created *.nib* file into a new directory. Select Save in the File menu, and in the Name entry field enter a new directory name followed by a slash and a file name, *HelloWorld/HelloWorld.nib*. Click OK or press Return. (A panel appears asking you to confirm the creation of the path *~/HelloWorld* if it does not already exist. Answer *Create* to the prompt.)

Select the Project menu option under the File option. The Project Inspector panel appears with a message asking if a project file should be created in the directory. Click OK. This step creates the *Makefile*, *HelloWorld.iconheader*, *HelloWorld_main.m*, and *IB.proj* files.

2.2.2 Menu

Working in Interface Builder, perform the following steps to configure the HelloWorld menu:

1. Modify the menu. Delete the Info... and Edit items by selecting them and clicking Delete in the Interface Builder Edit submenu. (Under version 2.0 of NeXTstep, select Hide first then select Edit to get around a bug in Interface Builder.)

2. Place additional menu items in the menu by clicking the menu icon at the top of the Palettes panel. Select an Item cell from the palette, and place it in the menu. The Item cell appears in the menu resized to match the existing items. Add another Item by repeating the process or by selecting the new Item cell in the menu and copying and pasting.

Figure 2.2 *HelloWorld menu*

3. Change the text in the top Item cell to Hello World by double clicking in the cell and typing *Hello World*. Pressing Return or clicking another cell causes the menu to resize to the correct size and show all the text.

4. Change the text in the second item cell to Clear by double clicking, and typing *Clear*. Hide and Quit remain as they are.

2.2.3 Placing a View Within a Window

The following steps place a view in the window:

1. Resize the window and move it to where you want it to appear when the application launches.

2. Move to the Inspector panel and change it from Project Inspector to Attributes Inspector (the pop-up list at the top of the panel does this). Select the window by clicking in it below the title bar. Change the title of the window from MyWindow to Hello World through the Attributes Inspector in this panel and select OK.

3. Change the Palette panel to sliders/buttons/text fields by selecting the appropriate button.

4. Drag the CustomView object into the window.

5. Enlarge the CustomView in the window until it can contain the "Hello World" message.

When the application runs, the view won't appear as it does in the CustomView in Interface Builder. The background of the view will match the background of the window.

Figure 2.3 *CustomView*

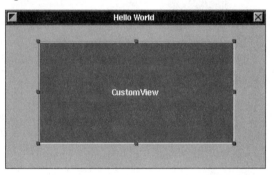

2.2.4   WorldView

The following steps turn the CustomView into a WorldView:

1. Double-click the Classes icon in the Objects panel at the lower left. A Classes in HelloWorld panel appears.

2. Scroll through the Object and Responder classes and select the View class. The subclasses of View are Box, Control, ScrollView, and Text. Do not select any of these.

3. Move to the Operations button and select Subclass. A subclass named MyView appears in the panel next to View.

4. Change the name of MyView to WorldView in the text entry under the icon at the right of the panel.

   WorldView should be a subclass of View, not a subclass of Box, Control, ScrollView, or Text.

Figure 2.4 *Classes in HelloWorld*

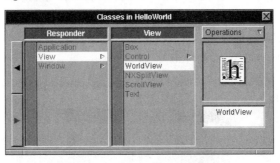

Once the WorldView subclass has been created, change the Custom-View in the window from a View class to a WorldView class.

1. Move to the Attributes Inspector of the Inspector panel.

2. Select the CustomView in the window. The Attributes panel shows CustomView as a View class.

3. Change the class from View to WorldView, and select OK or press Return. The CustomView in the window is renamed WorldView, as shown in Figure 2.5.

Figure 2.5 *WorldView*

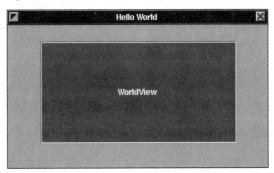

2.2.5 Adding Method Names

The next step is to make the connection between the menu items and the methods that will be called in the WorldView class. To form these connections graphically they must first be defined within Interface Builder.

1. Select the WorldView object in the window.

2. Change the Inspector panel from an Attributes Inspector to a Class Inspector. An outlet/action panel appears with the single action **printPSCode:** in gray. Method names for the WorldView object are entered as actions and will appear next to the **printPSCode:** method, as shown in Figure 2.6.

Figure 2.6 *Class Inspector*

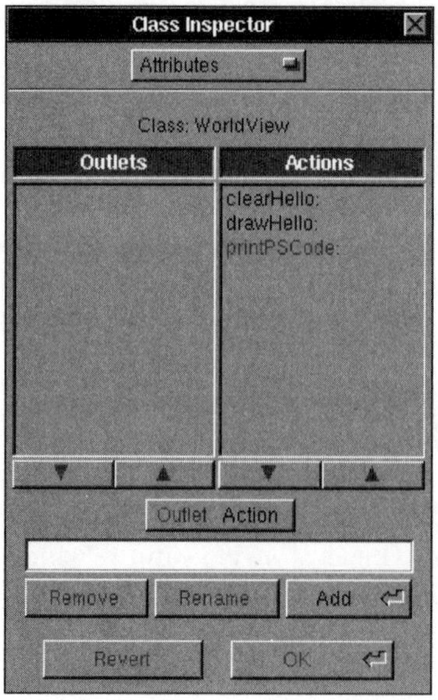

3. Select Action in the Outlet/Action button. Enter the method name **drawHello** and press Return (or select the Add button). (It's not necessary to add a colon after the name because Interface Builder appends one if it doesn't appear.)

4. Enter the method name **clearHello**, and press Return or select the Add button.

Now that the method names in the WorldView class are defined within Interface Builder, you can make the connection between a menu cell and a method name.

2.2.6 Connections

Making a connection between objects within Interface Builder means that a message expression is placed in the *.nib* file. This message is sent from one object to the other when the appropriate event occurs in the application. In this case, messages are sent to the WorldView object whenever you select the Hello World or Clear items in the menu.

Perform the following steps to make the first connection:

1. Hold down the control key while selecting the Hello World menu cell with the mouse. A small black square appears in the center of the cell with a black line attached.

2. Continue holding the mouse down and move to the WorldView object. As soon as the mouse nears WorldView, a black box surrounds the WorldView and connects it to the existing black line.

3. Release the mouse; the black lines and square remain. The Inspector panel automatically changes to a Connections Inspector with **drawHello:**, **clearHello:**, and **printPSCode:** appearing in the Actions of Destinations subview.

4. Select the **drawHello:** method, then select the Connect button. This forms the connection between the menu cell and the action so that a message is sent to the **drawHello:** method in WorldView when the menu cell is selected.

Repeat the same steps with the Clear menu cell, selecting **clearHello:** instead of **drawHello:**.

Note   *Select the Connect button or press Return after choosing the action; otherwise the connection does not take effect.*

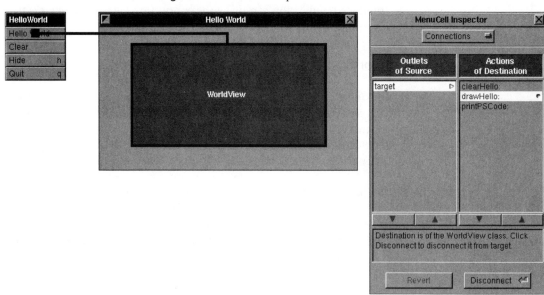

Figure 2.7 *Connections Inspector*

2.2.7   Unparsing the WorldView Class

The following steps create initial *WorldView.h* and *WorldView.m* files:

1. Move to the Classes in HelloWorld panel, and select the WorldView class.

2. Move to the Operations button, and select the Unparse option.

3. Answer *OK* to the two prompts. The first *OK* confirms the creation of the files. The second confirms the inclusion of the files in the *Makefile*. (Only create the files once. Subsequent creations overwrite the files destroying any changes made to the files.)

4. Save the *.nib* file you created with the Save item in the File menu, and hide or quit Interface Builder.

2.2.8   HelloWorld Source Files

Launch the Edit application or another editor, and open the *WorldView.h* and *WorldView.m* files. Example 2.1 shows how these files appear. Objective-C statements must be inserted in the files in order to make WorldView perform the operations described at the beginning of this chapter.

Example 2.1 *WorldView files created by Interface Builder*

Interface file WorldView.h

```
/* Generated by Interface Builder */

#import <appkit/View.h>

@interface WorldView:View
{
}

- drawHello:sender;
- clearHello:sender;

@end
```

Implementation file WorldView.m

```
/* Generated by Interface Builder */

#import "WorldView.h"

@implementation WorldView

- drawHello:sender
{
    return self;
}

- clearHello:sender
{
    return self;
}

@end
```

WorldView.h

The following steps modify the interface file, *WorldView.h*:

1. Add an instance variable to keep track of whether to display "Hello World." This instance variable should be declared as a Boolean value and called *drawHello*.

2. Add a declaration for the **drawSelf::** method. The WorldView inherits this method from the View class. The WorldView class overrides this method in order to draw Hello World in the window when the program is running.

```
- drawSelf:(NXRect *)r :(int) count;
```

3. Save the file.

With the addition of comments, the interface file should be similar to Example 2.2. The bold text signifies new additions (other than the comments).

Example 2.2 *Completed WorldView.h*

```
/*
 * WorldView.h
 *
 * The instance variable drawHello is toggled between YES and NO
 * and indicates whether the "Hello World" string should be
 * displayed in the view.
 */

#import <appkit/View.h>

/*
 * WorldView is a subclass of View. It inherits all View's instance variables
 * and methods.
 */

@interface WorldView:View
{
   BOOL drawHello;
}

- drawHello:sender;
- clearHello:sender;
- drawSelf:(NXRect *)r :(int) count;

@end
```

WorldView.m

The following steps modify the implementation file, *WorldView.m*:

1. In *WorldView.m*, add the two lines in bold to the **drawHello:** method, before the *return* statement:

```
- drawHello:sender
{
    drawHello = YES;
    [self display];

    return self;
}
```

2. Add the two lines in bold that appear in the following code to the method **clearHello:**, also before the *return* statement:

```
- clearHello:sender
{
    drawHello = NO;
    [self display];

    return self;
}
```

The first line of each method toggles the Boolean instance variable, *drawHello*, between *YES* and *NO* (*YES* for drawing Hello World and *NO* for not drawing it). The next line sends a message to *self* (the WorldView object's id) telling it to perform the **display** method. The **display** method is defined in View and is inherited by WorldView. Drawing in a view occurs by placing the drawing instructions in the **drawSelf::** method, thereby overriding the inherited **drawSelf::** method. The **display** method initiates the drawing but the **drawSelf::** method does the actual drawing.

To override the **drawSelf::** method, insert **drawSelf::** after **clearHello:**. The drawing consists of clearing the previous drawing by filling the view with light gray and displaying "Hello World" if *drawHello* is *YES*.

Example 2.3 *WorldView.m **drawSelf::** method*

```
- drawSelf:(NXRect *) r: (int) count
{
    PSsetgray(NX_LTGRAY);
    PSrectfill(bounds.origin.x, bounds.origin.y,
        bounds.size.width, bounds.size.height);

    if (drawHello)
    {
        PSsetgray(NX_BLACK);
        PSmoveto(50.0, 70.0);
        PSselectfont("Times-Roman", 40.0);
        PSshow("Hello World");
```

```
    }
    return self;
}
```

The drawing uses the single operator calls in the Client Library. These calls are used for a simple drawing like that found in this example. Drawings that are more complex, frequent, or time critical, use pswrap, user paths, and more performance-oriented drawing approaches such as those described later in this book.

Clearing any previous drawing consists of two operations: setting the color and filling the view. The *bounds* structure that appears in the **PSrectfill( )** call is an instance variable of the View class that gives the origin, width, and height of the view. **PSrectfill( )** fills the view with the current color in the PostScript graphics state, light gray. The gray level selected matches the background of the window, so it doesn't matter if WorldView is smaller than the window.

The next group of lines shows the text "Hello World" in the view if *drawHello* equals *YES*. The gray level is set to black and a current point is set in the PostScript graphics state. The PostScript operator **selectfont** establishes the current font in the graphics state (40 point, Times-Roman). The **show** operator displays the string "Hello World" in the current font at the current point in the current color.

Note   *The point (50.0, 70.0) is relative to the lower left corner of the view placed within the window in Interface Builder. A different point might be necessary for a differently sized or differently placed view.*

Include the **#import <dpsclient/wraps.h>** line, add comments, and save the file. The complete file appears in Example 2.4.

Example 2.4 *Completed WorldView.m*

```
/*
 * WorldView.m
 *
 * WorldView is a subclass of View. It simply displays and clears a message in
 * the view. The one lesson this example shows is the modification of
 * "drawSelf::" and the call to "display". The method, "drawSelf::", should
 * not be called directly.
 *
 * Rather, "display" should be called. The display message performs
 * some necessary overhead such as bringing the View into focus by
 * constructing a clipping path around its frame rectangle and making its
 * coordinate system the current coordinate system for the application. The
 * display method then messages drawSelf::. These steps are repeated for
```

```
 * each of the View's subviews.
 *
 * Note: Any instance variables that need to be initialized before the first display
 * should be done in the "init" or "initFrame:" method. In this case,
 * drawHello is already a null value at its creation so no initialization
 * has to be performed.
 */

#import "WorldView.h"
#import <dpsclient/wraps.h>

@implementation WorldView

- drawHello:sender
{
    drawHello = YES;
    [self display];

    return self;
}

- clearHello:sender
{
    drawHello = NO;
    [self display];

    return self;
}

/*
 * The first two lines clear the view. The remainder display the
 * message in the view.
 */
- drawSelf::(NXRect *) r: (int) count
{
  PSsetgray(NX_LTGRAY);
  PSrectfill(bounds.origin.x, bounds.origin.y,
      bounds.size.width, bounds.size.height);

  if (drawHello)
  {
    PSsetgray(NX_BLACK);
    PSmoveto(50.0, 70.0);
    PSselectfont("Times-Roman", 40.0);
    PSshow("Hello World");
  }
  return self;
}
@end
```

2.2.9 The Make Command

The **make** command can be activated from Interface Builder (in the File submenu) or from the shell. Type *make* in the shell to create the executable file *HelloWorld*. (The application name can be set explicitly in the Project Inspector. By default, it takes the name of the *.nib* file.)

After the make has completed successfully, that is, after compiler time errors have been resolved, the application can be launched. (The **make** option in Interface Builder creates a debug version of *HelloWorld*, *HelloWorld.debug*, under gdb, the GNU debugger.)

2.2.10 Running HelloWorld

Type *HelloWorld* in the shell or double-click the file in the Workspace Manager™ to start the application. The application should work as described in the beginning of this chapter. (If you use the **make** option in Interface Builder, the application is named *HelloWorld.debug*.)

2.2.11 Common Problems

- Selecting a menu item does nothing.

  Menu items must be connected to their appropriate methods within Interface Builder. Press Return or press Enter after the method has been selected for the connection to take effect. Selecting the method is not enough. In addition, the two methods entered in the Class Inspector must have the same spelling as those in the *WorldView.h* and *WorldView.m* files.

- The string "Hello World" is either clipped or does not appear.

  The point (50.0, 70.0) might not position the text in the correct spot. Try making adjustments to the point to position the text within the view. The color of the text must be different from the color of the background. Additionally, the text must be drawn after the background.

2.3 Drawing in a View

A View is an object in the Application Kit that provides a structure for drawing on the screen (and for handling mouse and keyboard events). Most drawing done within an application is encapsulated within some derivative of View objects. The Windows, Panels, Buttons, and

TextFields either contain View instances or are subclasses of View. (Windows and Panels contain View instances. Buttons and TextFields are subclasses of Views.)

Note   *An instance that contains ids to other instances is an example of an instance hierarchy. Each instance in the relationship controls a different aspect of an operation. The Control and Cell relationship and the Window and View relationship are two examples of this type of hierarchy. The instances in the hierarchy do not have to belong to the same or related classes; they can belong to unrelated classes.*

The methods provided in the View class handle much of the overhead for drawing. The actual drawing takes place in the **drawSelf::** method of the subclass. This method should not be called directly. Instead, send a message to **display**, which in turn sends a message to **drawSelf::**.

The Window object in HelloWorld contains two views, a *frame view* and a *content view*. The frame view consists of the border, title bar, and resize bar. The content view consists of the area inside the border and bars. The frame view is private to all but the window and shouldn't be altered. The content view is public. It can contain other views and can be replaced by another view. In HelloWorld, the content view is kept as a subview of the window, and WorldView is made a subview of the content view.

The Display PostScript system uses the Cartesian coordinate system to specify location on the screen. The origin is at the lower left of the screen. The positive y-axis is at the top and the positive x-axis is to the right. Each unit or *point* in the default coordinate system is equal to 1/72 of an inch. (The coordinate space for the 17-inch NeXT monitor uses 1/92 of an inch.)

An important feature of the PostScript coordinate system is that the origin can be moved to another location. As a result, instructions that are used in one location can be used in another by moving or *translating* the origin of the coordinate system. For example, in drawing two identical buttons, only one set of PostScript language instructions is needed to describe the look of the buttons. The different positions are accomplished by translating the origin.

The same concept applies to views. A view has a width, height, and position on the screen, as shown in Figure 2.8. It also has its own coordinate system so that drawing within the view is relative to the view only and not to its position on the screen or within a window. The default origin for the view is its lower left corner. The instance variable *bounds*, contains the origin (which is usually the point (0.0, 0.0)) and the width and height of the view. These values, *bounds.origin.x*, *bounds.origin.y*, *bounds.size.width*, and *bounds.size.height*, are passed as arguments to **PSrectfill( )** in order to clear the view.

Figure 2.8 *Screen and view orientations*

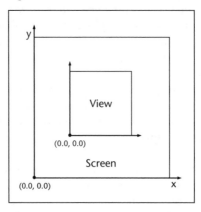

The display of HelloWorld includes a call to **PSmoveto( )**, with the point (50.0, 70.0). This point is about an inch up and half an inch to the right of the view's bottom left corner. Note that the origin when drawing is the lower left of the *view*, not the lower left of the *window*.

By default, a view sets a clip path around the dimensions of its frame. Anything that is outside the frame does not appear. As a result, moving to a point of (50.0, -30.0) and performing the **PSshow( )** won't display any text. Likewise, the point (-90.0, 110.0) shows only a portion of the text.

Figure 2.9 shows the results of using different coordinates when displaying HelloWorld. The dotted border is the clipping path and the outlined text indicates text you won't see on the screen.

Figure 2.9 *HelloWorld string positioning*

Figure 2.9 *HelloWorld string positioning*

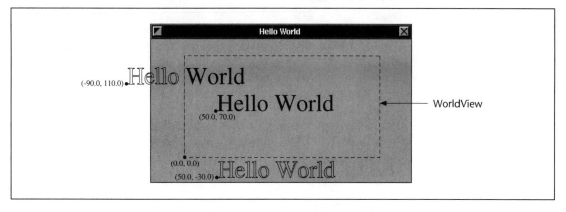

2.3.1 Sending a Message to Display

To draw in a view, you must override the **drawSelf::** method in the View subclass. Drawing is accomplished by sending a message to **display** and not to **drawSelf::**. In the HelloWorld example, both **drawHello:** and **clearHello:** send messages to **display**. This method is found in the View class and sets the state for drawing in the view.

The **display** method brings the view into focus, which means that the view's coordinate system is installed as the current coordinate system in the graphics state, and a clipping path is created around its frame rectangle. (The coordinate system is discussed in Chapter 3.)

After the view is in focus, **display** sends a message to **drawSelf::**. Then **display** messages are sent to all the subviews of the current view. A view that has its subviews do all the drawing doesn't need to override **drawSelf::**. The **display** message of the superview sends a message to all subviews.

Note   *You can send messages to **drawSelf::** directly without going through the **display** method. The only caveat is to bracket the messages to **drawSelf::** with **lockFocus** and **unlockFocus** messages. The **display** message, however, is applied recursively to each subview whereas the **drawSelf::** message is not. (The **lockFocus** and **unlockFocus** methods ensure that the View draws in the correct coordinates and to the correct device. The **display** method includes messages to these two methods.)*

2.4 Conclusions

- Interface Builder is an application supplied with the NeXT Computer that helps developers quickly create a user interface for an application.

- A Window is an Application Kit class that manages and coordinates windows for an application. Each instance corresponds to a physical window.

- A View is an Application Kit class that supports drawing to the window server and to a stream context. It also provides a structure for handling mouse and keyboard events.

- Most drawing in a NeXTstep application is performed by subclassing the View class and placing the drawing instructions in the **drawSelf::** method of the subclass.

CHAPTER 3

The Coordinate System

A key feature of the PostScript language is its device independence. One way that device independence is achieved is through a coordinate system that is independent of the resolution of any monitor. The PostScript interpreter maps paths defined in this coordinate system to device pixels as part of the rendering process.

The PostScript language coordinate system enables you to perform linear distortions such as scaling and rotating text and graphics, which allows scalable fonts, text on a curve, and intricate objects rotated at any angle. This chapter provides background on the coordinate system and on the PostScript imaging model.

This chapter also discusses paths and their relation to pixels. The StrokeAdjust application is used to show the effect stroke adjustment has at the pixel level. Although these details are less important on high-resolution devices, stroke adjustment can make a significant difference on low-resolution devices; differences in line placement can cause noticeable differences in line widths. The PostScript interpreter can adjust lines to a uniform width despite differences in line placement. *Automatic stroke adjustment* is the default behavior for the Display PostScript system and can be turned on and off.

Automatic stroke adjustment is not available in PostScript Level 1 interpreters, so some applications might need to include stroke adjustment procedures in their output stream when printing on low-resolution devices (300 dpi). An example appears in Chapter 14, "Printing Issues."

3.1 User Space and Device Space

The PostScript language coordinate system is actually composed of two coordinate systems. One system, *user space*, is used for all drawing instructions. This system looks consistent across all devices. Any point drawn appears in the same location in user space in one device as it does in any other.

The second coordinate system, called *device space*, does not share this property. A point on one device can, and most often will, appear in a different location on a different device. Device space is used to address actual pixels within the image area. Since devices vary in resolution and imaging direction, different device space coordinate system representations are necessary and contain different origins, axes orientations, and unit lengths.

You don't need to be aware of the differences in device spaces or, for the most part, be concerned with device space because the PostScript interpreter translates user space to device space automatically. As a result, the application is not concerned with printing or displaying to different types of devices. One set of drawing instructions drawn with respect to a single coordinate system is sufficient. The interpreter handles the translation from user space to device space for a given device, deciding which pixels are turned on and which ones are not.

In Figure 3.2, the user space is on the left and two different device spaces appear on the right. The first device space is from the NeXT MegaPixel Display™. Its device space coordinate system matches the user space coordinate system. The second space is from the Apple® LaserWriter® II NTX. Its origin and unit length are different from the user space. In both cases, the interpreter manages the mapping from user space to device space.

Figure 3.1 *User space to device space mapping*

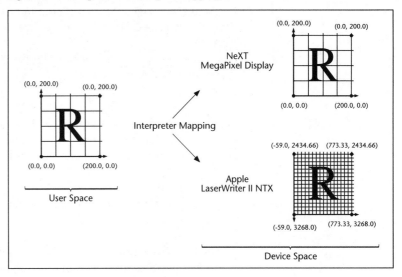

The standard or default user space has its origin in the lower left corner of the page with the positive y-axis extending upward and the positive x-axis extending to the right. The length of a unit along the x-axis and along the y-axis is 1/72 of an inch.

Note   *The unit size, 1/72 of an inch, is close to the size of a printer's point (1/72.27 inch), which is a standard measuring unit in the printing industry.*

The NeXT MegaPixel Display, the Apple LaserWriter II NTX, and the View object in the NeXT Application Kit have the same default user space. In each case, the dimensions of the display or page (the image area) might be different, but the origin, axes orientation, and unit size are all the same. (One exception to this is the NeXT 17-inch monitor. Seventy-two units on this monitor equals 72/92 of an inch instead of a full inch. This reduction is constant across the entire screen, so it is not an important concern for the developer.)

3.2 Transformations

The conversion from one coordinate system to the other is specified by a transformation matrix called the *current transformation matrix* (CTM). The CTM can be altered and changed to cause a different mapping from user space to device space. It specifies how the x and y values for a point in one coordinate space are mapped into the x and y values of the corresponding point in device space.

Applications can draw in a common coordinate system with the PostScript language interpreter handling the particulars of the actual device. One page description will suffice for all devices.

Note   *A page description is a self-contained PostScript language description of a document, which is generated at one time for execution at some arbitrary later time.*

One way to understand the alteration of the CTM is to visualize the user space as changing in one of the following ways. The PostScript language system contains operators to perform these transformations.

- The **translate** operator moves the origin to a different location on the display area leaving the orientation of the axes and the unit size unchanged.

- The **rotate** operator rotates the coordinate system about the origin by the specified angle, altering the orientation of the axes.

- The **scale** operator alters the units of the axes independent of each other, changing the length of a unit. For example, the coordinate system can be scaled so that a unit in the y direction is actually twice the size of a unit in the x direction.

Figure 3.2 *User space transformations*

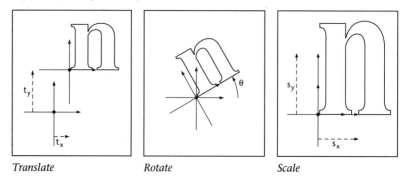

Translate   Rotate   Scale

These transformation types provide many ways to simplify drawing and produce interesting results. For example,

- A single path description can appear at any angle by rotating the user space before displaying the path.

- The origin of the user space can be moved to the upper left corner of the page, and the user space scaled so the y axis is positive toward the bottom of the page. This facilitates filling with text from the top of the page. (The Text class in the Application Kit uses this orientation.)

- A single circle description can display any type of oval by scaling and rotating the circle before displaying it.

For an explanation of the matrix mathematics involved with transformations of the CTM, refer to section 4.3, "Coordinate Systems and Transformations," in the *PostScript Language Reference Manual, Second Edition.*

3.3 Paths

A *path* in the PostScript language is a set of line, arc, and/or Bézier curve segments. These segments can be continuous (a single **moveto** operator) or disjointed (multiple **moveto** operators interspersed within the set). The segments within a path have no width, and the shape formed by the path has no fill until the path is rendered with a painting operator, such as **stroke** or **fill**.

At the time of rendering, values for the current graphics state variables are used to determine which pixels to turn on. Only when you execute **stroke** or **fill** are the line width or color settings taken into account.

Executing **fill** fills the inside of the path with the current color. The fill does not extend outside the path, although any pixel that the path passes through is colored.

Stroking a path extends the width of the path by the current line width setting. One half of the line width extends on either side of the path. The line width is specified in units of points in the current user space so that any scaling operation has a corresponding effect on the line width.

The examples in Figure 3.3 show a path and its subsequent stroking and filling. The path is a mathematical representation of an arc. The stroked path and the filled path are the pixel representations in device space.

Figure 3.3 *Path, stroked path, and filled path*

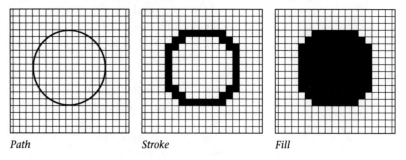

Path   *Stroke*   *Fill*

The placement of the path within a pixel is a factor in determining which pixels to turn on when stroking. Figure 3.4 shows four instances where a vertical path falls at different locations within a pixel column. In the first case, a line width setting equivalent to one point in device space results in a one pixel line. In the second, third, and fourth cases, a line width setting equal to one point results in a two-pixel line. In the first case, the line width does not extend across pixel boundaries; in the others, it does.

Figure 3.4 *Mapping of line widths to device space*

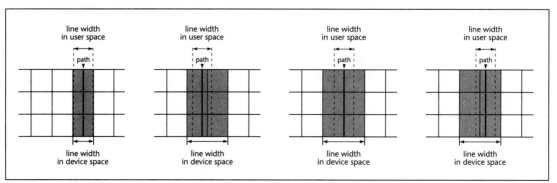

3.4 StrokeAdjust Application

The StrokeAdjust application shows the effect that line position relative to pixel boundaries has on the actual pixel width of lines. Lines with the same width may turn on a different number of pixels. For high-resolution devices, the location of a path within a pixel may not matter because the pixel size is so small that an additional pixel is difficult to detect. For lower resolution devices, such as a display or a 300-dpi printer, an additional pixel in width is very noticeable and can cause unattractive results when a grid or some other symmetrical group of lines is displayed.

Figure 3.5 *StrokeAdjust application*

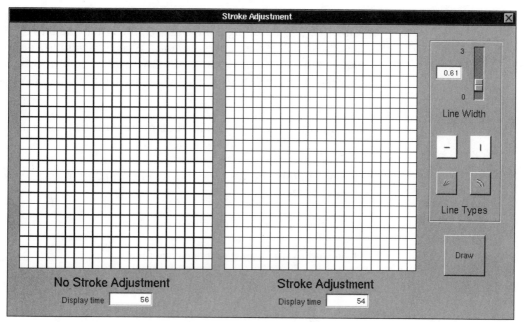

In Figure 3.5, the grid on the left shows the inconsistent line weights. The line width is set to 0.61, but the actual line width might vary by a pixel because the paths for the grid fall at different locations in device space. As the line width increases and decreases, the number and locations of the variations differ.

The grid on the right takes advantage of the stroke adjustment feature in Level 2 and in the Display PostScript system. This feature adjusts the location automatically to produce lines with uniform pixel width. It works by adjusting the placement of every path so that the paths fall at precisely controlled locations within pixels. This adjustment is, by default, turned on in displays and turned off in Level 2 printers; it can be turned on or off on both types of devices with the **setstrokeadjust** operator. When outputting to PostScript interpreters without automatic stroke adjustment, you might want to redefine the path construction operators to manually adjust the path placement.

The next section explains the algorithm for adjusting the path. For more information about stroke adjustment, see Technical Note #5111, "Emulation of the **setstrokeadjust** Operator."

3.5 Printing to Level 1 Devices

The Display PostScript system can perform stroke adjustment automatically. The default setting is on. Once set, the system handles the adjustment so that lines have uniform widths. When you print to a device that does not have automatic stroke adjustment, other adjustments might be required depending on the nature of the application. In Level 2 devices, the default setting is off.

A summary of the emulation for the stroke adjustment found in Display PostScript and Level 2 follows.

1. Convert the user space coordinates of each point to device space coordinates.

2. Subtract .25 from each device space value.

3. Round to the nearest whole device pixel.

4. Add .25 to each device space value.

5. Convert from device space coordinates back to user space coordinates.

The repositioning of the endpoints at the .25 mark within a pixel seems unusual, but if the pixel *boundary* is chosen, all the lines are of even pixel width. If the *midpoint* of each pixel is selected, all the lines are of odd pixel width. The choice of .25 as well as .75 provides for equal distribution of even and odd pixel widths. These are illustrated in Figure 3.6.

Figure 3.6 *Positioning of path coordinates within pixels*

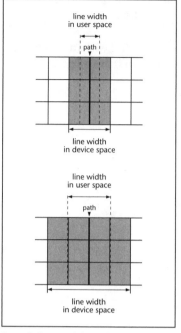

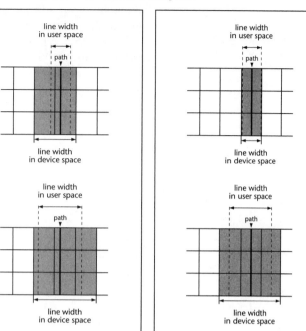

Rounded to pixel boundary: even pixel widths

Rounded to .25 pixel: even/odd pixel widths

Rounded to midpoint: odd pixel widths

The PostScript language procedures for the Level 1 stroke adjustment emulation appear in Chapter 14, "Printing Issues." These procedures are incorporated into a procedure set, which is then placed in the prolog of a page description.

3.6   Conclusions

- The PostScript language allows linear distortions such as scaling, rotating, and translating of text, graphics, and images.

- The PostScript language imaging model achieves device independence by using two coordinate systems: device space, which is tied to the device and user space, which is independent from the device and consistent across all interpreters. The PostScript interpreter handles the mapping from user space to device space.

- Stroke adjustment is a Level 2 and Display PostScript system feature that automatically adjusts paths to device space to produce consistent pixel widths for lines with the same line widths.

- Developers must adjust paths to device space in Level 1 implementations to provide the stroke adjust capability in these devices.

CHAPTER 4

Single Operator Calls and Wraps

The Display PostScript system uses a client-server architecture. The clients send drawing instructions to the server either through single operator calls or through wraps. The server maintains a context for each client. Although a client can have multiple contexts, one context per client or application is recommended. The context contains the memory space, stacks, and input/output facilities.

In this chapter, two mechanisms for communicating with the server are explored: using *single operator calls* from the Client Library and using *wraps* created with the pswrap translator facility. At the same time, the examples illustrate binding and delayed stroking, which are techniques for improving drawing performance.

The Client Library contains the procedures needed to communicate with the PostScript interpreter. One subset of the Client Library is a collection of C language function calls (*single operator calls*) that interface with single PostScript language operators. An example is **PSmoveto( )**. This function takes an x and y coordinate and makes it the current point in the graphics state.

The pswrap translator, on the other hand, encapsulates a custom sequence of PostScript language operations (a wrap) that are callable as a C function. Example 4.1 is a sample pswrap source file and the C function call. This wrap takes two coordinates as arguments, constructs a path between the coordinates, and strokes the path to draw the line on the screen.

Example 4.1 *Sample wrap definition*

```
/* Wrap definition - examplewraps.psw */
defineps PSWDrawLine(float x1, y1, x2, y2)
    x1 y1 moveto
    x2 y2 lineto
    stroke
endps
```

Sample wrap invocation

```
/* Wrap call in a C language program */
#import <dpsclient/wraps.h>
#include "examplewraps.h"

main( )
{
    . . .
    PSWDrawLine(100.0, 100.0, 200.0, 200.0);
    . . .
}
```

In this chapter, a simple application called LineDraw is used for examples. We show several ways to draw lines using either single operator calls or wraps. The timings provided allow you to compare methods. In the course of introducing single operator calls and wraps, the groundwork is provided on the client-server architecture of the Display PostScript system and its use of contexts.

Wraps reduce display time by 20% over single operator calls (1966 milliseconds versus 2276 milliseconds in Table 4.1). Each message to the server incurs some small but fixed performance cost. Reducing the number of messages reduces the number of times you incur this cost.

Binding procedures within the wraps and performing much of the data presentation on the client side are also considered. One of the best ways to reduce display time is to delay stroking until it becomes necessary, either because of a change in a line attribute or the completion of all the paths. When all lines have the same width and color, this technique improves display time by 50% over a wrap that strokes every line and 60% over single operator calls.

In addition, lines that are equivalent to one pixel wide in device space have been made a special case within the Display PostScript system, and as a result print and display much faster than wider lines. A line width setting of 0.15 or less is suggested to obtain the benefits of this feature without the device dependence of a zero line width.

Note   *The special case of 0.0 line width always results in a one pixel line, regardless of the CTM.*

4.1   Client-Server Model

The Display PostScript system uses a client-server network architecture: The interpreter is the server and each application is a client. The client and server are usually separate processes on the same machine, but the client can also exist on a remote machine. The client sends PostScript language code to the server through either single operator calls or wraps. Data can be returned from the server in the form of return arguments. The Client Library implements client-server communication transparently with respect to the low-level communication protocols used by different windowing and operating systems.

Each client within the Display PostScript system operates within a *context*. A context can be thought of as a virtual printer. It has its own set of stacks, input/output facilities, and memory space. Separate contexts enable multiple applications to share one PostScript interpreter running as a process in the server. Figure 4.1 illustrates the Client-Server architecture.

Although the Display PostScript system can support multiple contexts for a single client (application), one context is usually sufficient for all drawing within an application and simplifies programming overhead. A single context can handle multiple windows and views (the Application Kit object specifically designed for drawing on the screen).

An example of where an additional context is suitable is the imaging of imported EPS files. The NXEPSImageRep object in the Application Kit uses a separate context when imaging EPS files. This protects the application context and simplifies error recovery if an imported file contains PostScript language errors.

Figure 4.1 *Client-Server architecture*

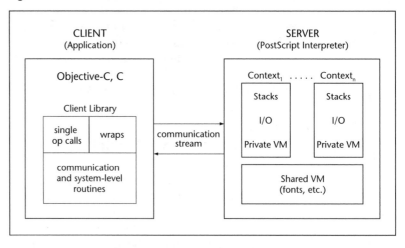

The server handles the scheduling associated with executing contexts in time slices. Each client has access to a separate and private portion of *virtual memory space* within its context. An additional portion of memory, called *shared VM*, is shared among all clients and holds system fonts, among other items. Private VM can also hold fonts but they are private to the client.

The structure of a context is the same across platforms. Creating and managing a context, however, can be different. In the case of the NeXT computer, the application object within the Application Kit manages the handling of contexts. For the most part, context operations are transparent. The main concern for the NeXT developer is the execution of PostScript language operators within a context. (Appendix A, "Client Library," contains information on managing contexts. Refer to section A.4 for detailed information on creating, setting, and destroying contexts.)

4.2   Single Operator Calls

The Client Library manages the communication channel with the server. An important portion of the library is two sets of functions that invoke single PostScript language operators. These sets are almost identical in function. The only difference is that the first group (found in *dpsops.h*) takes as its first argument an explicit context handle in which to execute the operator. Those in the second group (found in *psops.h*) do not take a context parameter because the operators execute within the current context.

Since most applications in the NeXT environment use only one context, the second group of functions is most commonly used. Use the Display PostScript version of the operators if you switch frequently between contexts to avoid having to explicitly set each context before writing to it. Each PostScript language operator has a corresponding single operator call in both *dpsops.h* and *psops.h*. Examples of each for the operator **moveto** appear in Example 4.2.

Example 4.2 *Sample single operator invocation*

```
DPSmoveto(DPSContext ctxt; float x, y);

PSmoveto(float x, y);
```

Some single operator functions require operands but do not take arguments; an example is **PSadd( )**. Two operands are needed but no arguments are taken. These types of operators use operands from the operand stack. In these cases, place the operands on the stack either in a wrap that appears before the function call or through an operation that leaves data on the stack. Look up the description of single operator calls initially to get the arguments right.

Another way to place data on the stack is by using the **PSsend...** set of single operator functions: **PSsendboolean( )**, **PSsendchararray( )**, **PSsendfloat( )**, **PSsendfloatarray( )**, **PSsendint( )**, **PSsendintarray( )**, and **PSsendstring( )**. Each of these functions takes appropriate arguments and places them on the stack. Other functions can then be used to perform operations on those arguments. You can use a corresponding set of **PSget...** functions to retrieve objects from the operand stack.

A single operator call is a simple wrap for a single PostScript language operator. Single operators can be used for such simple drawing as filling in a rectangle or drawing a few lines. Use custom wraps to embody groups of PostScript language operations that frequently appear together, such as **setcolor** and **setlinewidth**. Each Client Library call incurs some processing overhead within the system, so combining operations into wraps reduces the total execution time.

For the most part, don't use the server if the same operation can be done entirely within the client. For example, to obtain the angle formed by a given x and y value, use the UNIX® function **atan( )**, instead of the **PSatan( )** operator in the Client Library. Although **PSatan( )** provides the same answer, the UNIX call is more efficient. The PostScript language is better suited for *imaging* than for *processing* because it is interpreted rather than compiled.

4.3 Wraps

The pswrap translator takes a set of PostScript language instructions and produces a C function. In other words, it groups a set of PostScript language operators into a single procedure call, which then can be used within an application. This approach is similar to providing a C function interface to a FORTRAN library. Arguments can be passed to and received from the server. The single operator calls found in the Client Library are a special set of predefined wraps.

The pswrap translator is a stand-alone program that works like a compiler. It produces a source-level C language file containing the function calls and an include file containing the external declarations.

The translator takes the text representation of the PostScript language code and converts it into a C source file of calls to the Client Library routines. The Client Library formats the arguments into a binary format (a more efficiently executed representation) at run time and sends them to the server. Figure 4.2 illustrates the pswrap translator process.

Figure 4.2 *pswrap translator process*

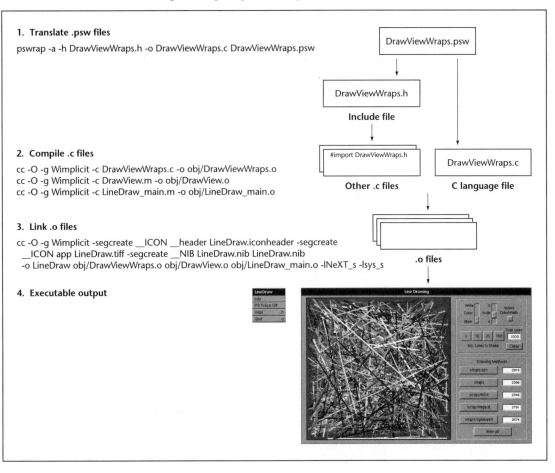

The pswrap translator has an invocation in the shell, as shown in Example 4.3.

Example 4.3 *pswrap translator invocation in the shell*

pswrap [-ar] [-o outputCfile] [-h outputHfile] [-s length] [inputFile]

-a uses ANSI C procedure syntax
-o specifies the outputCfile (default is standard out)
-h generates the external declarations in the header file specified
-s Max length of string input in PS program
-r Wrap can be used in a shared lib, generates extra code, use only if necessary
outputCfile is the source file name desired (the .c extension should be included)
outputHfile is the header file name desired (the .h extension should be included)
inputFile is the .psw or .pswm file (default is standard input)

The *Makefile* generated by Interface Builder invokes pswrap as long as the wrap file is included in the Project Inspector. The header (*.h*) and source (*.c*) files don't need to be included in the Project Inspector. However, declare the header file as an import in the files that call the wraps. In the LineDraw application, *WorldView.m* imports *DrawViewWraps.h*, the header file for *DrawViewWraps.psw*. (The *Makefiles* provided by Interface Builder invoke pswrap whenever the *.psw* file changes. Other *Makefiles* might not do this.)

4.4 Wrap Declarations

This section briefly describes the wrap syntax used in the examples. (See Appendix B, "pswrap," for a more comprehensive explanation of the wrap syntax.)

Each wrap definition contains three parts:

- *defineps/endps* pairing

- C function definition (including argument types)

- PostScript language code

4.4.1 defineps/endps Pairing

Each wrap is enclosed between a *defineps* and *endps*. (Both should appear at the beginning of a new line.) All the text between the pairing, except for the procedure call definition, must be PostScript language code. The text is processed by the translator and converted into C code. All text not included between the pairings passes to the source level C language file untouched. As a result, comments inside each *defineps/endps* should be PostScript language comments (%). Comments outside each *defineps/endps* should be C language comments (/* ... */).

Note   *PostScript language comments are not sent to the server or stream context. Use **DPSPrintf( )**, **DPSWritePS( )**, or **DPSWriteData( )** to send comments.*

4.4.2 Procedure Call Definition

The call definition contains the procedure name and the argument list in parentheses. The procedure type is *void*, but this is implicit and should not be included as part of the definition. No other return type is possible. By default the function names are external, but they can be declared static by placing *static* on a separate line immediately before *defineps*.

Arguments can be passed to the server and returned from the server if included arguments are declared within parentheses immediately following the procedure name. (Parentheses are required even for wraps without arguments.)

4.4.3 PostScript Language Code

All text included between a *defineps* and an *endps* should be PostScript language operators or arguments declared in the function definition. The pswrap translator performs the conversion of the text into binary objects but does not validate the operations. Errors in the body of a wrap won't be caught during translation but will cause exceptions at run time.

4.5 LineDraw Application

The purpose of the LineDraw application is to draw lines and time the results. This application contains one example of using single operator calls and four using variations of wraps. The wraps can be found in *DrawViewWraps.psw*, the invocation in *DrawView.m*.

Table 4.1 summarizes times, in milliseconds, obtained from the LineDraw application for drawing 1000 lines in the worst-case and best-case situations.

Table 4.1 *Times for single operator calls and wraps*

Best Case (uniform width and color)		Worst Case (random width and color)	
Drawing times for 1000 lines in milliseconds, from best to worst			
Wraps with Optimized Stroking	845	Wraps with Binding	2584
Wraps with Binding	1895	Wraps	2639
Wraps	1966	Wraps with Optimized Stroking	2645
Wraps with Interpreter Loop	2103	Wraps with Interpreter Loop	2792
Single Operator Calls	2276	Single Operator Calls	2958

LineDraw defines six arrays of floating point numbers to store the values that are used to draw the lines: *X, Y, X1, Y1, C,* and *W.* The arrays store the starting x and y coordinates, the ending x and y coordinates, and the color and line width for each line. These arrays are populated when you select certain controls in the interface.

The starting x and y point and the ending x and y point for each line is generated with the **rand( )** function and modified to fall with the bounding rectangle of the view in the application. The color and line width can be set to specific values for each set of lines or generated randomly, again modified to fall within certain ranges. The ability to display sets of lines with uniform color and line widths as well as randomly generated color and line widths provides the best and worst cases for display times.

Each example of the displaying lines has been placed in a separate method. These methods are sent a message by the **drawSelf::** method if the appropriate button for the specific drawing operation is selected. The Draw button sends a message to a method in the DrawView class, which in turn sends a message to **display.**

4.5.1   PSWMarkTime( ) and PSWReturnTime( )

PSWMarkTime( ) and **PSWReturnTime( )** are used in all of the drawing methods to obtain the processing time for each example. **PSWMarkTime( )** defines **StartTime** and assigns it the value of the PostScript language operator **realtime** at the time of the wrap invocation. **PSWReturnTime( )** gets the current real-time value and subtracts **StartTime.**

The difference is returned from the server to the client in the output argument, *ElapsedTime.* Output arguments appear after the input arguments in the wrap declaration and are separated from the input arguments by a vertical bar (|). A call to **NXPing( )** is inserted immediately after the **PSWMarkTime( )** in order to flush the buffer to the server. This ensures the immediate execution of the **realtime** operation. An **NXPing( )** is unnecessary after the **PSWReturnTime( )** because a return argument automatically flushes the buffer.

Note   *NXPing( ) is a NeXTstep equivalent of the Client Library function DPSWaitContext( ).*

Example 4.4 *Wraps used for timing measurements*

PostScript language code

```
/* Wrap definitions - DrawViewWraps.psw */
defineps PSWMarkTime( )
  /StartTime realtime def
endps

defineps PSWReturnTime( | int *ElapsedTime)
  realtime StartTime sub
  ElapsedTime
endps
```

C language code

```
/* Wrap calls - DrawView.m */
int ElapsedTime;

PSWMarkTime( );  NXPing( );
/* code segment to time */
. . .
PSWReturnTime(&ElapsedTime);
```

Whenever an output argument is encountered within a wrap, the topmost value on the operand stack is removed and placed in the address that the output argument provides. Any attempt by a subsequent PostScript language operator to use the value will either use the wrong value or produce a stack underflow error message. If an output argument is used multiple times within a wrap, its value upon return is the last value assigned.

4.5.2   Single Operator Calls

The single operator calls in the Client Library are used like other C language function calls. The calls are contained in the **drawSingleOps** method. This method is sent a message within the **drawSelf::** method. (The **setIntValue** message displays the drawing time in a field in the application interface.)

Single Operator Calls	
Drawing times for 1000 lines in milliseconds	
Best Case *(uniform width and color)*	2276
Worst Case *(random width and color)*	2958

Example 4.5 *Drawing with single operators*

C Code

```
-drawSingleOps
{
  int ElapsedTime, counter;

  PSWMarkTime( ); NXPing( );
```

```
PSsetgray(BGCOLOR);
PSrectfill(0.0, 0.0, bounds.size.width, bounds.size.height);
PSsetgray(BGSTRCOLOR);
PSsetlinewidth(BGSTRWIDTH);
PSrectstroke(0.0, 0.0, bounds.size.width, bounds.size.height);
for (counter = 0; counter < TotalLines; counter++)
{
  PSsetlinewidth(W[counter]);
  PSsetgray(C[counter]);
  PSmoveto(X[counter], Y[counter]);
  PSlineto(X1[counter], Y1[counter]);
  PSstroke( );
}

PSWReturnTime(&ElapsedTime);
[displaySingleOpTime setIntValue:ElapsedTime];

return self;
}
```

PSWMarkTime( ) and **PSWReturnTime( )** are wraps used for timing. The other calls are single operator calls from the Client Library, more specifically *psops.h*. The view is first cleared by drawing over the previous drawing with the background color and then stroking the border. The names in all capitals are predefined literals. The values passed to **PSrectfill( )** and **PSrectstroke( )** are the origin and dimensions for the bounding rectangle for the view.

The **for** loop draws one line each iteration. Some of the functions in the loop take arguments, such as **PSsetgray( )**. Others do not, such as **PSstroke( )**. The number and type of arguments for each call are found in the include files for the single operator calls. For an explanation of the function of the operators, see the *PostScript Language Reference Manual, Second Edition.*

4.5.3   Simple Wraps

Simple Wraps	
Drawing times for 1000 lines in milliseconds	
Best Case *(uniform width and color)*	1966
Worst Case *(random width and color)*	2639

The second way of drawing lines uses simple wrap definitions. The wrap definitions appear first followed by their invocation in the DrawView class method **drawWraps**. The first wrap clears the view and the second creates and strokes a line path.

Example 4.6 *Drawing with wraps*

PostScript language wraps

```
/* Wrap definitions - DrawViewWraps.psw */
defineps PSWEraseView(float BGColor, BGStrColor, BGStrWidth, BGrect[4])
  BGColor setgray
  BGrect rectfill
  BGStrColor setgray
  BGStrWidth setlinewidth
  BGrect rectstroke
endps

defineps PSWDrawLine(float LineWidth, LineColor, X, Y, X1, Y1)
  LineWidth setlinewidth
  LineColor setgray
  X Y moveto X1 Y1 lineto stroke
endps
```

C language code

```
/* Wrap call - DrawView.m*/
-drawWraps
{
  int ElapsedTime, counter;
  float ViewRect[4];

  PSWMarkTime( ); NXPing( );
  ViewRect[0] = ViewRect[1] = 0.0;
  ViewRect[2] = bounds.size.width;
  ViewRect[3] = bounds.size.height;
  PSWEraseView(BGCOLOR, BGSTRCOLOR, BGSTRWIDTH, ViewRect);

  for (counter = 0; counter < TotalLines; counter++)
  {
    PSWDrawLine(W[counter], C[counter], X[counter], Y[counter],
        X1[counter], Y1[counter]);
  }

  PSWReturnTime(&ElapsedTime);
  [displayWrapTime setIntValue:ElapsedTime];

  return self;
}
```

Use the float array *ViewRect* to pass the bounding rectangle of the view to the wrap in one structure rather than as four individual values, simplifying the call. In the wrap declaration, the array is specified as a float array of size 4. The individual elements in an array can be used within a wrap by specifying an index, or the entire array can be specified by not including an index. (See Appendix B, "pswrap," for more information. In **PSWEraseView( )**, the entire array is placed on the operand stack.

As in the single operator example, the **for** loop draws one line per iteration. The coordinate points for the line and the color and line width for each line are passed to the wrap. The wrap sets the color and line width in the graphics state of the PostScript interpreter and creates and strokes the path.

4.5.4   Wraps with Binding

Wraps with Binding	
Drawing times for 1000 lines in milliseconds	
Best Case *(uniform width and color)*	1895
Worst Case *(random width and color)*	2584

The wraps with binding example is similar to the simple wraps example except that PostScript language *procedures* are defined and called instead of individual *operators* within the wrap. The necessary PostScript language operators appear in the procedures.

A wrap called **PSWDefs( )** defines the procedures. It is called in the **initFrame:** method of the DrawView class so that the definitions exist in the server when the wraps invoke them. These procedures are created so that they can be bound using the **bind** operator. Binding replaces each executable operator name with its value. During execution of the procedures, the interpreter encounters pointers to the executable code that implements the operators rather than the names of the operators.

Whenever the interpreter encounters a name, it looks up the name in the dictionaries on the dictionary stack. Name lookups are fast but they represent noticeable processing overhead. Binding forces the look up of the names of the operators at definition time instead of every time the procedure is executed.

Binding makes a greater difference for frequently called sequences of code. In this case, the view is not erased frequently, so the savings is negligible for the PostScript language procedure **EVB**. The savings is larger for **DLB**, however, since this sequence is invoked many more times.

The two procedures **EVB** and **DLB** in Example 4.7 have been assigned short names. In print drivers, the reduction in data communications overhead using short names can reduce processing time by up to 30%. In Display PostScript, the overhead of name length is insignificant due to pswrap name optimizations and the binary encoding scheme. If a stream might be converted to ASCII and sent to a printer, short names for procedures are worthwhile.

Note   *The wrap names have not been reduced. The wrap is a C language function rather than an executable PostScript language name. Long wrap names make the application code easier to read and have no performance impact.*

Example 4.7 *Drawing with wraps (bind procedures)*

PostScript language wraps

```
/* Wrap definitions - DrawViewWraps.psw */
defineps PSWDefs( )
. . .
  /EVB { % BGrect BGStrWidth BGStrColor BGColor
    setgray 2 index rectfill
    setgray setlinewidth rectstroke
  } bind def

  /DLB { % X1 Y1 X Y LineColor LineWidth
    setlinewidth setgray
    moveto lineto stroke
  } bind def
  . . .
endps

defineps PSWEraseViewBind(float BGColor, BGStrColor, BGStrWidth, BGrect[4])
  BGrect BGStrWidth BGStrColor BGColor EVB
endps

defineps PSWDrawLineBind(float LineWidth, LineColor, X, Y, X1, Y1)
  X1 Y1 X Y LineColor LineWidth DLB
endps
```

C language code

```
-initFrame:(const NXRect*) frameRect
{
    [super initFrame:frameRect];
    ...
    PSWDefs( );

    return self;
}

/* Wrap call - DrawView.m */
-drawWrapsBind
{
  int ElapsedTime, counter;
  float ViewRect[4];

  PSWMarkTime( ); NXPing( );
  ViewRect[0] = ViewRect[1] = 0.0;
```

```
ViewRect[2] = bounds.size.width;
ViewRect[3] = bounds.size.height;
PSWEraseViewBind(BGCOLOR, BGSTRCOLOR, BGSTRWIDTH, ViewRect);

for (counter = 0; counter < TotalLines; counter++)
{
  PSWDrawLineBind(W[counter], C[counter], X[counter], Y[counter],
      X1[counter], Y1[counter]);
}

PSWReturnTime(&ElapsedTime);
[displayWrapBindTime setIntValue:ElapsedTime];

return self;
}
```

4.5.5   Wraps with Interpreter Loop

Wraps with Interpreter Loop	
Drawing times for 1000 lines in milliseconds	
Best Case *(uniform width and color)*	2103
Worst Case *(random width and color)*	2792

The fourth example draws lines in a loop within the PostScript language rather than the C language. As the **DLRB** procedure shows, many stack operations such as **roll**, **dup**, and **exch** are necessary. The resulting drawing time shows that this method is slow when compared to other methods. You should avoid extensive programming with the PostScript language not only because of the slower performance but also because of the unnecessary complexity. The client should handle as much of the data presentation as possible.

Example 4.8 *Drawing with wraps (interpreter loop)*

PostScript language wraps

```
/* Wrap definitions - DrawViewWraps.m */
defineps PSWDefs( )
. . .
  /DLRB { % i - number of times to loop
    0 1 3 -1 roll 1 sub { % for
      dup PSW exch get setlinewidth
      dup PSC exch get setgray
      dup PSX exch get PSY 2 index get moveto
      dup PSX1 exch get PSY1 2 index get lineto
      stroke pop
    } for
  } bind def
  . . .
endps

defineps PSWDrawLineRepeatBind(float W[i], C[i], X[i], Y[i], X1[i], Y1[i]; int i)
  /PSW W def
  /PSC C def
```

```
        /PSX X def /PSY Y def
        /PSX1 X1 def /PSY1 Y1 def
        i DLRB
    endps
```

C language invocations

```
/* Wrap call - DrawView.m */
-drawWrapsRepeat
{
    int ElapsedTime;
    floatViewRect[4];

    PSWMarkTime( ); NXPing( );
    ViewRect[0] = ViewRect[1] = 0.0;
    ViewRect[2] = bounds.size.width;
    ViewRect[3] = bounds.size.height;
    PSWEraseViewBind(BGCOLOR, BGSTRCOLOR, BGSTRWIDTH, ViewRect);
    PSWDrawLineRepeatBind(W, C, X, Y, X1, Y1, TotalLines);

    PSWReturnTime(&ElapsedTime);
    [displayWrapRepeatTime setIntValue:ElapsedTime];

    return self;
}
```

Example 4.8 erases the view with a wrap from Example 4.7. In the wrap that displays the lines, **PSWDrawLineRepeatBind( )**, the six arrays that define the lines are passed to the server which then performs the loop for each line. This case shows the use of dynamically sized arrays within wraps. The arrays and their size are passed as arguments. In the wrap declaration, the array size variable is used to specify the size of the arrays.

Example 4.9 *Variable array adjustment size*

```
definps PSWDrawLineRepeatBind(float W[i], C[i], X[i], Y[i], X1[i], Y1[i]; int i)
```

The variable array size, shown in Example 4.9, provides a good deal of freedom when passing data to the server. Other chapters provide examples where passing large, dynamically sized arrays can provide significant time savings. In example 4.8, the benefit is lost because of the stack manipulations necessary to display the lines.

4.5.6 Wraps with Optimized Stroking

Wraps with Optimized Stroking

Drawing times for 1000 lines in milliseconds

Best Case *(uniform width and color)*	845
Worst Case *(random width and color)*	2645

This method of drawing lines is similar to the Wraps with Binding example except that the stroking of the lines takes place only after the line width or color has changed. The path is extended (with **moveto**s and **lineto**s) without stroking as long as the width and color are the same. If the width or color changes or the number of lines end, the resulting path is stroked and the path begun anew.

The PostScript language operator, **stroke**, paints a line over the current path in the current color using the current line attributes (width, line cap, etc.) in the graphics state. As long as the color or line attributes do not change, significant stroke overhead can be eliminated by collecting a series of disconnected subpaths and performing a single stroke operation on the entire series.

A random ordering of the line types does not show any advantage over stroking every line. Grouping lines according to the same line attributes, however, is the fastest of all the methods explored in this chapter.

This method of drawing is useful when displaying a grid or other drawings with lines of uniform color and line attributes. There also might be some advantage to ordering lines within an application's data structures according to similar line attributes, assuming that there are no layering issues.

Example 4.10 *Drawing with wraps (optimized stroking)*

PostScript language wraps

```
/* Wrap definitions - DrawViewWraps.psw */
defineps PSWDefs( )
  . . .
  /MLB { % X1 Y1 X Y
    moveto
    lineto
  } bind def

  /SLB { % LineColor LineWidth
    setlinewidth
    setgray
    stroke
  } bind def
  . . .
endps
```

```
defineps PSWMakeLineBind(float X, Y, X1, Y1)
  X1 Y1 X Y MLB
endps

defineps PSWStrokeLineBind(float LineWidth, LineColor)
  LineColor LineWidth SLB
endps
```

C language calls

```
/* Wrap call - DrawView.m */
-drawOptimizedStroke
{
  int ElapsedTime,counter;
  float ViewRect[4];

  PSWMarkTime( ); NXPing( );
  ViewRect[0] = ViewRect[1] = 0.0;
  ViewRect[2] = bounds.size.width;
  ViewRect[3] = bounds.size.height;
  PSWEraseViewBind(BGCOLOR, BGSTRCOLOR, BGSTRWIDTH, ViewRect);

  for (counter = 0; counter < TotalLines; counter++)
  {
    PSWMakeLineBind(X[counter], Y[counter],
        X1[counter], Y1[counter]);

    if (counter >= TotalLines -1 ||
        C[counter] != C[counter + 1] ||
        W[counter] != W[counter+1])
    {
      PSWStrokeLineBind(W[counter], C[counter]);
    }
  }

  PSWReturnTime(&ElapsedTime);
  [displayOptimizedStroke setIntValue:ElapsedTime];

  return self;
}
```

Note   *The PostScript interpreters in most printers have a 1500-point path length limit. For printer compatibility, place a ceiling on the number of points allowed when you draw a path. The limit is significantly larger in the Display PostScript system.*

The optimization technique for stroking should not be used for filling. The performance is not improved and the results are visually unpredictable due to the interactions between the PostScript language fill rule and overlapping subpaths. It is best to draw and fill each object individually. (Group rectangles in **rectfill** and **rectstroke** whenever possible.)

4.6   Small Width Lines

Small Width Lines	
Drawing times for 1000 lines in milliseconds	
0.15 Point Line Width *(uniform color)*	530
2.0 Point Line Width *(uniform color)*	845

Line widths equivalent to one pixel in device space display faster than other line widths because the interpreter contains optimizations for these lines. A line width setting of 0.15 is suggested to obtain the benefits of this feature without the absolute device dependence of a zero line width.

A zero line width is, by definition, one pixel on all devices. A one-pixel line is visible on a low-resolution display but is barely visible on a 300 dpi printer and is almost invisible on a 1200 dpi typesetter. A line width setting of 0.15 produces a one-pixel line on devices with resolutions of 400 dpi or less but is still visible on higher resolution devices.

Small line widths are better for uses such as displaying a wire frame drawing of an image. In this instance, a line width setting of 0.15 displays much faster than one that doesn't use the optimization feature.

4.7   Conclusions

- Use the PostScript language and the Display PostScript server for imaging but not for programming. Any operation that can be performed more easily in the client should be performed there.

- Use wraps to group together frequently invoked sets of PostScript language operators.

- Procedures defined in the PostScript language server must be included in the prolog of a page description to be used in the script of that description. If you use the **bind** operator, define variables in the procedure beforehand. Otherwise, previously defined values might be bound into the procedure if the page description is included in another document.

- Delaying the stroking of similar sets of lines until all the lines have been constructed can dramatically reduce display time.

CHAPTER 5

Path Construction and Rendering

Chapter 4 of this manual describes using single operator calls and wraps to render paths. This chapter further explores the issue of efficiently rendering paths by using *user paths* (a Display PostScript system extension to the PostScript language).

User path operators can be invoked by single operator calls or by wraps and provide advantages that conventional path construction operators do not. The following are the primary benefits of user paths:

- They are more efficient to interpret and execute.

- They provide a convenient way to send an arbitrary path to the server.

- They are compact and minimize data transmission when the client and server are on different machines.

- They can be cached.

A user path is represented as a PostScript language array that consists of path construction operators and their corresponding operands expressed as literal numbers. That is, a user path is a complete and self-contained path description. A number of Display PostScript system rendering operators can act on user paths to perform standard PostScript language operations such as stroking or filling. A user path can be described either as a standard PostScript language procedure or in an encoded format that consists of an array of two elements: an array of operands and a string of operators.

In this chapter, the Dial application highlights three ways of drawing hash marks around the inner edge of a dial; two use standard path construction operators and the third uses user paths.

The first method rotates the same line description for each mark on the dial using wraps. The second calculates the beginning and ending coordinates for the lines using trigonometric functions and then sends them to the server using wraps. The third method is similar to the second but it makes use of user paths and the NeXT procedure **DPSDoUserPath( )** to send the paths to the server. Each group of hash marks is sent as a single large user path reducing the number of operators sent to the server and taking advantage of the delayed stroking technique mentioned in Chapter 4.

A user path is the most efficient means of path construction in the Display PostScript system. User paths can be sent to the server in a wrap, but **DPSDoUserPath( )** serves the same purpose and provides additional benefits.

DPSDoUserPath( ) encodes the operands as encoded number strings, a more efficient number format, and provides an emulation of user paths and their rendering operators when printing to Level 1 devices. The encoded number string format is shown in Example 5.3, and the conversion into Level 1 path construction operators by the **DPSDoUserPath( )** procedure is shown in Chapter 14, Example 14.2.

Note   *You can declare and send encoded number string arguments in wraps. The pswrap translator recognizes a numstring type in the wrap declaration. The translator includes instructions in the wrap that format the int, float, or char array arguments passed to the wrap at run time into encoded number strings. Including numstring in the declaration is all you need to obtain the performance edge of encoded number strings. In Chapter 7, Example 7.4 contains a wrap with the numstring declaration. The encoded number string argument is a Level 2 feature, however, and is not supported in Level 1 devices. As a result, you must send conventional number formats to Level 1 devices.*

Figure 5.1 *Dial application*

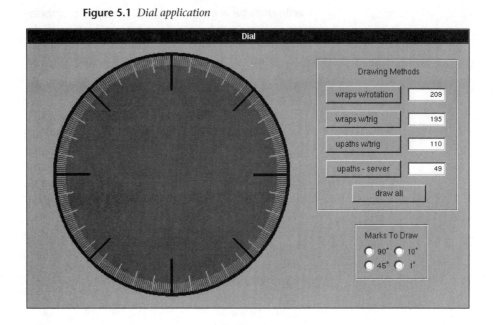

5.1′ User Path Uses

A user path can provide an advantage over conventional path construction in a number of instances, such as when the path is known ahead of time. Instead of creating a wrap to construct the path, use an encoded user path to store the path in a compact form. When it comes time for rendering, invoke the user path with the desired user path rendering operator.

For example, a user path might be used to retain the descriptions of clock hands. Instead of drawing the hands within a wrap using **moveto**, **lineto**, and **curveto** operators, you can create two initialized arrays for each path containing the operands and operators, and send them to the server with **DPSDoUserPath( )**. Example 6.2 in Chapter 6 shows this approach.

Even if the path is created dynamically, user paths can improve performance. As the Dial application shows, it is faster to place a large path in a user path just before sending it to the server than it is to send each segment individually.

Graphics applications can make use of this feature by retaining a user path definition for each object or by converting the internal path representation to a user path immediately before drawing. Since dynamically sized arrays can be sent to the server, an application can maintain two large buffers (one for operands and one for operators) to transmit user paths to the server. Both Example 5.7 in this chapter and the Scrolling application in Chapter 9 use this technique.

5.2   User Path Definition

A user path is an array that consists of path construction operators and their coordinate operands expressed as literal numbers. User path rendering operators such as **ustroke** and **ufill** take a user path as an argument and perform the appropriate rendering operation. Example 5.1 shows one of the formats for a user path description with the **ustroke** operator.

Example 5.1 *ASCII user path description*

```
{
   0 0 200 200 setbbox
   175 100 moveto
   200 100 lineto
   100 175 moveto
   100 200 lineto
   25 100 moveto
   0 100 lineto
   100 25 moveto
   100 0 lineto
} ustroke
```

5.2.1   Path Description

The path description can be represented two ways. The first format, Example 5.1, consists of an ASCII path definition enclosed within { } braces, which creates an executable PostScript language array. The second format, Example 5.2, is a two-part array containing an array or string of encoded numbers and a string of encoded path construction operators. The < > brackets create a PostScript language string object whose elements are encoded with hex digits.

The operators are executed sequentially with the operands for the operators taken from the encoded number grouping. Example 5.2 shows the same user path description as Example 5.1 except the path description is in the encoded format.

Example 5.2 *Encoded user path description*

```
[
  [
    0 0 200 200 75 100 200 100 100 175 100 200
25 100 0 100 100 25 100 0
  ]
  <000103010301030103>
] ustroke
```

Example 5.3 contains the same user path as in Example 5.2 except that it has encoded number string operands instead of a number.

Example 5.3 *Encoded user path descriptions with number string operands*

```
{<9500001400000000000000000000000c8000000c8000000af0000006400000
0c8000000640000006400000af00000064000000c800000019000000640000
000000000006400000006400000019000000640000000000><0001030103010301
03>]ustroke
```

5.2.2 User Path Construction Operators

Table 5.1 lists the allowed path construction operators. The second column lists the operands for each operator, the third lists the corresponding encoding value in decimal, and the fourth column lists the NeXT literal definition for the encoding (contained in *dpsNeXT.h*).

Table 5.1 *User path construction operators and encodings*

Operators	Operands	Encoding	NeXT Encoding
arc	$x\ y\ r\ ang_1\ ang_2$	7	dps_arc
arcn	$x\ y\ r\ ang_1\ ang_2$	8	dps_arcn
arct	$x_1\ y_1\ x_2\ y_2\ r$	9	dps_arct
closepath		10	dps_closepath
curveto	$x_1\ y_1\ x_2\ y_2\ x_3\ y_3$	5	dps_curveto
lineto	$x\ y$	3	dps_lineto
moveto	$x\ y$	1	dps_moveto
rcurveto	$dx_1\ dy_1\ dx_2\ dy_2\ dx_3\ dy_3$	6	dps_rcurveto
rlineto	$dx\ dy$	4	dps_rlineto
rmoveto	$dx\ dy$	2	dps_rmoveto
setbbox	*llx lly urx ury*	0	dps_setbbox
ucache		11	dps_ucache

Readers who know the PostScript language will be familiar with all the path construction operators except **setbbox**, **arct**, and **ucache**. The **ucache** operator is optional, but it must appear as the first operator in the path description if included. The **ucache** operator forces the Display PostScript system to save the result of executing the user path in a cache. This cache is analogous to the font cache that saves rendered font glyphs. If the PostScript interpreter encounters a user path that is already in the cache, it substitutes the cached results instead of reinterpreting the path definition.

Additional processing is required to place the path in the cache, so you should use the cache only for paths that are rendered frequently. Although caching works with translated user paths, it does not work for rotated or scaled user paths. In these instances, the path must be reinterpreted and re-cached. The costs and benefits of the user path cache as well as timing studies and guidelines for its use are discussed more fully in Chapter 9, "Drawing Issues and Scrolling."

The **setbbox** operator is required and immediately follows **ucache** (or appears as the first operator if **ucache** is not used). **setbbox** requires four operands that make up the bounding box enclosing the entire path. The operands specify the lower left and upper right coordinates of the bounding box, *not* the NeXT representation of a rectangle as an origin followed by a size.

All coordinates specified as operands for successive operators must lie within this bounding box. Otherwise, a **rangecheck** error is generated. The bounding box reduces the number of calculations the interpreter must perform and improves path rendering performance.

In this case, a bounding box that is closer in size to the actual bounding box performs only slightly better than a bounding box that is larger. Increasing the bounding box for **setbbox** by a thousand points in each direction for the user path approach increases the execution time by 4 to 5 milliseconds off a base time of approximately 200 milliseconds. The bounding box values, however, can be used by the interpreter to determine whether an image lies within a clipping region. In these cases, the differences can be more significant.

The **arct** operator is a user path replacement operator for **arcto**. The operators are identical except that **arct** does not push any results on the operand stack whereas **arcto** pushes four numbers. The **arcto** operator cannot be used in user path definitions because it pushes results on the stack.

5.3 User Path Rendering Operators

The Display PostScript system extensions to the PostScript language include operators that interpret and operate on user paths. These operators are also available in all devices that support PostScript Level 2. The rendering operators are:

ufill	**inufill**
ueofill	**inueofill**
ustroke	**inustroke**
ustrokepath	
uappend	

The operators in the first column, except for **uappend**, perform the same functions on a user path that their corresponding operators perform on regular paths. For example, **ufill** takes the user path off the operand stack, interprets it, and then paints the area enclosed by the user path with the current color. The operators in the second column are used for hit detection.

The **uappend** operator interprets a user path definition and appends the result to the current path in the graphics state. It should only be used for special circumstances because it's less efficient than rendering the path directly. Use **ustroke, ufill**, etc., whenever possible rather than appending the path with **uappend** and then calling **stroke**.

User path rendering operators make a temporary adjustment to the user space by rounding the origin components to the nearest integer values. This ensures that a single user path description produces uniform results regardless of its position on the page or display due to translation of the user space. The results of rendering a user path might be slightly different from the results of rendering a conventional path that uses Level 1 operators, but using the same approach for all path construction minimizes, if not eliminates, this effect.

5.3.1 Clipping with a User Path

The list of rendering operators does not include a **uclip** operator. Clipping with a user path can be done by using the **uappend** operator to append the path to the current path, then using the **clip** operator to clip the current path. Example 5.4 shows this sequence.

Example 5.4 *Clipping with a user path*

```
newpath <user path> uappend clip newpath
```

5.4 Dial Application

The Dial application draws a dial with hash marks appearing around its inner edge. Hash marks are drawn at 90, 45, 10, and 1 degree rotations. Three methods are used to draw the marks. Timing results allow comparisons between the types of drawing and the number of hash marks drawn. In the code segments, the wraps are shown first followed by their invocations in the DrawView class methods.

In the Dial application, each type of hash mark has different size and color attributes. The source code contains literal definitions for each of the attributes for the hash marks. In the code examples, CLR1 and WID1 are literals for the line color and line width for one type of hash mark. The values are NX_LTGRAY and 0.5. The variable, *maxdim*, is an instance variable in the DialView class that is the diameter of the dial. The literal, LEN1, is the scale factor for the hash mark (10.0/11.0) and DEG1 is the degrees between hash marks (1.0). The *viewcenter* variable holds the x and y locations for the center of the dial.

The *pts* and *ops* arguments in the user path example are pointers to arrays equal to the maximum size of the path description sent to the server. They are allocated at initialization time and hold each user path description for its transmission to the server.

Figure 5.2 *Hash marks in the Dial application*

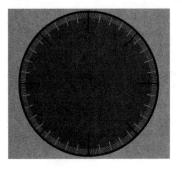

5.4.1 Wraps with Rotation

Wraps with Rotation	
Display times in milliseconds	
4 Lines	6
8 Lines	12
36 Lines	31
360 Lines	209

The first method uses the same line description for all the marks but rotates the user space each time to render the line at a different angle around the dial. Example 5.5 first sets the color and line width settings. It rotates the user space by the specified degree, then calls the wrap to perform the **moveto/lineto**. After all the lines have been constructed, the path is stroked by calling **PSstroke( )**.

Example 5.5 *Wraps with rotation*

PostScript language code

```
defineps PSWDefs( )
. . .
  /RML { % X1 Y1 X0 Y0 Ang
    rotate moveto lineto
  } bind def
. . .
endps

defineps PSWRotate_MakeLine(float Ang, X0, Y0, X1, Y1)
  X1 Y1 X0 Y0 Ang RML
endps

defineps PSWSetColorWidth (float Color, Width)
  Color setgray Width setlinewidth
endps
```

C language code

```
static void drawWrapsRotate(clr, wid, startlen, endlen, deg)
  float clr, wid, startlen, endlen, deg;
{
  int   angle;

  PSWSetColorWidth(clr, wid);
  for (angle = 0; angle < 360; angle += deg)
    PSWRotate_MakeLine(deg, startlen, 0, endlen, 0);
  PSstroke( );
}

- drawRotate
{
  . . .
  drawWrapsRotate(CLR1, WID1, maxdim * LEN1, maxdim, DEG1);
  . . .
}
```

This type of drawing is the easiest to implement. One static path
description can be used for all the drawings within a set. With only a
few paths and rotations, the difference in performance is insignificant,
making it an acceptable drawing method, particularly for a smaller
number of lines.

5.4.2 Wraps with Trigonometric Calculations

Wraps with Trigonometric Calculations	
Display times in milliseconds	
4 Lines	5
8 Lines	11
36 Lines	30
360 Lines	195

The second method performs trigonometric calculations on the client side to find the precise coordinates for the line segments. These coordinates are then sent to the server within a wrap to create the line. Again, stroking occurs after the all the lines in the group have been made. This is illustrated in Example 5.6.

Example 5.6 *Wraps with trigonometric calculations*

PostScript language code

```
defineps PSWDefs( )
. . .
  /ML { % X1 Y1 X0 Y0
    moveto lineto
  } bind def
. . .
endps

defineps PSWMakeLine(float X0, Y0, X1, Y1)
  X1 Y1 X0 Y0 ML
endps
```

C language code

```
static void drawTrigLines(clr, wid, x, y, startlen, endlen, deg)
  float clr, wid, x, y, startlen, endlen, deg;
{
  int  angle;

  PSWSetColorWidth(clr, wid);
  for (angle = 0; angle < 360; angle += deg)
    PSWMakeLine(x + (float) cos(angle * RADIANS) * startlen,
        y + (float) sin(angle * RADIANS) * startlen,
        x + (float) cos(angle * RADIANS) * endlen,
        y + (float) sin(angle * RADIANS) * endlen);
  PSstroke( );
}

- drawTrig
{
  . . .
  drawTrigLines(CLR1, WID1, viewcenter.x, viewcenter.y,
  maxdim * LEN1, maxdim, DEG1);

  . . .
}
```

The times given by this method show little advantage over rotation of a single path description. This comparison shows that rotating the user space has some overhead associated with it but that it is not significant at low frequencies. The disadvantage of calculating the coordinates is that it can get complex.

This test case uses one of the simplest paths possible, a single line segment. A path with multiple line segments and curves and arcs could be difficult to process. Unless the performance advantage outweighs the complexity, you might prefer rotating the user space over calculating the positions on the client side.

In addition, wraps are less efficient for constructing than user paths, so for more intensive drawing cases, use user paths instead of wraps.

5.4.3   User Paths with Trigonometric Calculations

User Paths with Trigonometric Calculations	
Display times in milliseconds	
4 Lines	5
8 Lines	11
36 Lines	28
360 Lines	110

The last method takes the trigonometric approach a step further by placing each line segment into a user path and sending the user path to the server after they have all been placed. In this case, the array is populated each time the hash marks are drawn, then sent to a wrap with a dynamic index size. A description for each set of hash marks can be saved in an initialized array in a source file, eliminating the **for** loop and the calculations in Example 5.6. Calculating the marks around the dial, though, is easy and inexpensive, so it's more practical to generate the points dynamically.

The resulting times of a user path are significantly faster for a large number of lines. The benefit is derived from the elimination of interpreter loop overhead during the path construction. User paths combine a restricted data format with an optimized rendering pipeline to eliminate much of the data manipulation that path construction operators such as **moveto** and **lineto** perform.

The total processing time for drawing eight hash marks isn't enough to produce a noticeable difference between user paths and wraps. For 360 hash marks, however, user paths represent a time savings of almost 40% over the wrap method (195 milliseconds versus 110 milliseconds). Unlike the previous method, using user paths to reduce the number of operators outweighs the complexity of performing the trigonometry.

In this method of drawing, the user path is sent to the server with **DPSDoUserPath( )**. The calling sequence for this procedure appears in Example 5.7. (Refer to the NeXT documentation for the complete specification.)

Example 5.7 *DPSDoUserPath( ) invocation*

```
void DPSDoUserPath(
    void *coords, int numCoords, DPSNumberFormat numType,
    char *ops, int numOps, void *bbox, int action)
```

The *coords* argument is a pointer to an array of coordinate points with *numCoords* identifying the number in the array. The *numType* argument specifies the type of the numbers passed in the *coords* and *bbox* arrays. The three identifiers are *dps_float*, *dps_long*, and *dps_short*.

The *ops* argument is a pointer to a character array or string containing the user path construction operators, and the *numOps* argument identifies the number of operators in the array or string. The *bbox* argument is a pointer to a four-element number array that contains the values for the **setbbox** operator. The *action* argument is an identifier for a user-path rendering operator. Examples are *dps_ufill* and *dps_ustroke*.

Note   *The bbox argument describes the bounding box of the user path by specifying the lower left and upper right coordinates. This representation is different from the NeXT rectangle structure of an origin followed by a size.*

Example 5.8 *User paths with trigonometric calculations*

C language code

```
/*
 * Calculate the start and end points and place in user path
 * format. Send the entire user path at once using the
 * DPSDoUserPath( ) call.
 */

static void drawUpathsTrig(pts, ops, clr, wid, x, y, startlen, endlen, deg, bbox)
    float pts[ ];
    char ops[ ];
    float clr, wid, x, y, startlen, endlen, deg;
    float bbox[4];
{
    int i , j, angle;

    i = j = 0;
    for (angle = 0; angle < 360; angle += deg)
    {
        pts[i++] = x + (float) cos(angle * RADIANS) * startlen;
        pts[i++] = y + (float) sin(angle * RADIANS) * startlen;
        ops[j++] = dps_moveto;

        pts[i++] = x + (float) cos(angle * RADIANS) * endlen;
        pts[i++] = y + (float) sin(angle * RADIANS) * endlen;
```

```
        ops[j++] = dps_lineto;
    }

    PSWSetColorWidth(clr, wid);
    DPSDoUserPath(pts, i, dps_float, ops, j, bbox, dps_ustroke);
}


- drawUpathsTrig:(int) cell;
{
    float bbox[4];
  . . .
    bbox[0] = bounds.origin.x;
    bbox[1] = bounds.origin.y;
    bbox[2] = bounds.origin.x + bounds.size.width;
    bbox[3] = bounds.origin.y + bounds.size.height;
  . . .
    drawUpathsTrig(
        pts, ops, CLR1, WID1, viewcenter.x, viewcenter.y,
        maxdim * LEN1, maxdim, DEG1, bbox);
  . . .
}
```

5.4.4   Retaining User Paths in the Server

Retaining user path descriptions in the server is not highlighted as a method, but you might want to do it with this type of drawing. Storing a user path in the server is a matter of creating a user path description or using a static user path description, placing a name object on the stack, and sending the description to the server using **DPSDoUserPath( )** with *dps_def* as the *action* argument. This assigns the user path description (the value) to the name object (the key).

The drawing invocation is a matter of executing the description with the appropriate user path operand. Example 5.9 shows how this process works. Storing a description in the server eliminates the need to send the description to the server each time, which might be more efficient. This has benefits in a networked environment when the client and server are running on different machines or in other cases where data transmission is an issue. It is advantageous only for paths that are large, frequently drawn, and do not change. The wrap places the string on the stack as a literal to use as a key for the user path definition.

Example 5.9 *Defining and drawing user paths in the server*

PostScript language code

```
defineps PSWPlaceName(char *str)
  /str
endps

defineps PSWDrawUserPath (char *str)
  str ustroke
endps
```

C language code

```
/*
 * This definition is for the name of the user path array in
 * the server. A user object could be used as well.
 */
static char *upath1 = "upath1";

...
PSWPlaceName(upath1);
DPSDoUserPath(pts, i, dps_float, ops, j, bbox, dps_def);
...


...
PSWDrawUserPath(upath1);
...
```

5.5   Comparison of Times

Table 5.2 lists times in milliseconds for drawing hash marks using the three methods in the Dial application.

Table 5.2 *Times for constructing paths*

Method	4 Lines	8 Lines	36 Lines	360 Lines
Display times in milliseconds				
Wraps with Rotation	6	12	31	209
Wraps with Trigonometric Calculations	5	11	30	195
User Paths with Trigonometric Calculations	5	11	28	110

The two examples in Table 5.2 that show slower results should not necessarily be discounted. For types of drawing different from that shown with the dial, these methods might be preferred because either the methods are easier to implement or the drawing is not too extensive.

5.6 Conclusions

- A user path is a Level 2 and Display PostScript extension that provides the most efficient way to construct and render paths in the PostScript language. User paths offer a compact and convenient way to draw previously existing or dynamically created paths.

- A user path is a complete and self-contained path description that consists of path construction operators and their coordinate operands expressed as literal numbers.

- The bounding box for a user path description is composed of the lower left and upper right coordinates. It is not the origin and size dimensions associated with the *NXRect* structure.

CHAPTER 6

User Objects and Graphics State Objects

The Display PostScript system contains features designed specifically for drawing in a display environment. Using the Clock application, this chapter examines two of these features, user objects and graphics state objects, which are useful for managing other objects within a display.

A *user object* is an integer identifier of a PostScript language object in the server. User objects refer to objects in the server using integer keys rather than name keys. PostScript language objects, such as arrays, strings, dictionaries, or graphics states, can be referenced by user objects. User objects are more convenient to store and manipulate in C than PostScript language variable names, which must be stored as strings.

Note   *A user object is different from a user path. The first is an identifier to an object in the server, and the second is a path description.*

A *graphics state* is a collection of parameters that determine how and where a path is rendered. A *graphics state object* (or *gstate*) is a PostScript language data type that encapsulates the values of the parameters that make up a graphics state. Gstates provide more flexibility than the graphics state stack for setting the current graphics state. A gstate can be installed as the current graphics state by performing a **setgstate** operation, circumventing the **gsaves** and **grestore** operations normally used within a page description.

Gstates allow switching between states and can improve performance in uses such as scrolling. There is some memory cost associated with using them. Their principal use, however, is as a handle to the device. The current device in the graphics state determines where imaging occurs, in a window or offscreen buffer. By managing a list of gstate objects associated with different devices, an application can easily and efficiently switch between devices using the **setgstate** operator.

Although user objects and graphics state objects provide a slight performance advantage over conventional methods, their primary usefulness is in simplifying object management in the server.

The Clock application used in this chapter examines three additional drawing techniques:

- Using an offscreen buffer eliminates redrawing the clock face every tick.

- Storing the user path descriptions of the clock hands in the server eliminates retransmitting the descriptions each time a hand is drawn.

- Scaling the View object and then redefining the graphics states for the hands scales the clock hands within the view without explicitly scaling each graphics state or user path description fragment.

Storing user path descriptions in the server is addressed in Chapter 5, "Path Construction and Rendering." This technique can improve performance by approximately 20% over retransmitting the user paths with each redrawing. Although the performance difference is not as significant here, the primary reason they are stored in the server is that it simplifies the drawing invocation. Since the description of the clock hands doesn't change, it is better to store them in the server rather than to transmit them every time.

The Clock application differs from the Dial application in that the Clock application uses user objects rather than character strings to refer to the user paths in the server.

6.1 Clock Application

A simple clock illustration, as shown in Figure 6.1, is used to highlight the techniques discussed in this chapter.

Figure 6.1 *Clock*

The clock is composed of a view within a window. The view has six visual components:

clock face   hour hand
seconds hand   minute hand
seconds hand shadow   alarm hand

Figure 6.2 *Clock components*

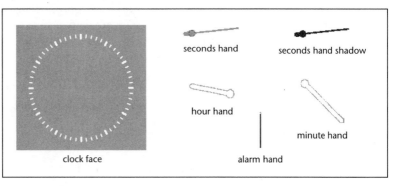

Almost all the hands have a different offset from the center of the clock face and a different color and line width attribute. The path descriptions are stored in the server as user objects. The drawing position, color, and line width for each hand are encapsulated in a graphics state object that is also stored in the server as a user object.

Using a gstate to manage information eliminates translating each hand before drawing. This approach provides a slight performance gain, but its principal advantage is that it provides cleaner, more manageable switching between drawing states.

6.2 User Objects

In the examples shown in Figure 6.2, graphics state objects are retained as *user objects*. User objects provide an efficient way to refer to PostScript language objects in the server. The traditional way is to use a key, which is normally a name object.

When referring to PostScript objects in the server in the Display PostScript system, initialized character arrays or string literals can be used and sent as arguments with wraps. This approach may become difficult to manage if more than a few objects are used. User objects allow you to tag objects with an integer instead of a name, saving space and allowing you to dynamically provide identifiers in both the client application and in the server.

Note   *Use names to refer to objects when writing PostScript language by hand because the dictionary lookup mechanism has been optimized for names. However, referring to objects as names becomes a problem when referring to PostScript objects in the client program.*

Example 6.1 is taken from the Dial application. It uses initialized character strings to refer to user paths in the server. The character strings are sent to the server first to define the user path and then again to refer to the user path when rendering.

Example 6.1 *Defining a name object*

PostScript language code

```
defineps PSWPlaceName(char *str)
  /str
endps

defineps PSWDrawUserPath (char *str)
  str ustroke
endps
```

C language code

```
/*
 * This definition is for the name of the user path array in
 * the server. A user object could be used as well.
 */
static char *upath1 = "upath1";

...
PSWPlaceName(upath1);
DPSDoUserPath(pts, i, dps_float, ops, j, bbox, dps_def);
...


...
PSWDrawUserPath(upath1);
...
```

```
...
/upath1
[(<5780 byte string> ) ( <721 byte string>)] def
...


...
upath1 stroke
...
```

Example 6.2 shows the sequence used in the Clock application to define user paths as user objects. The operands and operators for the user paths are stored in one of the client files as initialized float and character arrays. They can also be stored in a section of a Mach-O segment. For each user path, an array of points and an array of operators are sent to the server within a wrap and placed on the stack as a single array of two elements.

The **DPSDefineUserObject( )** procedure is used to define the user object. A zero (0) is passed as an argument prompting the procedure to create a new object identifier. Subsequent references to the user paths use this object.

Example 6.2 *Defining a user object*

PostScript language code

```
defineps PSWSetUpath (float Pts[Tot_Pts]; int Tot_Pts;
        char Ops[Tot_Ops]; int Tot_Ops)
   [Pts (Ops)]
endps

defineps PSWUpathFill(userobject UPath)
   UPath ufill
endps
```

C language code

```
/*
 * These are the user path operands and operators for the clock hands.
 * They are sent and stored in the server.
 */
static float ptsSec[ ] = { -10, -30, 10, 170, -1.5, 0, 0, 145,
      3, 0, 0, -145,4, 0, 0, -20, 0, -20, 5.5, 360, 180, 0,
      20, 4, 0, 0, 0, 0, 0, 10, 360, 0};
static char opsSec[ ] = {dps_setbbox, dps_moveto, dps_rlineto,
      dps_rlineto, dps_rlineto, dps_rlineto, dps_rlineto, dps_arcn,
      dps_rlineto, dps_rlineto, dps_closepath, dps_moveto, dps_arcn,
      dps_closepath};
```

```
int upathSec;

...

PSWSetUpath(ptsSec, sizeof(ptsSec)/sizeof(float),
    opsSec, sizeof(opsSec)/sizeof(char));
upathSec = DPSDefineUserObject(0);
...


...
PSWUpathFill(upathSec);
...
```

PostScript language trace

```
...
[[32 number array] <14 byte string>]
21exch
defineuserobject
...


...
21 execuserobject ufill
...
```

User objects are recommended for gstates, dictionaries, large arrays
or strings, user paths, and other objects stored in the server that can
be directly invoked from the client application. User objects can also
identify procedures, but procedures are usually called from within
wraps instead of from the client application directly.

User objects are stored in the userdict dictionary in an array called
UserObjects. This array is defined as read-only, and specific operators
(**defineuserobject**, **execuserobject**, and **undefineuserobject**) are available
for placing, executing, and removing objects in the array.

The **defineuserobject** operator takes two arguments, a nonnegative
integer index and the object to be defined. The object to be defined
is placed in the array at the position specified by the index. If the index
already exists, the new object replaces the existing one. If the index
does not exist, the number of entries in the array is extended to include
the new index. The **UserObjects** array is created in private VM.

In the NeXT implementation, do not call **defineuserobject** directly.
Many Application Kit methods define user objects, and any integer keys
you select might overwrite those already used by Application Kit
methods. Use **DPSDefineUserObject( )** instead.

This procedure handles the allocation of new identifiers and recycles existing identifiers. Pass a zero (0) to the procedure to create a new identifier. Pass the current identifier to reassign it. When a user object identifier is assigned to another object, the first object is made available for garbage collection as long as no other references to the object exist. The first does not need to be explicitly freed with the **undef** operator. (The **undef** operator is a Display PostScript operator that explicitly frees memory for a previously defined PostScript object.)

The user objects in the graphics state objects for the hands of the Clock are not redefined. When the graphics state for a hand changes, the new structure is copied into the old structure because a graphics state is a composite object. The user object retains a pointer to this structure.

Figure 6.3 is the **UserObjects** array for the Clock application. Entries 0-13 have been allocated by Application Kit objects used in the application. Entries 14-22 have been allocated by the ClockView object for the gstates and user paths for the hands.

Figure 6.3 *UserObjects array for the Clock application*

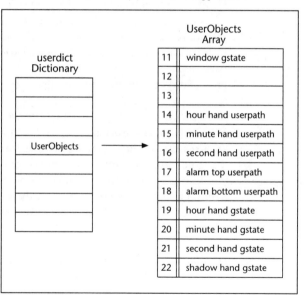

If user object identifiers are passed in single operator calls and wraps as type **userobject**, the Client Library performs an **execuserobject** on the identifier. Example 6.3 shows a sample **userobject** type.

Example 6.3 *Sample userobject type*

```
defineps PSWUpathFill(userobject UPath)
  UPath ufill  % An execuserobject is unnecessary
endps
```

6.2.1 Printing Issues with User Objects

The NeXT Print Package provides user object emulation, but you must define user objects in the page description in order to use them. The definition can occur in one of three sections in the description: the setup section for the document, the setup section for each page, or the script for each page. (Refer to Appendix G, "Document Structuring Conventions," in the *PostScript Language Reference Manual, Second Edition* for a further description of these sections.)

The document setup section is the usual location for the definitions because it has a global scope. Anything defined in this section can be referred to throughout the document.

Defining user objects within the page setup section brackets the definitions within the page level **save/restore** pairing. Because the page **restore** removes the definitions, they must be defined in the page setup section of every page. (The page-level **save/restore** pair ensures that any page can be extracted from the document, combined with the document prolog and document setup, and printed successfully.)

Defining user objects within the page section not only runs into the page level **save/restore** pairings but also into any downloadable font **save/restore** pairings. Placing **save/restore** constructs around downloadable fonts reclaims PostScript server virtual memory and enables you to use an unlimited number of downloadable fonts. User objects defined within a page section not only must be redefined for each page but potentially for each set of downloadable fonts. (Typically, three or more fonts can be included within a **save/restore** pairing.)

Note   *Defining user objects in the prolog rather than the document setup section creates problems for print managers that strip prologs out of files. Some print managers store procedure sets in printer memory and, therefore, strip out prologs in order to print faster and save space.*

6.3   Graphics States

Painting operators such as **stroke** and **fill** and character rendering operators such as **show** and **xyshow** cause an image to be transferred to the page or screen. These operators use parameters to decide which pixels to turn on and which ones to leave off. This set of parameters makes up a graphics state. The current graphics state defines the environment in which printing operators execute. See section 4.2, "Graphics State," in the *PostScript Language Reference Manual, Second Edition.*

Table 6.1 contains a list of device-independent parameters that make up a graphics state, as well as their default values.

Table 6.1 *Device-independent graphics state parameters*

Parameter	Definition
alpha[†]	A value that represents the amount of transparency the current color will have. Default: 1.0, opaque.
clipping path	The path that defines the current boundary against which output is cropped. Default: frame rectangle for a Window or View.
color	The color that will be used during painting operations. Several color models can be specified. Default: 0, black.
dash pattern	A description of the dash pattern to be used when lines are rendered by the **stroke** operator. Default: a solid line.
font	The set of graphic shapes (characters) that define the current typeface. Default: undefined.
instance drawing mode[†]	A Boolean value that determines whether the temporary drawing mode, called instance drawing, is on or off. Default: false, off.
line cap	A number that defines the shape of the endpoints of any open path that is stroked. Default: 0, square butt end.
line join	A number that defines the shape of joins between connected segments of a stroked line. Default: 0, mitered joins.
line width	The thickness in user coordinates of lines to be drawn by the **stroke** operator. Default: 1.0 in user space coordinates.
miter limit	The limit of the length of line joins for line segments connected at a sharp angle. Default: 1.0.
path	The path that would be rendered by a fill or stroke operation. Default: undefined.
position	The current position in user space, also known as the current point. Default: undefined.

| stroke adjustment | A Boolean value that determines whether automatic stroke adjustment is on or off. Default: true, on. |
| transformation matrix | The matrix that maps positions from user space to device space. Default: default CTM. |

† NeXT specific

Table 6.2 contains a list of device-dependent parameters that make up a graphics state, as well as their default values.

Table 6.2 *Device-dependent graphics state parameters*

Parameter	Definition
device	A set of internal primitives for rendering graphical objects in a particular area of raster memory. Default: specified at context creation time.
flatness	A number that reflects the accuracy with which curves are rendered. Smaller numbers give smoother curves at the expense of more computations. Default: 1.0.
halftone phase	A shift in the alignment of halftone and pattern cells in device space to compensate for window system operations that involve scrolling. Default: 0, 0.
halftone screen	A collection of objects that define the halftone screen pattern for gray and color output. Default: a device-dependent, type 3 halftone dictionary.

The NeXT drawing guidelines instruct that the current graphics state must be the same when leaving a View object as when entering except for the color, position, path, font, and line width. The **display** method of a view encapsulates the **drawSelf::** message between **gsave** and **grestore** operations through the use of the **lockfocus** and **unlockfocus** methods. As a result, the gstate is automatically restored when using **display**. Any drawing that bypasses **display** should use the **lockfocus** and **unlockfocus** methods to focus the view and restore the graphics state to its initial state after drawing.

A view typically inherits the graphics state left by its superviews. It is important to set the correct parameters before drawing. In addition, a view must explicitly set the color, position, path, font, and line width since these parameters are not guaranteed to be a specific value.

6.3.1 Graphics State Stack

Managing graphics states in devices without graphics state objects involves moving graphics states on and off the graphics state stack with **gsave** and **grestore** operations. The graphics state stack is appropriate in a printing environment since the drawing is highly structured. The **gsave** and **grestore** operators isolate major changes in the current graphics state, with minor changes accomplished by setting and resetting parameters.

Most states in a page description are based on the previous state and are used for only one instance. It makes little sense to initialize them, store them, and install them when needed, as is done with graphics state objects. In a page description, it is often easier to change the parameters as the drawing proceeds.

Note   *In some cases, it is more efficient to use the operand stack to save and reset previous parameter values than it is to use a **gsave/grestore** nesting. For example, a **currentlinewidth/setlinewidth** can encapsulate a change to the line width without a **gsave** and **grestore**, as shown in the following line of code:*

```
currentlinewidth 0.5 setlinewidth stroke setlinewidth
```

6.3.2 Graphics State Objects

Changing the parameters in a graphics state is important in a display environment. Many graphical objects are drawn repeatedly within the same or different windows with each object sharing little resemblance to other objects. The clipping paths, coordinate systems, and drawing attributes can be different from one window or view to another window or view. It is, therefore, more efficient to retain graphics states in the PostScript server virtual memory for significant and frequently invoked drawing objects.

When the objects are drawn, the graphics state can be installed with one operator instead of storing and resetting each parameter individually. Gstates offer an alternative to managing gstates with **gsave** and **grestore**.

In the NeXT Application Kit, graphics state objects are used principally for Window objects. These objects often have distinct coordinate systems as well as clipping paths.

In addition, and in what is really the key to graphics state objects, windows reserve space in raster memory. The device component in the graphics state serves as the link to this memory. When the gstate is set with a **setgstate** operation, the device in the Window object's gstate becomes the current device, installing the raster memory for the window as the drawing buffer. Using a gstate for a window provides a convenient and efficient way to install a coordinate system, a clipping path, and the window's raster memory.

In addition, NeXT compositing operations use gstates to locate the source image in raster memory and set its transformation matrix as the CTM. The NeXT NXImage class allocates a gstate by default. The View class, on the other hand, does not, so a gstate must be allocated explicitly for a view when compositing from it. Using the window's gstate as an argument to the NeXT composite operations won't give the effect you want if the CTM of the window and view are not identical.

Note   *Compositing is a method of accumulating separately rendered images into a final image. It encompasses simple copying as well as more sophisticated operations that take advantage of transparency.*

Gstates are optional for views. Since views don't reference raster memory, they don't benefit from gstates as significantly as windows. The principal reason for using a gstate is to install a particular graphics state at the time the view is focused instead of inheriting the state from the previous view. In other words, a gstate can be allocated and initialized with a specific set of parameters. When the view is focused, the parameters in its graphics state are installed as the current parameters.

Although more rare and not recommended (for reasons outlined in the following paragraphs), gstates can also be used for images within views. This approach is used for the hands of the clock, making the drawing of each hand easier and slightly faster. Each hand has a separate translation and color. A gstate is used to retain these values, so they do not have to be set explicitly before each hand is drawn.

A gstate takes up about two hundred bytes of virtual memory (with a NULL current path), so there is some cost to using a graphics state object. Using a gstate for each graphical object in a drawing application uses up an appreciable amount of memory in the server. In addition, parameters that change are likely to change frequently, requiring constant resetting of the gstate in the server. Creating a page description that can be printed to devices without gstate support requires a relatively inefficient emulation of gstate operators.

Instead of using gstates to hold the parameters for each graphical object, use structures entirely within the client. Immediately before drawing each object send these parameters to the server, changing the settings in the current graphics state.

Because the path and clipping path are saved in the gstate, set these parameters to the values you want when the gstate is defined. (Typically, these paths are empty.) Defining a gstate with a nonempty path installs the path as the current path when the gstate is made the current gstate. Any subsequent rendering operator prior to a **newpath** operator renders the path in the current color, line width, etc.

The same treatment applies to a clipping path: any nonempty clipping path clips subsequent drawings. You can use a gstate to retain a path, but it is not recommended. Using a cached user path or an offscreen buffer is a better approach for painted paths.

An example of gstates in action is scrolling. The movement of the scrollbar must coincide with the scrolling of the text or graphic. This is done by quickly alternating between the Scroller and the ClipView. A gstate is used for the ClipView, which allows the quick installation of the clipping path and the coordinate system with a single operation. This installation provides a critical performance advantage over creating the clipping path and making the coordinate system adjustments individually.

6.3.3   Allocating Graphics States in Views

The default instance of a view does not have a gstate associated with it, but one can be allocated with the **allocateGState** method of the View class. If a gstate is specified, it is installed as the current graphics state during the **lockFocus** message. If no gstate is specified, the window's gstate is installed and adjusted to reflect the view's coordinate system and clipping path.

The PostScript language trace in Example 6.4 shows the operations sent to the server for a custom view contained in a window. The instructions are sent by methods of the View class. The view object has set the clipping to *YES* but has not allocated a gstate.

1. The **lockFocus** method performs a **gsave** and installs the window's gstate as the current graphics state. (The Application Kit stores the gstate in the server as a user object.)

2. A clipping path is installed around the bounds of the view.

3. The user space is translated to the lower left of the view's bounding box.

4. After the drawing instructions, the **flushgraphics** and **grestore** operators are invoked by the **unlockFocus** method. (The **grestore** makes the previous graphics state the current graphics state.)

Example 6.4 *Setting the graphics state without a gstate*

PostScript language trace

```
gsave
11 execuserobject setgstate
52 38 302 152 rectclip
52 38 translate

< drawing instructions placed within drawSelf:: would appear here >

flushgraphics
grestore
```

When a view allocates a gstate, the PostScript language instructions look like those in Example 6.5. The view's gstate is installed, which, in this instance, is stored as user object 20 instead of the window's gstate (11). No clipping path or translation occurs because the values are part of the gstate.

Example 6.5 *Setting the graphics state with a gstate*

PostScript language trace

```
gsave
20 execuserobject setgstate

< drawing instructions placed within drawSelf:: would appear here >

flushgraphics
grestore
```

6.3.4 Initializing a View's Graphics State

A view instance can allocate a gstate to store particular values for the graphics state parameters. These values are installed as the current values in the graphics state when the view is focused with the **setgstate** operator. This is appropriate when the initial settings differ from those inherited from the last graphics state upon focusing. Performance savings, though, are minimal. This approach is more for convenience or special circumstances.

The parameters of a gstate can be initialized in a two-step process:

1. Override the **initGState** method in the View class. The appropriate single operator or wrap calls to configure the graphics state parameters are placed in this method.

2. Send a message to the **notifyToInitGState** method with a *YES* argument, then allocate a gstate by sending a message to the **allocateGState** method.

Calling **notifyToInitGState** causes the **initGState** method to be invoked when a gstate is created (at the time it is first needed, which is usually the next time the view is displayed).

Example 6.6 shows the steps that initialize a gstate. The PostScript language trace that results is generated from a combination of the View methods and the single operators placed in the **initGState** method.

Example 6.6 *Initialize the gstate in a View object*

C language code

```
/*
  * Called next time the view lockFocuses after
  * receiving the notifyToInitGState message
  */
- initGState
{
  PSsetlinewidth(2.0);
  PSsetgray(0.5);
  PSsetlinejoin(2);

  return self;
}

/*
  * Placed either in the initFrame: method or
  * in some other initial method
  */
[self notifyToInitGState:YES];
[self allocateGState];
```

PostScript language trace

```
gstate
19 exch defineuserobject
2.0 setlinewidth
0.5 setgray
2 setlinejoin
19 execuserobject currentgstate
pop
```

In the trace,

- The **gstate** operator creates a graphics state object.

- The second line defines the gstate as a user object. The next three lines set the gstate parameters (the results of the single operator calls in the **initGState** method).

- The current gstate operation copies the new gstate into the old gstate structure. A gstate is a composite object, so the user object points to the structure for the gstate. Since the user object identifier points to the same structure as before, it doesn't need to be redefined. (A gstate is a composite object, so the user object points to the structure for the gstate.)

The **pop** removes the gstate left on the stack by **currentgstate**.

You can redefine a view's graphics state object with the following steps. They produce the same trace as the previous trace except that the old gstate is installed as the current gstate and is not reallocated.

1. Lock the focus to the view.

2. Change the gstate parameters (by making single operator or wrap calls).

3. Copy the current gstate into the old gstate structure with the **currentgstate** operator.

4. Remove the gstate from the stack with the **pop** operator.

5. Unlock the focus.

The source code and the PostScript language trace appear in Example 6.7.

Example 6.7 *Redefining the gstate in a View object*

C language code

```
[self lockFocus];
    PSsetlinewidth(0.5);
    PSsetgray(0.25);
    PSsetlingjoin(1);
    PScurrentgstate([self gState]);
    PSpop( );
[self unlockFocus];
```

PostScript language trace

```
gsave
19 execuserobject setgstate
0.5 setlinewidth
0.25 setgray
1 setlinejoin
19 execuserobject currentgstate
pop
grestore
```

In Example 6.7, **gsave** and **setgstate** are invoked by **lockfocus** and **grestore** is invoked by **unlockfocus**.

6.3.5   Printing Issues with Graphics State Objects

Gstates are difficult to emulate using Level 1 operators. One example of an emulation is to store the values of the parameters in an array. When defining a gstate, the current graphics state parameters are placed into the array. When setting a gstate, the values in the array are taken out of the array and made the current graphics state parameters.

This solution has memory and performance problems as well as being very difficult to implement. As a result, we do not recommend using graphics state objects in the printing process. You should set parameters explicitly, and use the **gsave** and **grestore** operators when printing to manage the graphics state.

6.4 Offscreen Buffers

In the Clock application, the clock face is drawn at initialization and whenever the window is resized. Instead of drawing directly into the view, the application draws the clock face into an offscreen buffer or bitmap, an NXImage object. For each tick, the offscreen buffer is composited into the window, then the hands are drawn on top of the image. The clock uses a window with a buffered backing, so the window is not flushed onto the screen until the drawing has been completed, resulting in no discernible drawing flicker.

Figure 6.4 *Clock face*

Example 6.8 shows the C language code for drawing the clock face.

Example 6.8 *Drawing the clock face*

C language code

```
/*
 * Invoked at initialization and whenever the window is
 * resized. The frame size of the view is used instead of
 * the bounds size because the bounds size does not
 * reflect the correct size after scaling relative to a
 * an outside object.
 */
- drawFace
{
  NXsize size;
  if (imageId)
  {
    [imageId getSize:&size];
    if (size.width < frame.size.width ||
        size.height < frame.size.height)
      [imageId setSize: &frame.size]
  }
  else
  {
    imageId = [[NXImage newSize:frame.size]
```

```
        setFlipped:NO];
    }

    [imageId lockFocus];

    /* Draw the clock face. */
    . . .
    [imageId unlockFocus];

        return self;
}

/*
    * Invoked whenever the clock is drawn. The bounds
    * argument is an instance variable in view that
    * defines the size and position of the view.
    */
- drawSelf:(NXRect *)r :(int)count
{

    . . .
    [imageId composite:NX_COPY toPoint:&bounds.origin];
    . . .

    return self;
}
```

It is wasteful to use an offscreen buffer to hold an image like a rectangle because **rectfill** is a simple and efficient operation. Offscreen buffers are recommended for complex images that remain unchanged for a long time. A 400 by 400 point clock face takes approximately 3/10 of a second to draw. Since it remains the same unless the window is resized, it makes more sense to draw it into an offscreen buffer, then composite it into the window before drawing the hands.

Offscreen buffers for the hands are not appropriate because the hands are rotated. Since images cannot be rotated easily, an offscreen buffer is necessary for every position of each hand, using more than 200,000 buffers. Storing the user path descriptions for the hands in the server provides the optimal solution to imaging the hands.

6.4.1 Printing Issues with Offscreen Buffers

The highest quality results are obtained for each device by directly executing the PostScript language operators that describe each graphic or image. Offscreen buffers can be printed using the **image** operator, but they are limited to the resolution of the screen. Offscreen buffers should be used only during interactive display, not for the printing process. When printing, you should render the graphics with PostScript operators to obtain the best results for a particular device.

6.5 Storing Data in the Server

Deciding which items make good candidates for storing in the server is really a matter of judgement. Gstates and dictionaries are not visible outside the server, so they must reside in the server. Data structures such as arrays, strings, and user paths can be retained in either the client or the server.

The determination as to whether to keep structures in the server comes down to several factors: the size of the structure, the frequency of its execution, the number of times the structure changes, and the client-server network transmission overhead. In most cases, these structures do not belong in the server, but in some cases, it makes sense to store the data in the server rather than to keep passing it from the client.

The hands of the clock are objects that can be retained in the server. They have moderately sized descriptions, are called repeatedly, and do not change. Once the descriptions are sent to the server, the client has no need for them.

Calling a wrap to draw the user path and passing the appropriate user object identifier is the only client responsibility. The declaration, definition, and invocation are shown in Example 6.2. Interactive applications, such as drawing programs or word processing, have little use for storing data in the server; the data changes too frequently to be worth managing identical copies in both the server and the client.

6.6 Scaling a View

The Clock application scales the view in which the hands reside in order to scale the hands. The coordinate systems for the hands are based on the coordinate system of the view. As a result, the scale of the view is captured in the redefinition of the graphics state for each hand. Scaling the view instead of each image provides an easy way to globally scale a drawing that contains multiple images.

Figure 6.5 *Clock scaled to different sizes*

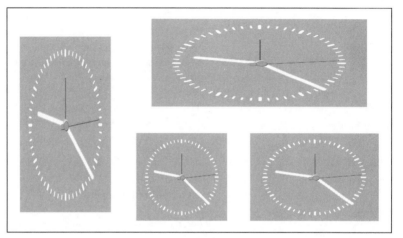

The coordinate system of a View object can be altered with the **scale::**, **moveTo::**, and **rotate::** methods available in the View class. These methods have the same effect on the current transformation matrix in the graphics state object of the view or window as the **scale, translate**, and **rotate** operations have when performed with a wrap or single operator call. Instead of redefining the gstate to incorporate the new CTM, a matrix is concatenated to the CTM after the gstate has been installed through a **lockFocus** message.

Note   *These methods change the graphics state relative to its present state. Doubling the scale of a view that has been scaled to one half its scale returns the view to its initial scale. As a result, some instance variables might be needed or some ratios made between the frame size and the bounds size in order to scale to an absolute value.*

The code segment in Example 6.9 shows how the **scale::** method is used to distort the clock without changing each element in the clock. Resizing a window also resizes the content view, which in this case is the ClockView. Because of this, it is possible to override the **sizeTo::** method in the View class and insert a message to the **scale::** method. When the window resizes, not only will the ClockView resize, but it will scale in order to fill the entire content region. The clock face is redrawn and the gstates for the hands are redefined at this time.

Example 6.9 *Scaling the view when the view resizes*

C language code

```
/*
 * The width and height arguments make up the
 * new frame size. The xframe variable holds the
 * previous size. The ratio of the two provides the
 * new scale.
 */
- sizeTo:(NXCoord)width :(NXCoord)height
{
    NXRect  xframe;

    xframe = frame;
    [super sizeTo:width :height];

    if (xframe.size.width && xframe.size.height)
    {
        [self scale:width/xframe.size.width :height/xframe.size.height];
        [self drawFace];
        [self defineGStates];
    }

    return self;
}
```

The **sizeTo::** method changes the sizes of both the *frame* and the *bounds* instance variables, while the **scale::** method changes the scale of the *bounds*. As a result, when the window is made smaller, the **sizeTo::** makes the *frame* and the *bounds* smaller, but **scale::** returns *bounds* to its previous size.

When referring to the size of a view, use the dimensions that are relative to a particular object. The *frame* size should be used by external objects to obtain the unaffected dimensions, while the *bounds* size should be used by the view internally to reflect its size in its own coordinate system. To resize the offscreen buffer for the clock frame, use the *frame* variable because it holds the true size. To move to the center of the view to place the hands, use the *bounds* variable because it provides the value in the altered coordinate system.

Note *The HitDetection application uses the **sizeTo::** and **scale::** methods to zoom in and zoom out of a document. See Chapter 8, "Hit Detection, Scaling, and Redrawing."*

6.6.1 Printing Issues with Scaling the Coordinate System

Printing a scaled view prints a scaled image. Applications that use a scaled or rotated view for the sake of zooming or rotating a page must set the graphics state of the view to its default scale before rendering a normal-sized and scaled image.

6.7 Conclusions

- User objects provide a convenient mechanism for referring to PostScript objects in the server using an integer identifier instead of a name identifier.

- A graphics state is a collection of parameters that determine how and where a path is rendered.

- A graphics state object (gstate) is a PostScript language data type that encapsulates the values for a particular graphics state.

- A graphics state object allows indiscriminate switching between drawing states and devices.

- The device component in a graphics state for a window serves as a link to the raster memory. Using the **setgstate** operation with a window or view, gstate installs the raster memory of the window as the drawing buffer. The NeXT **composite** operation also uses a gstate argument as a link to the raster memory for the source image.

- Simplify complex drawings by isolating portions of an image that do not change frequently, drawing them in offscreen windows or NXImage objects, and compositing them to the main drawing window when needed.

CHAPTER 7

Drawing Small Objects

Previous chapters have looked at ways of drawing lines either randomly or around a dial, timing each variation, and explaining and comparing the results. This chapter takes a similar approach by using the ControlPoint application to look at and compare seven ways to display a large number of control points (or any arbitrary object).

Using the ControlPoint application, however, the issue is not only the display time for each approach, but also the consistency between each of the control points and the device independence of each approach. Control points are typically very small; the ones used in this application are five points across. At such small sizes, a one-pixel variation in how a path maps from user to device space can have a significant impact on appearance.

This chapter introduces techniques that display a large set of small images efficiently, as well as consistently and device independently, by looking at seven ways of displaying up to 1000 randomly selected control points.

You can display four different shapes of points: a filled square, an open square, a cross, and an x. The areas highlighted for each approach include the display time, the algorithm to display n points, the control point description, the consistency between two or more points, and the device independence of the point.

The ControlPoint application is shown in Figure 7.1.

Figure 7.1 *ControlPoint application*

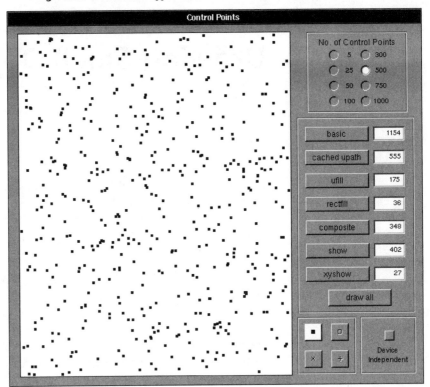

The approaches used to draw control points are

- Basic drawing, which uses **rmoveto**s and **rlineto**s within wraps

- User paths with cache, which represents each control point as a cached user path, translating to each point location before rendering

- User paths, which places a set of user path subpaths (one for each control point) into a large array and then executes a single **ufill** or **ustroke**

- Rectangle operations, which passes an array of rectangles to the **rectfill** and **rectstroke** operators (only for rectangular control points)

- Compositing an image, which draws the control point into an offscreen buffer and then composites the image at each control point location

- The **show** approach, which takes advantage of the font-caching mechanism by turning the control points into a Type 3 font program and using the **show** operator to display the points

- The **xyshow** approach, which behaves like **show** except the **xyshow** operator is used instead of **show**.

The fastest, simplest, and most consistent approaches are the rectangle operators and the **xyshow** operator. Both approaches are significantly faster (by at least a factor of four) than the other approaches. Drawing 500 squares takes approximately 38 milliseconds using **rectfill**, 27 milliseconds using **xyshow**, and 175 milliseconds using the next closest approach, user paths.

The calling sequence for the rectangle operations and **xyshow** is much simpler, and displaying consistent control points across different device resolutions surpasses the other methods. For drawing rectangles, **rectfill** and **rectstroke** are recommended. For drawing any other shapes, **xyshow** is recommended. (The **rectstroke** operator is slightly slower than **xyshow** for a stroked rectangle, but the convenience of the rectangle operators outweighs the minor performance differences.)

Both approaches have a few drawbacks. The rectangle operators are used only for rectangular control points; circles, stars, crosses, and x's cannot be represented. In addition, both methods display only a one-color image at a time. If you want multicolored control points, the methods must be repeated with a different color and shape.

Compositing is more than eight times slower than the **rectfill**, **rectstroke**, and **xyshow** operators, but it allows for multicolored and hand-tuned control points. However, in compositing, different bitmap images must be used for different display resolutions if you want the control points to scale with the display resolution.

The other four approaches, basic drawing wraps, user path caching, user path descriptions in large arrays, and **show** operations, are not suited for displaying a large number of control points. They have poorer performance and require greater complexity than the other three approaches. In addition, these approaches also have problems producing suitable images at extremely small point sizes.

7.1 Consistency and Device Independence

Rendering consistency and device independence are closely related. Consistency means that successive instances of the same control point or character appear the same regardless of the actual point location in the device space. Device independence means that the same description produces the same results on different resolution displays. At low resolutions and at small point sizes, these two issues are paramount because display anomalies are much more visible.

The Type 1 font format uses a hinting mechanism to produce consistent rasterizations in these instances. Other techniques outside the Type 1 font algorithms have a similar but less sophisticated capability for simple renderings.

Lack of consistency in drawing is readily noticeable on a single display. Lack of device independence is more subtle because it takes two devices with different resolutions for it to become apparent. Although device independence for display images receives little attention, it is becoming more important as more displays become available.

The same description might produce different results because the paths fall at different locations within a pixel in device space, as shown in Figure 7.2.

Figure 7.2 *Inconsistent control points*

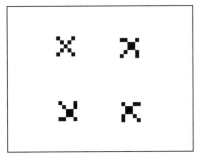

Same display, different locations

The different mappings from user space to device space turn on different pixels, as shown in Figure 7.3.

Figure 7.3 *Device-dependent control points*

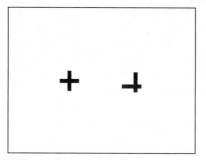

Different displays, same location

In the ControlPoint application, an array that contains 1000 point locations is created at initialization. These locations fall randomly at different locations within a pixel. Since the control points are five points across or less, small variations in the position of the control point can produce a noticeable difference in the appearance of the point.

In the case of the NeXT MegaPixel Display, one way to have the points appear consistently is to round the control point locations to the nearest integer. This works for the MegaPixel Display because of the one-to-one mapping from the default user space to device space. The correspondence means that a point location in user space maps to the same location in device space.

Relying on default mapping, though, is discouraged. Scaling or other transformations of the user space disrupt mapping, and other displays will have different resolutions and different mappings. Casting the drawing to one type of display produces problems when the drawing is performed on a different resolution display.

Some PostScript language operators perform a rounding adjustment automatically but round to device space and not to user space; the rectangle operators and the character **show** operators are two examples. Rounding to device space produces consistent rectangles and letters regardless of where the current point falls within a pixel. In the case of characters, the letters are consistent but not necessarily of good form.

The path locations might turn on undesired pixels. Type 1 font programs employ hints to constrain the paths and produce readable characters. Type 3 font programs can incorporate minor adjustments to produce a similar hinting capability.

The user path operators also round to device space, but they round the entire drawing, not each subpath. User path operators such as **ufill** and **ustroke** perform a temporary adjustment to the current transformation matrix (CTM) by rounding the origin to the nearest device boundary. This adjustment ensures that multiple renderings of the same path appear the same when the paths are placed at different locations by translating the user space.

The approach in this chapter that uses **ucache** to cache a single control point description benefits from this adjustment. The other user path approach, which puts the control point descriptions into a large array, does not. The change in position is done by moving explicitly to the new location and not through translation. As a result, the paths are not adjusted to device space.

By the nature of its operation, compositing a bit map aligns the image to pixel boundaries producing a consistent image. This image, though, is tied to one resolution and is not device independent.

Another technique for producing an acceptable control point for a single display is to hand tune the points in the path construction until an acceptable looking control point is produced. Adjusting the numbers by fractions of points can produce the control point you want. Problems arise, though, when these numbers are used on a different display with a different mapping to device space. The numbers for one device might not match another device and would produce inexact renderings.

A better solution is to round to device space, so the paths are always aligned with pixel boundaries. The basic drawing and font methods show techniques for doing this. Note that these methods use an algorithmic solution that is not tied to a particular device. (They are based on the stroke adjustment algorithm referred to in Chapter 3.)

In the case of basic drawing, the rounding doubles the display time. In the case of using a font, the description is only executed once, and the font machinery caches the resulting image. The roundings performed in the character description have no impact on performance. Rounding to device space, though, should be used only when necessary; for example, for small and exacting images. Larger images don't benefit as much from this exact positioning to device space.

7.2   ControlPoint Application

The ControlPoint application demonstrates techniques for drawing small control point shapes and measures the speed of each technique. The remaining sections of this chapter examine how these techniques are implemented in Objective-C on the NeXT computer.

The application creates an array of random locations at which to draw control points. You can display and time the drawing of a set of 5 to 1000 points. Four types of control points can be displayed. Each drawing technique uses a different way to describe the individual control points as well as a different algorithm for displaying the points.

For each approach, the control point drawing instructions, the display algorithm, and the PostScript language trace (the operations performed by the server) are listed for five points. A corollary to using time as an indication of performance is to look at the complexity of the source and the size of the trace. The three most favorable methods have the simplest calling sequence as well as the simplest and smallest traces. Reducing the amount of information sent to the server reduces both the transmission time and the processing time.

Several data structures are used by all the methods. The first variable, *XYArray*, is an array that holds 2000 coordinate values (randomly selected to fall within ControlView, the view that displays the points). Each consecutive pair of numbers make up a control point location. The values are sent in the wraps or placed in the arrays as the point locations for the following approaches.

An instance variable *indexOfPoints* provides the starting index into the array. The instance variable *numberOfPoints* contains the number of points to be displayed. The value is obtained from the tag of the selected radio button for the No. of Control Points control in the interface.

Some methods use two other arrays to send large data blocks to the server. The array *XYBuffer* holds any float numbers sent to the server. *XYBuffer* is used for the user path methods, the rectangle method, and the **xyshow** method to send the control point locations. Another array, *OpsBuffer*, holds the path construction operators for the user path method as well as the character values for **xyshow**.

7.2.1 Basic Drawing

The basic drawing approach displays control points by making calls to wraps. One call is made for each point. Four PostScript language procedures are used, each one describing a different type of control point. Only the procedure for the current shape is called.

Example 7.1 shows the wraps for the control points as well as two procedures to adjust the point locations to device space SA and RSA. The **PSWSetIndependent( )** and **PSWSetDependent( )** wraps activate and deactivate these two procedures. The wraps are invoked when the device-independent button is toggled in the ControlPoint interface. When the button is selected, the procedures are executed. When the button is not selected, the dummy procedure, **NOP**, is executed.

Example 7.1 *Control point descriptions*

```
/* This wrap is called in the initFrame: method to define and bind the
 * procedures. The procedures are invoked within another wrap.
 * The first 3 procedures, NOP, SA, and RSA, are used to adjust the
 * point positions to consistent locations in device space.
 */
defineps PSWDefsContPts ( )
 /NOP { } def

 /SA { % x y sa x' y'
   transform
   0.25 sub round 0.25 add exch
   0.25 sub round 0.25 add exch
   transform
 } bind def

 /RSA { %dx dy rsa dx' dy'
   dtransform
   round exch
   round exch
   idtransform
 } bind def

 /BRF{ %X Y
   sa moveto -1.5 -1.5 rsa rmoveto 0 3 rsa rlineto
   3 0 rsa rlineto 0 -3 rsa rlineto -3 0 rsa rlineto
   closepath
 } bind def

 /BRS{ %X Y
   sa moveto -2 -2 rsa rmoveto 0 4 rsa rlineto
   4 0 rsa rlineto 0 -4 rsa rlineto -4 0 rsa rlineto
```

```
    closepath
  } bind def

  /BX { % X Y
    sa moveto -2 -2 rsa rmoveto 4 4 rsa rlineto
    0 -4 rsa rmoveto -4 4 rsa rlineto
  } bind def

  /BC{ % X Y
    sa moveto 0 2 rsa rmoveto 0 -4 rsa rlineto
    -2 2 rsa rmoveto 4 0 rsa rlineto
  } bind def
endps

defineps PSWSetIndependent ( )
  /sa /SA load def
  /rsa /RSA load def
endps

defineps PSWSetDependent ( )
  /sa /NOP load def
  /rsa /NOP load def
endps
```

Example 7.2 shows the algorithm used to display the points for the basic drawing approach. This algorithm makes use of a wrap call, **PSWBasic( )**, that is passed the name of one of the four procedures in Example 7.1, as well as either a **fill** or **stroke** painting operator. The procedure name and operator to use are obtained with the **getBasicProc** and **getBasicOp** methods.

These methods return pointers to the strings containing the names of the procedure and painting operators. The local variable *basicProc* points to either *BRF, BRS, BX,* or *BC*. The local variable *basicOp* points to either **fill** or **stroke**. (Other ways to invoke these procedures are possible but not used here in order to use a single approach across all drawing methods.)

Example 7.2 *Basic drawing*

PostScript language code

```
defineps   PSWBasic(float X, Y; char *Figure, *Op)
    X Y Figure Op
endps
```

C language code

```
/* The drawing will center around the point passed in.*/
- drawBasic:(int)cell
{
  int   i;

  char *basicProc, *basicOp;

  basicProc = [controlPoint getBasicProc];
  basicOp = [controlPoint getBasicOp];
  ...
  PSWEraseView( );
  PSsetlinewidth(0.15);

  for (i = indexOfPoints; i < indexOfPoints + (numberOfPoints*2);
      i = i+2)
    PSWBasic(XYPoints[i], XYPoints[i+1], basicProc, basicOp);
  ...

  return self;
}
```

PostScript language trace

```
39.540001 478.549988 BRF fill
200.600006 197.649994 BRF fill
310.220001 339.709991 BRF fill
92.360001 474.529999 BRF fill
204.139999 492.670013 BRF fill
```

Using conventional path construction operators is not recommended for this type of drawing. Comparing times shows that this is the slowest of all the methods because each wrap incurs overhead and because the wraps contain many PostScript operations. These two features combined generate a lot of unnecessary setup, data formatting, and operator execution.

In addition, this approach has difficulty producing consistent images unless expensive adjustment procedures are performed. Without adjustments, the random location of the current point within a pixel causes pixel variations across images. The procedures used to eliminate this problem by rounding to device space produce a consistent and device-independent solution, but at the expense of performance. Rounding to device space almost doubles the display time, a significant factor since this is the slowest approach explored.

Figure 7.4 *Basic drawing*

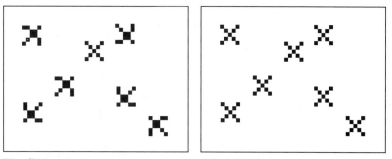

No adjustment   Adjusted to device space

7.2.2   User Paths

Although user paths draw much of the focus and recommendation in Chapter 5, they do not perform as well here as some of the other approaches for drawing control points. User paths are suited for both large, existing paths and dynamically created paths. The existing paths can be retained in a static array and both can be passed directly to the server. Both instances are straightforward, efficient uses of user paths, but for the type of drawing examined in this chapter, other approaches are more suitable.

In this section, we look at two cases of user paths. The first, user path cache, takes a single description and translates it to each control point location before rendering. The second places a set of user path descriptions for control points into a large array and performs a single **ufill** or **ustroke** operation (for a large number of control points, several waves are necessary). Both uses are unacceptable for drawing control points from performance and image quality standpoints.

Note   *For a description of a more appropriate use of the user path cache, see Chapter 9, "Drawing Issues and Scrolling."*

Drawing control points requires that the same description be drawn in a number of places. Translating to each control point location or placing a description for each control point into an array is not an efficient approach. The amount of data sent to the server and the limited ability to adjust the small sizes to device space makes these two methods less attractive than other approaches.

User Path Descriptions

Both cases use the same user path descriptions for the points (see Example 7.3). These descriptions are stored as float and character arrays in one of the application files. The first number in each array is the number of entries contained in the array. The information from these arrays is supplemented with other information and placed into other arrays before transmission to the server. (The supplemental information establishes a current point for these descriptions.)

Example 7.3 *Control point descriptions*

C language code

```
static float ptsrectfill[ ] = {8, -2, -2, 0, 4, 4, 0, 0, -4};
static char opsrectfill[ ] = {5, dps_rmoveto, dps_rlineto,
        dps_rlineto, dps_rlineto, dps_closepath};

static float ptsrectstroke[ ] = {8, -2, -2, 0, 4, 4, 0, 0, -4};
static char opsrectstroke[ ] = {5, dps_rmoveto, dps_rlineto,
        dps_rlineto, dps_rlineto, dps_closepath};

static float ptsX[ ] = {8, -2, -2, 4, 4, 0, -4, -4, 4};
static char opsX[ ] = {4, dps_rmoveto, dps_rlineto, dps_rmoveto,
        dps_rlineto};

static float ptsCross[ ] = {8, 0, 2, 0, -4, -2, 2, 4, 0};
static char opsCross[ ] = {4, dps_rmoveto, dps_rlineto, dps_rmoveto,
        dps_rlineto};
```

User Path Cache

User Path with Cache	
Display times of 500 points in milliseconds	
■ Filled	555
□ Open	571
+ Cross	575
× X	580

In this approach, a single generic control point is created that is centered around the location (0, 0). The user space origin is then translated to each control point location before rendering. The operands for the generic user path description (the bounding box, current point, and path values) are placed in *XYBuffer*. The literals for the **ucache**, **setbbox**, **moveto**, and path construction operators for the same point are placed in *OpsBuffer*.

In Example 7.4, the **getUserPtsArray**, **getUserOpsArray**, and **getUserOp** methods return the addresses of the user path description and the user path rendering operator. The variable *userPtsArray* holds the address of one of the four float arrays. The variable *userOpsArray* holds the address of one of the four character arrays. The variable *userOp* points to the character string *ufill* or *ustroke*. *FIGURESIZE* is the width and height of the largest control point, 4 points.

The user space is translated by performing a translate that is relative to the last translate performed. This relative translate is faster than an absolute translate encapsulated within a **gsave/grestore** nesting.

Note   *The user path and rectangle examples use the numstring data type to pass operands to the server. The numstring data type provides a 15-30% improvement over an ordinary PostScript array object; the savings occurs because unlike the PostScript array object, an encoded number string does not have to be scanned by the PostScript scanner. However, most Level 1 emulations of the user path and rectangle operators do not accept the numstring data type. When printing to Level 1 devices, use a wrap that does not include the numstring in the input declaration.*

Example 7.4 *Drawing with the user path cache*

PostScript language code

```
defineps PSWUserPath (float numstring Pts[Tot_Pts]; int Tot_Pts;
     char Ops[Tot_Ops]; int Tot_Ops; char *Op)
  [Pts (Ops)] Op
endps
```

C language code

```
- drawUserCache:(int)cell
{
  int    i, i_pt, i_op, j;

  char   *userOp, *userOpsArray;

  float  *userPtsArray;

  userPtsArray = [controlPoint  getUserPtsArray];
  userOpsArray = [controlPoint  getUserOpsArray];
  userOp = [controlPoint  getUserOp];

  . . .
  /*
  * Places a user path description for a generic control
  * point into the OpsBuffer and XYBuffer.
  */
```

```
i_op = i_pt = 0;
OpsBuffer[i_op++] = dps_ucache;

XYBuffer[i_pt++] = -FIGURESIZE/2;
XYBuffer[i_pt++] = -FIGURESIZE/2;
XYBuffer[i_pt++] = FIGURESIZE/2;
XYBuffer[i_pt++] = FIGURESIZE/2;
OpsBuffer[i_op++] = dps_setbbox;

XYBuffer[i_pt++] = 0;
XYBuffer[i_pt++] = 0;
OpsBuffer[i_op++] = dps_moveto;

for (j = 1; j <= userPtsArray[0]; j++)
  XYBuffer[i_pt++] = userPtsArray[j];

for (j = 1; j <= (int) userOpsArray[0]; j++)
  OpsBuffer[i_op++] = userOpsArray[j];


. . .
/*
* Performs an initial translate to the first location
* and then performs a relative translation thereafter.
*/
PSgsave( );
PStranslate(XYPoints[indexOfPoints], XYPoints[indexOfPoints+1]);

for (i = indexOfPoints; i < indexOfPoints + (numberOfPoints*2);
    i = i+2)
{
  PSWUserPath(XYBuffer, i_pt, OpsBuffer, i_op, userOp);
  PStranslate(XYPoints[i+2] - XYPoints[i],
      XYPoints[i+3] - XYPoints[i+1]);
}
PSgrestore( );
. . .

return self;
}
```

PostScript language trace

```
39.540001 478.549988 translate
[<9530000ec0800000c0800000408000004080000000000000000000000c0000
000c000000000000000404000004040000000000000000000000c0400000>
<0b0001020404040a>] ufill
161.059998 -280.899994 translate
[<9530000ec0800000c0800000408000004080000000000000000000000c0000
000c000000000000000404000004040000000000000000000000c0400000>
<0b0001020404040a>] ufill
```

109.619995 142.059998 translate
[<9530000ec0800000c08000004080000040800000000000000000000c0000
000c000000000000000404000000404000000000000000000000c0400000>
<0b0001020404040a>] ufill
-217.860001 134.820007 translate
[<9530000ec0800000c08000004080000040800000000000000000000c0000
000c000000000000000404000000404000000000000000000000c0400000>
<0b0001020404040a>] ufill
111.779999 18.140015 translate
[<9530000ec0800000c08000004080000040800000000000000000000c0000
000c000000000000000404000000404000000000000000000000c0400000>
<0b0001020404040a>] ufill
-65.979996 -281.380005 translate

The benefit of the user path cache is offset by performing a translate operation and then sending a user path description for each control point. As in the basic drawing case shown previously, two server operations are necessary for each control point.

A consistent image can be produced because the translation before each point adjusts the CTM uniformly. However, device-independent adjustments can't be made to the user path description to produce acceptable images at small sizes. The user path format limits the description to literal numbers and path construction operators. This restricted format precludes any attempt to round the points to device space with procedures like those used in the basic drawing method.

Figure 7.5 *Drawing with the user path cache*

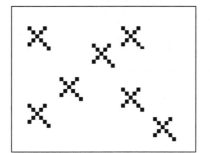

No adjustment

The user paths start in the same place in device space because of the adjustment to the CTM before each user path rendering operator. The individual path elements, though, cannot be adjusted because of the restricted user path format.

A Single Large User Path

User Path in a Large Array	
Display times of 500 points in milliseconds	
■ Filled	175
□ Open	100
+ Cross	75
× X	92

In the second case, a user path in a large array, placing a set of control points as user paths into a large array requires placing a **moveto** operation into the array followed by the path description for the point. Not only does this method require two large arrays, one for the points and another for the operators, it also calls for replicating the same user path descriptions many times in the arrays. The source code and the PostScript language trace appear in Example 7.5. The source code is tortuous and the trace large (when expanded to its full size): These two factors signal that it is not an acceptable approach.

The same wrap, **PSWUserPath( )**, is used to send the description and rendering operator to the server. The local variables *userPtsArray*, *userOpsArray*, and *userOp* also point to the same user path descriptions and operators. The bounding box of the user path is set to the size of ControlView's bounds, not to the size of a single control point, because all the points are drawn at their absolute locations. A **moveto** operation is placed into the user path description for each control point and followed by the description of the control point. This process is repeated for every control point.

Example 7.5 *Drawing with a single large user path*

PostScript language code

```
defineps PSWUserPath (float numstring Pts[Tot_Pts]; int Tot_Pts;
    char Ops[Tot_Ops]; int Tot_Ops; char *Op)
  [Pts (Ops)] Op
endps
```

C language code

```
- drawUserPath:(int)cell
{
  int   i, i_pt, i_op, j;

  char   *userOp, *userOpsArray;

  float *userPtsArray;

  userPtsArray = [controlPoint  getUserPtsArray];
  userOpsArray = [controlPoint  getUserOpsArray];
  userOp = [controlPoint  getUserOp];

  . . .

  XYBuffer[0] = bounds.origin.x;
  XYBuffer[1] = bounds.origin.y;
```

```
    XYBuffer[2] = bounds.origin.x + bounds.size.width;
    XYBuffer[3] = bounds.origin.y + bounds.size.height;
     OpsBuffer[0] = dps_setbbox;

    i = 0; i_pt = 4; i_op = 1;
    while (i < numberOfPoints * 2)
    {
      /*
      * This check sends the array to the server if the array
      * limit has been reached.
      */
      if ((i_pt + userPtsArray[0] > MAX_UPATHPTS) ||
          (i_op + (int) userOpsArray[0] > MAX_UPATHOPS))
      {
        PSWUserPath(XYBuffer, i_pt, OpsBuffer, i_op, userOp);
        i_pt = 4; i_op = 1;
      }

      XYBuffer[i_pt++] = XYPoints[indexOfPoints + i++];
      XYBuffer[i_pt++] = XYPoints[indexOfPoints + i++];
      OpsBuffer[i_op++] = dps_moveto;

      for (j = 1; j <= userPtsArray[0]; j++, i_pt++)
        XYBuffer[i_pt] = userPtsArray[j];

      for (j = 1; j <= (int) userOpsArray[0]; j++, i_op++)
        OpsBuffer[i_op] = userOpsArray[j];
    }
    PSWUserPath(XYBuffer, i_pt, OpsBuffer, i_op, userOp);
    . . .

    return self;
}
```

PostScript language trace

```
[( <220 byte string> )
<0001020404040a01020404040a01020404040a01020404040a01020404040a
>] ufill
```

Another drawback of this approach is that there is no way to adjust the positioning of control points in the array. Unlike the **ucache** method, the appearance of the control points can vary because the individual control points do not start in prescribed locations within device space. The user path rounding is only performed once, not for each point as in the previous case.

Figure 7.6 *Drawing with a single large user path*

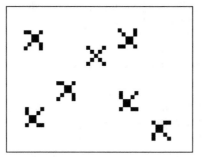

No adjustment

A less significant side effect occurring with user paths in a large array is that the subpaths (control points) are painted or stroked at that same time; that is, they appear on the screen simultaneously. All the other methods cascade the control points in a continuous procession. This is not a problem when drawing in a buffered window or when the number of operators is less than the recommended number per **ufill** or **ustroke**.

When drawing on the screen in an unbuffered window and when multiple rendering operators are necessary, the control points appear in waves. In the ControlPoint application, 1000 points causes three sets of points to appear with each set containing a few hundred points. The appearance of the three waves can be disrupting.

Note   *Arrays containing more than 2500 points can exceed either the path limit of the interpreter (version1.0 of Display PostScript) or the communications buffer in the Client Library resulting in run-time errors. As a result, an upper limit of 2500 points should be placed on user path arrays used for display. Applications that use the emulation provided by **DPSDoUserPath( )** to produce PostScript Level 1 language code should place the limit at 1500 points, the path limit for Level 1 printers.*

7.3   Rectangle Operations

Rectangle Operations	
Display times of 500 points in milliseconds	
■ Filled	36
□ Open	120
+ Cross	—
× X	—

The Display PostScript rectangle operators, **rectfill** and **rectstroke**, provide the simplest and second-fastest method of those presented in this chapter. The drawback is that this method can be used only for control points that have rectangular shapes.

The arguments for the rectangle operations can take three forms: four numbers describing a single rectangle, or an array or encoded number string describing an arbitrary number of rectangles. (See Example 7.6.)

Example 7.6 *Invocation for the **rectfill** operator*

PostScript language code

```
x y width height  rectfill
numarray   rectfill
numstring rectfill
```

Level 1 equivalent for the x y width height case

```
gsave
newpath
x y moveto
width 0 rlineto
0 height rlineto
width neg 0 rlineto
closepath
fill
grestore
```

The second and third forms perform the same function as the first except that the process is repeated several times.

Providing an array of rectangles for rectangle operations is much faster than calling operators multiple times, for the same reasons that user paths are faster than conventional drawing. Only one single operator call or wrap and only one PostScript language operator are necessary for displaying a large number of rectangles, minimizing the number of PostScript language operations executed. When the array of rectangles is replaced by individual calls to **rectfill**, the processing time increases tenfold from approximately 36 milliseconds to 350 milliseconds for 500 rectangles. Whenever possible, combine multiple rectangles, even different sizes, into a single operation.

In Example 7.7, *RECTOFFSET* positions the origin of the rectangle away from the control point center. *RECTSIZE* makes up the width and height of the rectangle. *RECTOFFSET* and *RECTSIZE* have values of 2 and 4, respectively.

Example 7.7 *Drawing with rectangle operators*

PostScript language code

```
defineps PSWRectDraw (float numstring XYScratch[j]; int j; char *rectOp)
  XYScratch rectOp
endps
```

C language code

```
/*
 * Here we have to calculate the offset from the center because
 * rectfill starts drawing at the location passed in.
 */
- drawrectOp:(int)cell
{
  int  i, j;

  char  *rectOp;

  rectOp = [controlPoint  getRectOp];

  . . .
  for (i = indexOfPoints, j = 0;
    i < indexOfPoints + (numberOfPoints*2); i = i+2, j = j+4)
  {
    /* Draw the rectangles if the array limit has been reached */
    if (j+3 > MAX_RECTANGLEPTS)
    {
      PSWRectDraw (XYBuffer, j, rectOp);
      j = 0;
    }

    XYBuffer[j] = XYPoints[i] - RECTOFFSET;
    XYBuffer[j+1] = XYPoints[i+1] - RECTOFFSET;
    XYBuffer[j+2] = RECTSIZE;
    XYBuffer[j+3] = RECTSIZE;
  }
  PSWRectDraw (XYBuffer, j, rectOp);
  . . .

  return self;
}
```

PostScript language trace

```
<95300014421828f643ee86664040000040400004347199a43442666404000
0040400000439a5c2943a91ae1404000004040000042b5b85243ec83d740400
00040400000434aa3d743f595c34040000040400000> rectfill
```

Note   *The NeXTstep C functions, **NXRectFill( )** and **NXRectFillList( )**, are not used in this example because corresponding **rectstroke** functions are not available.*

A limit of 500 rectangles per **rectfill** or **rectstroke** invocation is recommended. The **rectstroke** operator produces limitcheck errors in the first release of the Display PostScript system when passed an array of 600 or more rectangles.

7.4 Compositing

The next approach composites an image of a control point at each control point location. Although more than eight times slower than **xyshow**, compositing provides an advantage that **xyshow** does not: Multicolored control points can be used without having to render the control point multiple times. The other approaches require a separate invocation for each color in the control point.

The ControlPoint application uses an NXImage object to hold the image of the control point. Before the control point is drawn, the image is painted over with a white color and a transparent alpha. The transparent alpha of the image allows the portions of the drawing background covered by the image but not covered by the control points to show through.

Note   *The alpha value works with the NeXT compositing operation to provide different levels of transparency to pixels within an image. The values range from 0.0 for a transparent pixel to 1.0 for an opaque pixel. Most drawing is performed with an opaque value but a transparent value is useful for situations such as the one above, as well as for blending images. Transparency cannot be represented in a printed document so that all pixels have the equivalent of 100% opacity when printed.*

The basic drawing method is used to draw the control point in the image. The variable *basicProc* points to the name of the drawing procedure in the server while *basicOp* points to either **fill** or **stroke**.

Example 7.8 *Drawing the control point image*

C language code

```
- drawImage:imageId
{
  [imageId lockFocus];
    PSgsave( );
      PSsetalpha(0.0);    /* Transparent */
      PSsetgray(NX_WHITE);
      PSrectfill(0, 0, FIGURESIZE, FIGURESIZE);
      PSsetalpha(1.0);    /* Opaque */
      PSsetgray(NX_BLACK);
      PSWBasic(FIGURESIZE/2, FIGURESIZE/2, basicProc, basicOp);
    PSgrestore( );
  [imageId unlockFocus];

  return self;
}
```

Once the control point has been imaged, the only step required to display a point is to composite the bitmap at the point's location. An offset should be used so that the center and not the lower left or upper left corner of the image lies on the point location. Example 7.9 shows the source and trace for compositing a control point.

Example 7.9 *Drawing with compositing*

C language code

```
- drawComposite:(int)cell
{
  int    i;

  NXPoint  point;

  [controlPoint drawBitMap:imageId];


  . . .
  for (i = indexOfPoints; i < indexOfPoints + (numberOfPoints*2);
       i = i+2)
  {
    point.x = XYPoints[i] - FIGUREHALFSIZE;
    point.y = XYPoints[i+1] - FIGUREHALFSIZE;
    [imageId composite:NX_SOVER toPoint:&point];
  }
  . . .

  return self;
}
```

PostScript language trace

```
0 0 8 8 26 execuserobject 35.540001 474.549988 2 composite
0 0 8 8 26 execuserobject 196.600006 193.649994 2 composite
0 0 8 8 26 execuserobject 306.220001 335.709991 2 composite
0 0 8 8 26 execuserobject 88.360001 470.529999 2 composite
0 0 8 8 26 execuserobject 200.139999 488.670013 2 composite
```

The **composite** operator takes the gstate object of the image as one of its arguments. In the previous example, the gstate object is stored as a user object. The **26 execuserobject** retrieves the gstate object and places it on the stack. User objects and gstate objects are covered more thoroughly in Chapter 6, "User Objects and Graphics State Objects."

Since each control point requires a separate **composite** operator, the cumulative overhead of the calls accounts for the reduced performance in comparison to the rectangle operations and **xyshow**.

A major limitation of this approach is that it is device dependent. A bitmap is suitable only for one resolution. Whereas the other types of control point renderings are infinitely scalable, a bitmap does not scale particularly well, especially when the amount of data is small. As a result, if the size of a control point changes, a new image is necessary. The ControlPoint application draws the control point in the NXImage object using the basic drawing technique, which is acceptable since, like the font, the control point is rendered only once.

A *TIFF* file can also be stored in the *.nib* file for use as a control point image.

7.5 show and xyshow

The next two approaches use the font machinery to cache and display points. In each case, the character description is executed once, when the character first appears. Each subsequent display uses the description stored in the font cache. Rendering a character that is already in the font cache is up to 1000 times faster than converting it by scanning from the character description in the font.

The font cache does not retain color information; it stores the data as a mask. As a result, the color should not be set in the character descriptions. To produce color changes, change the current color in the current graphics state before invoking **xyshow**. If you want multicolored control points, repeat **xyshow** with a color change appearing between invocations, or use an NXImage object with the composite operation as described in section 7.4, "Compositing."

The font description used for **show** and **xyshow** does not appear in the following code segments but is covered in a later section. The **getChar** method returns the character that corresponds to the current control point. The **selectFont** method selects and scales the font. (*FONTSIZE* has a value of 5.) The **PSgsave( )/PSgrestore( )** nesting preserves the previous font.

7.5.1 show

show		
Display times for no adjustment and adjustment of 500 points in milliseconds		
■ Filled	402	407
□ Open	405	403
+ Cross	406	401
× X	407	403

The **show** operator is not recommended because each character requires a separate wrap to execute a **moveto** and a **show** operation. Control points do not appear together, so only a single character can be rendered per **show** operator. The font caching mechanism provides some benefit, but the advantage is offset by the overhead that each wrap incurs as well as the processing time required for each operator.

Example 7.10 *Drawing with the show operator*

PostScript language code

```
defineps PSWShow (float X, Y; char *Char)
  X Y moveto (Char) show
endps
```

C language code

```
- drawShow:(int)cell
{
  int  i;

  char fontchar[2];

  fontchar[0] = [controlPoint getChar];
  fontchar[1] = 0;
  [controlPoint selectFont:FONTSIZE];

  . . .
  PSgsave( );
    for (i = indexOfPoints; i < indexOfPoints + (numberOfPoints*2);
        i = i+2)
      PSWShow(XYPoints[i], XYPoints[i+1], fontchar);
  PSgrestore( );
  . . .

  return self;
}
```

PostScript language trace

```
39.540001 478.549988 moveto (a) show
200.600006 197.649994 moveto (a) show
310.220001 339.709991 moveto (a) show
92.360001 474.529999 moveto (a) show
204.139999 492.670013 moveto (a) show
```

7.5.2 xyshow

The **xyshow** operator works well for displaying control points. This operator takes a string of characters followed by an array or encoded number string of point displacements. The number of operations are minimal; in the case of the ControlPoint application, a single **xyshow** is used.

The size of the data necessary for **xyshow** is smaller than for either the rectangle operation approach or the user path approach. Only one character and two points are necessary to describe the control point for **xyshow**, whereas the rectangle operators need four points per control point and the user path description needs at least two points for each path construction operator plus an entry for the operator itself.

Note   *See Chapter 8, "Hit Detection, Scaling, and Redrawing," for a discussion of calculating the correct size of the control points during zooming.*

The array passed to **xyshow** contains the displacements relative to the previously placed character, not the absolute location of the character. The first two numbers in the array are the positions of the second character offset from the positions of the first. A current point must be established before executing **xyshow.** This relative positioning means that when a control point is moved, not only does the relative position for that point change, but also the relative position for the point immediately following.

Example 7.11 *Drawing with the **xyshow** operator*

PostScript language code

```
defineps PSWXYShow(float X, Y; char *CharString;
      float numstring XYCoords[j]; int j)
  X Y moveto  (CharString) XYCoords xyshow
endps
```

C language code

```
- drawXYShow:(int)cell
{
  int   i, j;

  char  fontchar;

  fontchar = [controlPoint getChar];

  /*
  * Place the characters into the character string for xyshow.
```

```
    * Terminate the string with a NULL character.
    */
    for (i = 0; i < numberOfPoints; i++)
      OpsBuffer[i] = fontchar;
    OpsBuffer[i] = 0;

    [controlPoint selectFont:FONTSIZE];

    . . .
    PSgsave( );
      /* Calculate the displacement from the previous character. */
      for (i = indexOfPoints+2, j = 0;
          i < indexOfPoints + (numberOfPoints*2); i++, j++)
        XYBuffer[j] = XYPoints[i] - XYPoints[i-2];

      /*
      * Provide a dummy set of displacements for the move after
      * the last character has been shown.
      */
      XYBuffer[j++] = 0;
      XYBuffer[j++] = 0;

      /* Establish a current point and then execute the xyshow. */
      PSWXYShow(XYPoints[indexOfPoints], XYPoints[indexOfPoints+1],
        OpsBuffer, XYBuffer, j);
    PSgrestore( );
    . . .

    return self;
}
```

PostScript language trace

```
39.540001 478.549988 moveto (aaaaa)
<9530000a43210f5cc38c733342db3d70430e0f5cc359dc294306d1ec42df8f5c
41911ec0 0000000000000000> xyshow
```

Unlike **rectfill** or **rectstroke**, **xyshow** can display different characters with a single operation. Two different types of control points can be drawn just by including different characters in the string that is passed to **xyshow**.

In both the **show** and **xyshow** cases, the consistency between images is handled by the font machinery. Each character is positioned at the same point within the device space to ensure that the same image is produced regardless of the user space point selected.

The font in the ControlPoint application employs the same procedure used in the basic drawing method to round the path placement to device space. This procedure provides device independence without sacrificing performance (the font cache reduces the number of times the description is executed). This approach works for the simple character descriptions that are employed. Applications that use more elaborate characters might consider the Type 1 font format. The following section contains details on the character descriptions used.

Figure 7.7 *Drawing with **xyshow***

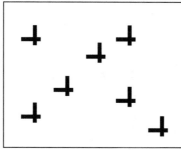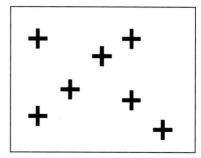

No adjustment (consistency handled by the font machinery)   *Adjusted to device space*

7.6   Creating a Type 3 Font

The most significant part of the **show** and **xyshow** approaches is to create a font of control points. The *PostScript Language Reference Manual, Second Edition* and the *PostScript Language Tutorial and Cookbook* provide more detailed information on how to create Type 3 fonts.

The font used in the example is a Type 3 font. A Type 1 font program can be created, incorporating hints to accommodate small point sizes and low resolutions. A description of this format is available in the *Adobe Type 1 Font Format* specification.

Each font program contains a number of key-value pairs. Some of these are used by the font machinery and must adhere to the correct syntax. Others are optional and user-definable. Each font must have the following keys: **FontMatrix**, **FontType**, **FontBBox**, and **Encoding**. In addition, each font must have a procedure called **BuildChar** whose job it is to render the character for the character code passed to it.

Note   *The **definefont** operator places an additional entry in the font dictionary. The key is FID and the value is an object of type fontID. In Level 1, the dictionary must be made large enough to accommodate this additional entry. In Level 2, dictionaries can grow beyond their initial capacity.*

Example 7.12 *Type 3 font definition for the four control points*

```
defineps PSWDefineFont(char *fontname)
  8 dict dup begin
  /FontName /fontname def
  /FontType 3 def
  /FontMatrix [.001 0 0 .001 0 0] def

  /FontBBox [-500 -500 500 500] def

  /Encoding 256 array def
    0 1 255 {Encoding exch /.notdef put} for

  Encoding
    dup (a) 0 get /Rectfill put
    dup (b) 0 get /Rectstroke put
    dup (c) 0 get /Ximage put
    (d) 0 get /Crossstroke put

  /CharProcs 5 dict def
  CharProcs begin
   /.notdef { } def
   /Rectfill {
      -300 -300 sa moveto 0 600 rsa rlineto
      600 0 rsa rlineto 0 -600 rsa rlineto
      closepath
      fill
   } def
   /Rectstroke {
      -400 -400 sa moveto 0 800 rsa rlineto
      800 0 rsa rlineto 0 -800 rsa rlineto
      closepath
      stroke
   } def
   /Ximage {
      -500 -500 translate
      1000 1000 scale
      5 5 true [5 0 0 5 0 0]
      {<88 50 20 50 88>} imagemask
   } def
   /Crossstroke {
      0 400 sa moveto 0 -800 rsa rlineto
      -400 0 sa moveto800 0 rsa rlineto
      stroke
```

```
      } def
    end

    /BuildChar { % font dict, char code
      500 0 -500 -500 500 500 setcachedevice
      exch begin
        true setstrokeadjust
        Encoding exch get
        CharProcs exch get
        exec
      end
    } def
    end
  /fontname exch definefont pop
endps
```

7.6.1   Required Keys

FontMatrix describes the mapping of the character to the user coordinate system. Just as the CTM uses a matrix to map to device space, a font program uses a matrix to map to user space. This process avoids having to scale the character descriptions in order to scale the font. If you want a 10-point font, the matrix is scaled by 10. If you want a 12-point font, the matrix is scaled by 12. (The font matrix is either scaled by the scalar argument passed to **scalefont** or is concatenated by the matrix argument passed to **makefont**.)

Most font programs, including the one in the ControlPoint application, use a **FontMatrix** of [0.001 0 0 0.001 0 0] and define the characters in terms of a 1000-unit character coordinate system. In other words, a character is drawn with the idea that 1000 points in the character coordinate system will equal 10 points in a 10-point font and 20 points in a 20-point font.

In the font for the control points, the characters are centered at the point (0, 0) and extend to the left and bottom as well as to the right and top. This centers the character on the current point when the character is drawn.

The use of a 1000-unit coordinate system is partially historical and partially structural. The Type 1 font format employs a number encoding scheme to reduce the amount of space necessary to store integer values between -1131 and 1131. Working with a 1000-unit coordinate system allows for a suitable drawing range while taking advantage of the compact number representation.

Type 3 font programs do not employ this encoding scheme, but most use the same **FontMatrix** for uniformity.

Figure 7.8 *Font space to user space to device space mapping*

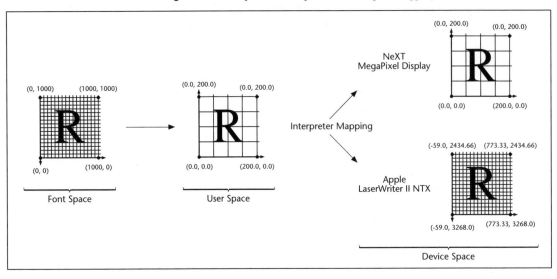

The **FontType** indicates where the information for the character description is found and how it is represented. Set the font type for a user-defined font to 3. The **FontBBox** gives the lower left and upper right coordinates for the bounding box that contains all the characters if they were to be imaged at the same point. The font machinery uses this array for setting clipping paths and making caching decisions.

The **Encoding** entry is an array of 256 names that maps the character codes to the procedure names. An application or a computer system might change a font's encoding vector to match its requirements. The index into the array is the character code. The entries of the array are procedure names that draw the characters. Therefore, juggling the entries changes the encodings.

In the ControlPoint font, the character codes for *a*, *b*, *c*, and *d* are used for the control points. The procedure names for the control points are placed in these locations of the encoding vector array. The **.notdef** procedure name is placed in all the other locations. Each character name has a procedure of the same name in the **CharProcs** dictionary. The **.notdef** procedure is used as a placeholder for unused characters.

The procedure for the character c draws an x using the **imagemask** operator. Image data can be incorporated into a Type 3 character description, but since the font cache doesn't represent color values, a mask must be used instead of an image. This approach is heavily device-dependent because of the limited ability to adjust the image to fit to device space.

Figure 7.9 *Encoding array and CharProcs dictionary*

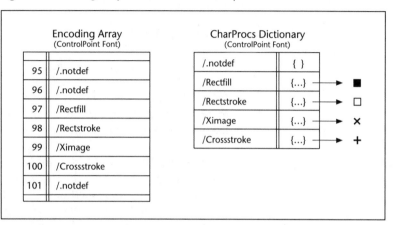

The elements of the string that pass to **show** and **xyshow** are treated as character codes. The character codes are used as indexes into the **Encoding** array to obtain a procedure name. The procedure name is then looked up in the **CharProcs** dictionary and its value executed. The **setcachedevice** in the **BuildChar** procedure sets the dimensions of the font cache, and the **setstrokeadjust** turns on stroke adjustment. Stroke adjustment is *off* by default when building a Type 3 font character.

7.6.2 Optional Keys

Optional keys typically used in font software are: **FontName, PaintType, Metrics, StrokeWidth, FontInfo, UniqueID, CharStrings,** and **Private.** The ControlPoint font only includes **FontName.** This name is separate from the name used to define the font and is provided for information only. The interpreter uses the name passed to it in the **definefont** operation to identify the font.

UniqueID provides a unique identifier for the system to identify characters that have already been created and cached. The font machinery uses this identifier to operate more efficiently across applications. Each font program that uses a **UniqueID** should have a different value. Font programs that have a **UniqueID** are cached across jobs while fonts that do not are cached for the immediate job.

UniqueIDs that are not unique can cause incorrect characters to appear. Adobe Systems Incorporated maintains a registry of **UniqueID** numbers. The font used in the ControlPoint application is localized to one application and relatively trivial, so a **UniqueID** is not used.

7.7 Printing Issues

The focus of this chapter has been the display of control points on the screen. The techniques used here can also be used to display an arbitrary number of objects as part of an application. An example would be to display stars within a star map. Such an application will more than likely want to print to a printer.

Only two methods are able to print without any adjustments: drawing with basic operators and using **show**. The PostScript language instructions produced by these methods are compatible with all PostScript language interpreters. User paths, rectangle operations, and **xyshow** need emulation procedures for Level 1 interpreters. Emulation for these operations are included in the NeXT print driver.

7.8 Comparison of Times Without Adjustment

Table 7.1 shows a comparison of display times, in milliseconds, without adjustment. These times are taken from the examples in this chapter.

Table 7.1 *Times for drawing small objects (without adjustment)*

Method	Filled	Open	Cross	X
Display times of 500 points in milliseconds				
Basic Drawing	1154	685	620	648
User Path with Cache	555	571	575	580
Large User Path	175	100	75	92
Rectangle Operations[†]	36	120	—	—
Compositing[†]	348	355	352	352
show	402	405	406	407
xyshow[†]	27	27	27	27

[†]*Indicates approaches acceptable from both a performance and image quality standpoint.*

7.9 Conclusions

- The amount of data and the number of PostScript language operators used in an operation have a direct correlation to its efficiency. Less data and fewer operators usually means a more efficient operation.

- The **rectfill**, **rectstroke**, and **rectclip** operators offer an efficient and convenient way to construct rectangles. The performance improvement is even more pronounced over Level 1 approaches when arrays of rectangles are passes to the rectangle operators.

- Turning symbols into characters in a Type 3 font format and using the **xyshow** operator reduces the number of operators needed to display the symbols while at the same time takes advantage of the font cache to quickly render the symbols.

- Multi-colored images require separate passes for each color when using **rectfill**, **rectstroke**, and **xyshow**. The slower performance for compositing an image lessens with each additional pass that is required.

- The **xyshow** operator takes relative distances as coordinates (the distance from the previous point) instead of the absolute point locations for the characters.

CHAPTER 8

Hit Detection, Scaling, and Redrawing

An application that allows you to draw on the screen handles a number of special circumstances that other applications do not. These include determining whether an object has been selected, enlarging and reducing the document, moving and redrawing selected objects, and scrolling through a document. This chapter, along with Chapter 9, "Drawing Issues and Scrolling," presents techniques to handle these issues.

In this chapter we examine hit detection, zooming, and redrawing. A brief description of Bézier curves is also provided. Chapter 9 provides more information on the user path cache and scrolling techniques. Performance is the driving force behind each of the techniques shown. A technique is acceptable only if it allows you to draw and redraw objects without a noticeable delay in response time.

The HitDetection application is used as an example of an interactive drawing application. Although it has limited functionality, its techniques can be applied to more ambitious projects.

You are provided with a scrollable drawing view that contains a single Bézier curve. The curve is selected by clicking the mouse when the cursor is at or near the curve. The application determines if the mouse point is near the curve by using the PostScript language operator **inustroke**. By choosing from a set of radio buttons, you can increase the sensitivity of the hit detection. (The radio buttons determine the size of the rectangle used to check for hit detection.)

Figure 8.1 *HitDetection application*

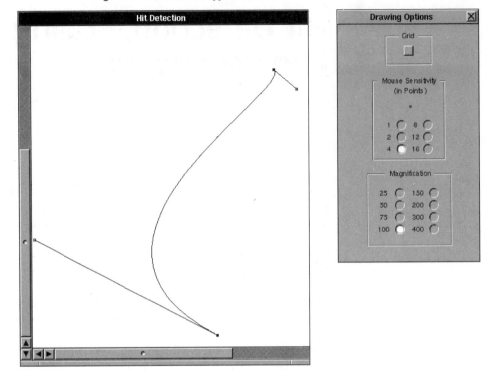

Once selected, you can grab a control point and change the shape of the curve, or grab the curve itself and move it to a different position in the view. Offscreen buffers decrease the amount of drawing done for each mouse movement. The view scrolls whenever the curve or a control point is grabbed and dragged outside the window. The image and the control points are constrained to the dimensions of the paper. (Some applications allow paths to go off the paper.)

A drawing application will more than likely allow magnification of the document. In this application, a set of magnification buttons allows you to enlarge and reduce the drawing field and image. Select the scale from the set of radio buttons and then mouse down somewhere within the view. The view zooms in or zooms out centered at the mouse down location.

This scaling action is accomplished in much the same manner as in the Clock application in Chapter 6. The **scale::** method sends a message to the view that contains the drawing, although in this case both the x and the y direction are scaled by the same amount. Scaling the coordinate system in which the curve resides is much easier than scaling the curve itself. Whenever a path appears, every point is transformed from user space coordinates to device space coordinates by the PostScript interpreter. As a result, it makes more sense to change the mapping than to change each point before the mapping. The **scale::** method provided in the View class accomplishes this action by altering the current transformation matrix, which maps the user space to device space.

8.1 Bézier Curves

The HitDetection application uses a Bézier curve as the selectable object. A Bézier curve in the PostScript language is described by four points. The first and last serve as endpoints of the curve and the second and third, even though they might not lie on the curve, influence the shape of the curve. Figure 8.2 shows a Bézier curve. Example 8.1 shows the parametric equation for the curve.

In the equations, the variable t ranges from 0 to 1. At each step in the range, each point has a varying amount of influence on the resulting x and y values. At $t = 0$, the value of x and y are the coordinates of the first point. As t increases, the values are pulled first toward the second point and then toward the third until, at $t = 1$, the values are the coordinates of the last point in the description.

Figure 8.2 *Bézier curve*

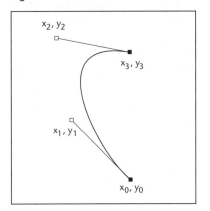

Example 8.1 *Parametric equation for the Bézier curve representation*

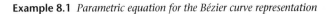

$$x(t) = (1-t)^3 x_0 + 3t (1-t)^2 x_1 + 3t^2(1-t) x_2 + t^3 x_3$$
$$y(t) = (1-t)^3 y_0 + 3t (1-t)^2 y_1 + 3t^2(1-t) y_2 + t^3 y_3$$

The curve is tangent to the line from the first to the second point at the first point, and tangent to the line from the third to the fourth point at the fourth point. This feature enables multiple Bézier curves to be joined with no loss in continuity. Other examples of Bézier curves appear in Figure 8.3.

Figure 8.3 *Bézier curve examples*

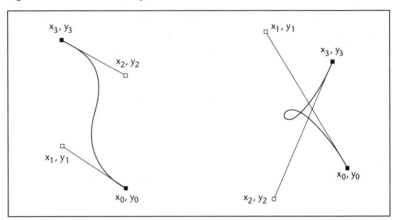

The operators **curveto** and **rcurveto** take six arguments. The current point is used as the first point in the Bézier description. The first two arguments form the second point, the next two the third, and the last two the fourth in the description.

The following are the PostScript language operators used to create Bézier curves:

$x_1\ y_1\ x_2\ y_2\ x_3\ y_3$ **curveto** –

$dx_1\ dy_1\ dx_2\ dy_2\ dx_3\ dy_3$ **rcurveto** –

The curve resulting from the four points lies within the convex shape formed by the points. The hit detection algorithm in HitDetection takes advantage of this characteristic by testing the bounding box formed by the points before continuing to a more exacting hit detection test using PostScript operators.

In HitDetection, the relationship between the first and second points is preserved when the position of the first point is changed. Likewise, the relationship between the fourth and third points is preserved when the fourth point is changed. When the second and third points are moved, the others are not affected. This action allows the size of the curve to grow or shrink while maintaining some of the shape of the curve. In addition, the previous image is kept as a reference during the move or redraw until the mouse button is released. Other interfaces for moving and changing the shape of a Bézier curve are equally valid.

Figure 8.4 *Bézier control point relationships*

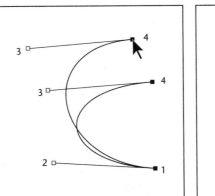 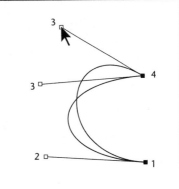

The relationship between the 3rd and 4th control points remains the same when the 4th control point is moved.

The 4th control point is unaffected when the 3rd control point is moved.

8.2 Hit Detection

The Display PostScript system contains six operators that determine whether a point is *on* or *in* a path. These operators were created specifically for interactive use and are

infill	**inufill**
ineofill	**inueofill**
instroke	**inustroke**

Each operator places a Boolean value on the stack. The operators **infill** and **ineofill** return *true* if any portion of the point or user path passed as an argument lies in the region painted by **fill** or **eofill** of the current path. The operator **instroke** returns *true* if any portion of the point or user path lies in the region painted by a stroke of the current path. The three operators in the second column are similar except they use a user path instead of the current path.

All the operators use the parameters in the current graphics state to determine whether the point or user path is in the correct region. This is especially important for **instroke** and **inustroke**, since the line width combined with the current path determine which pixels are used for the hit detection comparison. The line width for the hit detection check should be the same as when rendering the line.

HitDetection uses **inustroke** to determine whether the mouse point is on the Bézier curve. This operator takes two user paths and determines whether the first intersects the second. The first path contains the selection point; the second contains the description of the Bézier curve.

The selection point is a rectangle centered around the mouse point, with its size determined by a set of radio buttons provided in the user interface. The size of this rectangle determines the mouse tolerance or the distance the mouse can be from the curve and still select the Bézier.

Example 8.2 shows the invocation for the **inustroke** operator.

Example 8.2 *Invocations for the **inustroke** operator*

```
x y userpath inustroke bool
x y userpath matrix inustroke bool
userpath₁ userpath₂ inustroke bool
userpath₁ userpath₂ matrix inustroke bool
```

returns *true* if pixel at (x, y) or any pixels in userpath₁ would be painted by **ustroke** of the userpath (or userpath₂)

Example 8.3 shows a sample **inustroke** operator.

Example 8.3 *Sample **inustroke** operator*

```
{ % User path of the mouse rectangle
   247 230 251 234 setbbox
   247 230 moveto
   0 4 rlineto 4 0 rlineto
   0 -4 rlineto closepath
}
{ % User path of the Bézier curve
   156 171 331 290 setbbox
   218 171 moveto
   156 209 331 290 294 189 curveto
}
inustroke % true would be placed on the stack
```

The **inustroke** operator is not used to determine whether the mouse is *on* a control point. Because the control point and the mouse point are both rectangles, a quick test for intersecting rectangles can be made entirely within the client application. HitDetection uses the NeXT function **NXIntersectsRect( )** for this test. HitDetection also uses this procedure to check if the mouse point lies in the bounding box of the Bézier curve.

Using this procedure quickly determines whether a wrap should be sent to the server to perform the more sophisticated hit detection test. Performing a portion of hit detection or at least pruning the search tree in the client side of the application is recommended. The PostScript language hit detection operators are useful for objects such as curves and complex shapes, but it is usually more efficient to perform simple hit detection tests entirely within the client.

8.3 HitDetection Application

The code sequence to perform the hit detection appears in Example 8.5. Two objects take part in the check: a DrawingView object and a Bézier object. DrawingView manages the drawing in the window and responds to mouse down events. Bézier holds the points for the Bézier curve and sends the drawing and hit detection operators to the PostScript language server. A control point hit is checked first. Failing this test, a hit on the Bézier curve is checked.

A special structure called *UPath* has been created to hold user paths. It contains two pointers to arrays that contain the operands and the operators for the user paths as well as two integers that hold the number of elements in each array. The C declaration appears in Example 8.4.

Example 8.4 *C structure for representing user paths*

```
/*
 * The pts variable holds an array of floats that forms the
 * operands of the user path. The num_pts variable holds the
 * number of coordinates in the array. The ops variable
 * holds an array of characters that forms the operators of the
 * user path. The num_ops field holds the number of operators
 * in the array. (A null-terminated string is not sufficient
 * because 0 is a valid user path operator.)
 */
typedef struct _UPath {
    float   * pts;
    int       num_pts;
    char      *ops;
    int       num_ops;
} UPath;
```

The DrawingView class declares one of these structures as an instance variable *hitPoint*. This variable holds the user path for the hit detection rectangle. This user path is initialized when the DrawingView object is created, but several important components such as the mouse location and rectangle size are left until a mouse down occurs.

On a mouse down, after filling in the current mouse location and setting for the hit rectangle, DrawingView passes the user path to the Bézier object, which in turn sends this user path and the user path for the Bézier curve to the server in a wrap to perform an **inustroke** operation. This wrap, **PSWHitPath( )**, includes a return argument to hold the result of the **inustroke** operation. This value determines the next action, which is whether to display the control points.

Note   *Before sending a wrap to the server, a check is made to test whether the selection rectangle is in the bounding box of the Bézier curve. This check can prevent needlessly performing the **inustroke** operator. In a more sophisticated application, the search can be pruned further by testing the bounding box of the object and then the bounding boxes of each segment before proceeding with the call to the server.*

Example 8.5 *Hit detection method (DrawingView object)*

```
#define  NUM_POINTS_HIT   12
#define  NUM_OPS_HIT      6

/*
 * Instance variables - hitPoint holds the user path for
 * hit detection while drawUpath is a scratch buffer used for
 * several misc. purposes.
 */
@interface DrawingView:View
{
  ...
  UPath    hitPoint, drawUpath;
  ...
}

@implementation DrawingView

-initFrame:(NXRect *) frm
{
[super initFrame:frm];
  . . .
  NX_MALLOC(hitPoint.pts, float, NUM_POINTS_HIT);
  NX_MALLOC(hitPoint.ops, char, NUM_OPS_HIT);
  [self initializeHitPoint];
  . . .
```

```
    return self;
}

/*
 * The user path uses relative movements to reduce the number
 * of points that have to be inserted each mouse down.
 */
- initializeHitPoint
{
  int    i;

  for (i = 0; i < NUM_POINTS_HIT; i++)
    hitPoint.pts[i] = 0;

  hitPoint.num_pts = i;

  hitPoint.ops[0] = dps_setbbox;
  hitPoint.ops[1] = dps_moveto;
  hitPoint.ops[2] = dps_rlineto;
  hitPoint.ops[3] = dps_rlineto;
  hitPoint.ops[4] = dps_rlineto;
  hitPoint.ops[5] = dps_closepath;
  hitPoint.num_ops = 6;

  return self;
}

/*
 * A method in the DrawingView class. Invoked by the mouse down
 * event. The mouse point and the current hit setting dimensions
 * are placed in the hit point user path before invoking the
 * hitObject method of the Bézier object.
 */
- (BOOL) checkObject:(const NXPoint *) p
{
  BOOL   hit;

  float  hitsetting;

  hitsetting = [[NXApp  getDocument]  hitSetting];

  /*  Bounding Box */
  hitPoint.pts[0] = floor(p->x - hitSetting/2);
  hitPoint.pts[1] = floor(p->y - hitSetting/2);
  hitPoint.pts[2] = ceil(p->x + hitSetting/2);
  hitPoint.pts[3] = ceil(p->y + hitSetting/2);

  /*  Moveto */
```

```
    hitPoint.pts[4] = p->x - hitSetting/2;
    hitPoint.pts[5] = p->y - hitSetting/2;

    /*  Rlineto's */
    hitPoint.pts[7] = hitSetting;
    hitPoint.pts[8] = hitSetting;
    hitPoint.pts[11] = -hitSetting;

    hit = [objectId hitObject:&hitPoint];

    return hit;
}
```

Example 8.6 *Hit detection method (Bézier object)*

PostScript language code

```
/*
 *  The return value, Hit, is the result of the inustroke
 *  operation, either true or false.
 */
defineps PSWHitPath(float numstring HPts[Tot_HPts]; int Tot_HPts;
    char HOps[Tot_HOps]; int Tot_HOps; float numstring Pts[Tot_Pts];
    int Tot_Pts; char Ops[Tot_Ops]; int Tot_Ops | boolean *Hit)
  [HPts (HOps)]  [Pts (Ops)] inustroke  Hit
endps
```

C language code

```
/*
 *  Instance variable - the pts array in path contains the 4 bounding
 *  box coordinates plus the 4 points that describe the Bézier.
 */
@interface Bézier:Object
{
  UPath   path;  /* Holds the user path description for the Bézier. */
}
@end

@implementation Bézier

/*
 *  Check for hit detection on the object. This uses the
 *  inustroke operator to check for an intersection of the
 *  hit detection rectangle with the path of the Bézier.
 */
- (BOOL) hitObject:(UPath *) hitUpath
{
  int     hit = NO;
```

```
NXRect   aRect, bRect;

NXSetRect(&aRect, hitUpath->pts[0], hitUpath->pts[1],
    hitUpath->pts[2] - hitUpath->pts[0],
    hitUpath->pts[3] - hitUpath->pts[1]);
[self getBounds:&bRect  withKnobs:NO];
if (NXIntersectsRect(&aRect, &bRect))
{
  PSWHitPath(hitUpath->pts, hitUpath->num_pts, hitUpath->ops,
    hitUpath->num_ops, path.pts, path.num_pts, path.ops,
    path.num_ops, &hit);
}

return (BOOL) hit;
}
@end
```

PostScript language trace

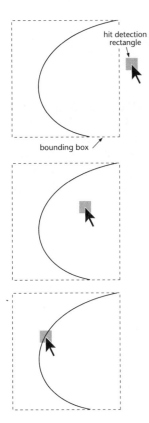

hit detection rectangle

bounding box

No trace. The mouse point lies outside the bounding box. No client-server message is sent.

[<9530000c433500004364000043390000436800004335000043640000000000
0004080000004080000000000000000000000c0800000> <00010404040a>]
[<9530000c4080000004188000043908000438880004390800041880000408000
00043210000432700004388800043538000043878000> <000105>] inustroke
% value returned ==> false

[<9530000c431d00004374000043210000437800004431d00004374000000000000
0004080000004080000000000000000000000c0800000> <00010404040a>]
[<9530000c4080000004188000043908000438880004390800041880000408000
00043210000432700004388800043538000043878000> <000105>] inustroke
% value returned ==> true

8.4 Zooming

A set of radio buttons in the HitDetection application enables you to scale the drawing view from 25% to 400%.

Note   *The user space in the PostScript language is, for the most part, infinitely scalable. The scale range in an application is only limited by the application's interface. The upper limit is 400% in this application, but the Scrolling application used in Chapter 9 allows scaling up to 1600%. Many Display PostScript applications allow the user to customize the list of scale factors because of the ease of zooming in the Display PostScript system.*

After you select the scale you want, the mouse icon changes to a zoom icon. When the you press the mouse button while in the DrawingView, the scale of the view changes to reflect the new scale. The View also scrolls so that the mouse location is the same after the zoom as before the zoom. This interface provides you with the same reference before and after the zoom.

HitDetection implements zooming by using the **scale::** method of the View class. The **scale::** method performs a PostScript language **scale** operation on the current transformation matrix (CTM).

A custom subclass of the View object (called DocView) has been created to make scaling and placement of the drawing view within the window easier. The DocView sits between the ClipView of the ScrollView and the DrawingView in the hierarchy. The DocView positions the Drawing-View in the center of the window and adds a drop shadow when the dimensions are smaller than the size of the window.

Figure 8.5 *ScrollView instance hierarchy in HitDetection*

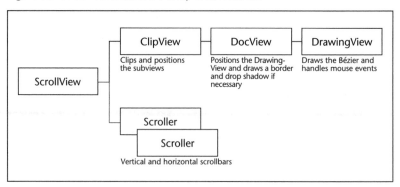

When the DrawingView receives a mouse down, it first checks to see if a zoom is taking place. If so, the point is passed to its superview, DocView. The DocView obtains the desired scale from the panel of buttons and then resizes and rescales the DrawingView. The resize is necessary because the scale does not change the frame of the DrawingView. The frame of the DrawingView must change to reflect its new size. The ratio of the old scale to the new scale determines the new size. Likewise, this ratio determines the new scale.

The scale ratio is necessary because the **scale** operation is relative to the current scale. The panel of radio buttons provides an absolute scale so a conversion must be made in order to end up at the desired absolute scale.

Example 8.7 *Zooming method (DocView object)*

```
/*
    * Instance variables - scale keeps track of the scale of the
    * drawing. Based off of 1.0 (a document at 100% will have a
    * scale of 1.0).
    */
@interface DocView:View
{
    ...
    float   scale;
    ...
}
@end

@implementation DocView

/*
    * Sizes the DrawingView from the old scale to the new scale.
    * The frame of the view is used because it provides the size
    * of the view in default coordinates. The bounds of the view
    * provides the size in scaled coordinates. As a result, the
    * bounds will always be the same regardless of the scale.
    */
- sizeView:viewId withScale:(float) newscale
{
    float    scalefactor, sizewidth, sizeheight;

    NXRect   viewFrame;

    [viewId  getFrame:&viewFrame];
    scalefactor = newscale/scale;
    sizewidth = viewFrame.size.width*scalefactor;
    sizeheight = viewFrame.size.height*scalefactor;
```

```
[viewId sizeTo:rint(sizewidth) :rint(sizeheight)];

    return self;
}


/*
 * Scales the DrawingView from the old scale to the new scale.
 * The scale method is relative so we use the ratio
 * of the old scale to the new scale to obtain the scaling factor.
 */
- scaleView:viewId  withScale:(float) newscale
{
    float    scalefactor;

    scalefactor = newscale/scale;
    [viewId scale:scalefactor :scalefactor];

    return self;
}
@end
```

In addition to scaling DrawingView during a zoom, DocView also places DrawingView in a specific location within the window. If DrawingView is smaller than the window, it is placed in the center of the window with a border and drop shadow placed around it. If DrawingView is larger, the view scrolls to the location where the mouse down occurred. The code segment for this is more involved than can be discussed here, but it can be found in the source code for the application.

Figure 8.6 *DrawingView at 50% scale*

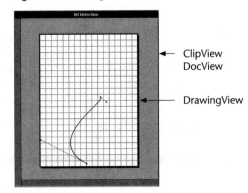

ClipView
DocView

DrawingView

When the DrawingView is scaled so that its frame is smaller than the frame of the ClipView, the frame of the DocView is sized to match the ClipView. In addition, the **drawSelf::** method of the DocView places a border and a drop shadow around the frame of the DrawingView.

Figure 8.7 *DrawingView at 100% scale*

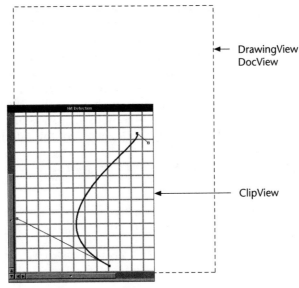

DrawingView
DocView

ClipView

When the DrawingView is scaled so that its frame is larger than the frame of the ClipView, the frame of the DocView is sized to match the DrawingView.

8.5   Control Points

Once an object has been selected, the control points and lines are drawn. Chapter 7, "Drawing Small Objects," compares six methods of displaying control points. In this application, an **xyshow** operator is used to display the points. Only four points appear, so there is little difference in performance between **xyshow** and any of the other methods.

The **xyshow** approach is used because of its simple interface. Two different control points appear: a filled rectangle and a stroked rectangle. Both types can be shown with one operation. If the rectangle operators are used, both a **rectfill** and a **rectstroke** operation are necessary. The font program created for the control points describes two different characters. At the time of display, the control point location and the characters are inserted into two separate arrays and then sent in a wrap that executes **xyshow.**

The code in Example 8.8 shows that the font size is altered to reflect the scale of the DrawingView. This change keeps the control points the same size regardless of the scale of the image. If the font size is not scaled, the control points are very large in a magnified DrawingView.

Making the control points the same size is a user interface issue. Some applications might allow the size to increase, but not at the same scale as the DrawingView. The algorithm used to display the control points and the font program that describes the control points are not included. Refer to sections 7.5, "show and xyshow," and 7.6, "Creating a Type 3 Font," in Chapter 7 for this information.

Example 8.8 *Constant control point size*

C language code

```
@implementation DocView
#define FONTSIZE    5

char fontname[ ] = "ControlPointsFont";

/*
 * Returns the size of the control point scaled to reflect the
 * current scale of the DrawingView. If the scaling were not done,
 * at 400%, a control point would look like an aircraft carrier.
 */
- (float) getControlPointSize
{
  return FONTSIZE * (1.0/scale);
}
@end

@implementation DrawingView

/*
 * Draw the control points and the control lines.
 */
- drawControl:(NXRect *)r  for:object
{
  PSselectfont(fontname, [superview getControlPointSize]);
  ...
```

```
        return self;
    }
    @end
```

PostScript language trace for control points at 400% scale

% unadjusted size

    /ControlPointsFont 5 selectfont

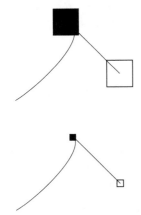

% adjusted size

    /ControlPointsFont 1.25 selectfont

8.6 Offscreen Buffers for Redrawing and Moving

One way to greatly improve drawing performance in any application is to draw only those areas or items that are necessary. This might mean drawing only the items that will be visible or only the items that change.

The Clock in Chapter 6 is an example in which only the items that change are drawn. The clock face is the same for each tick. The clock hands are the only items that change, so only they need to be redrawn. The rendering of the clock face is kept in an offscreen bitmap (an NXImage instance) and then composited into the main drawing window when needed. This saves having to redraw the clock face each tick. A similar technique is used in HitDetection to provide a fast response when redrawing or moving the curve.

In HitDetection, grabbing and dragging the curve moves the curve. Grabbing and dragging a *control point* alters the shape of the curve. HitDetection uses two offscreen buffers to reduce the amount of drawing needed when either of these events occur. (One is used for reshaping, two are used for moving.) These buffers are retained windows that are the same size as the drawing window. When the window is enlarged, the buffers are enlarged. The buffers stay the same size when the window is reduced.

Note   *The buffers are limited to the size of the visible portion of the DrawingView, which is slightly smaller than the size of the window. Larger buffers can be used, but it becomes difficult to keep track of the areas that are current and the ones that are not. In addition, buffers use an appreciable amount of memory. The larger the buffer the more likely that swapping into and out of memory will occur.*

One of the buffers holds the visible portion of the document before any change is made. In HitDetection, it holds the rendering of the Bézier curve and the grid, if displayed. In a more sophisticated application, this buffer would hold the rendering of all the visible objects. It's unnecessary to redraw unselected objects each time a selected object or a group of selected objects is altered or moved. Instead, the buffer containing the old image of the objects can be composited into the drawing window, and the new object or objects drawn on top. This is shown in Figure 8.8.

Figure 8.8 *Redrawing the curve using an offscreen window*

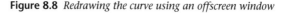

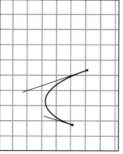
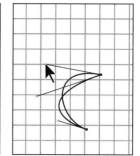

Offscreen Window 1: An offscreen window holds the contents before the change.

Portion drawn onscreen: The new Bézier is the only item in the window that must be redrawn.

Drawing Window: The offscreen window is composited into the drawing window, and the new Bézier is drawn on top.

In HitDetection, the contents of the first buffer are established at the time you move a control point or the curve. When this happens, the image in the drawing window is composited into the buffer. This image is then used in place of redrawing the old Bézier curve or, in a more sophisticated application, the unselected objects. The new curve is then drawn on top of this image in the drawing window.

This first buffer contains a ClipView that is synchronized with the ClipView in the drawing window. When the ClipView for the drawing window scrolls, the ClipView for the buffer scrolls. If this did not happen, the contents of the buffer would not be synchronized with the contents of the drawing window. In addition, the changes in the curve are made to a copy of the curve and not the original. If changes are made to the original, then the old Bézier disappears when the window scrolls because the description for the old curve no longer exists. Example 8.9 shows the event loop in HitDetection for changing the shape of the curve.

Example 8.9 *Redrawing the Bézier curve*

```
- redrawObject:(int) pt_num :(NXRect *)redrawRect
{
  id    copyId;

  BOOL tracking = YES;

  int   old_mask;

  ...

  NXEvent*event;

  /*
   * Composite the current image in the window into the first buffer.
   */
  [self  compositeBufferAlpha:NULL];

  /*
   *  Create a copy of the selected object. If we scroll we will need
   *  to redraw the old curve. If we do not create a copy we will
   *  not have an old curve.
   */
  copyId = [objectId  copy];
  [copyId  copyPts:objectId];
  ...

  old_mask = [window addToEventMask
          NX_MOUSEUPMASK|NX_MOUSEDRAGGEDMASK];
  event = [NXApp getNextEvent
          NX_MOUSEUPMASK|NX_MOUSEDRAGGEDMASK];
  if (event->type != NX_MOUSEUP)
  {
    while (tracking)
    {
      /* Get the point location and change in the copy. */
      ...
```

```
/* Scroll if necessary. */
...

/* Composite the old image and then redraw the new curve. */
PScomposite(rect_last.origin.x, rect_last.origin.y,
    rect_last.size.width, rect_last.size.height,
    [bufferAlpha gState], rect_last.origin.x
    rect_last.origin.y, NX_COPY);
[self drawObject:NULL for:copyId withUcache:NO];
[self drawControl:NULL for:copyId];

/* Flush the drawing so that it's consistent. */
[window flushWindow];
NXPing( );
...

    event = [NXApp getNextEvent:NX_MOUSEUPMASK|
        NX_MOUSEDRAGGEDMASK];
    tracking = (event->type != NX_MOUSEUP);
    }
    ...
}
[window setEventMask:old_mask];

[objectId free];
objectId = copyId;

...

return self;
}
```

During a move, the first buffer is the same as when reshaping. A second
buffer is used to hold a rendering of the curve. Only the location of the
curve changes, so as long as an image is available, it can be composited
to a new location throughout the event loop to simulate the move. The
first buffer (holding the old image and the grid) is composited first, and
the second buffer is composited on top. The background of the second
buffer is drawn with a white color and a transparent alpha so that only
the opaque portions of the image show through. A ClipView is not
needed for this buffer because unlike the first buffer, it doesn't need
to scroll with the drawing window. This is shown in Figure 8.9.

Figure 8.9 *Moving the curve using two offscreen windows*

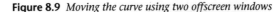

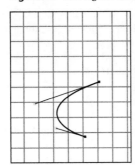 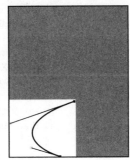 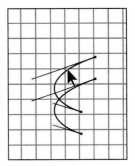

Offscreen Window 1:
An offscreen window holds
the contents before the
change.

Offscreen Window 2:
Another offscreen window
holds a rendering of the
Bézier. The background of
the image is transparent,
so it does not obscure any
drawing below.

Drawing Window:
The first offscreen window
is composited into the
drawing window and then
the second is composited on
top at the new location for
the Bézier.

When the Bézier curve is too large for the second buffer (common at an enlarged scale), it is drawn with a cached user path. The cached user path is translated to the new position during the event loop for the move to take advantage of the cache. (A user path that is translated to other locations has the same key in the cache, whereas a user path with different points does not.) Example 8.10 shows the event loop for the move.

Example 8.10 *Moving the Bézier curve*

```
- moveObject:(NXEvent *)event :(NXRect *)redrawRect
{
  BOOL tracking = YES, beta;

  int   old_mask;

  float scale;

  NXRect rect_now, rect_start, rect_last;

  ...


  /*
   * Composite the current image in the window
   * into the first buffer.
   */
  [self  compositeBufferAlpha:NULL];

  /* Check whether the object can fit in the second buffer. */
```

```
if (/* object can fit */)
{
  [bufferBeta  setDrawOrigin:rect_start.origin.x
      :rect_start.origin.y];
  [bufferBeta  lockFocus];
    PSsetgray(NX_WHITE);
    PSsetalpha(0.0);
    NXRectFill(&rect_start);
    PSsetalpha(1.0);
    [self  drawObject:NULL  for:objectId  withUcache:NO];
    [self  drawControl:NULL  for:objectId];
  [bufferBeta  unlockFocus];
  beta = YES;
}
else
  beta = NO;

...
old_mask = [window addToEventMask:
          NX_MOUSEUPMASK|NX_MOUSEDRAGGEDMASK];
event = [NXApp
getNextEvent:NX_MOUSEUPMASK|NX_MOUSEDRAGGEDMASK];
if (event->type != NX_MOUSEUP)
{
  while (tracking)
  {
    /* Get the point location and determine the new location. */
    ...

    /* Scroll if necessary. */
    ...

    /*
     * Copy the old image into the window. If using the second buffer, copy
     * it on top of the first buffer. Otherwise, translate and redraw.
     */
    PScomposite(rect_last.origin.x, rect_last.origin.y,
      rect_last.size.width, rect_last.size.height,
      [bufferAlpha gState], rect_last.origin.x
      rect_last.origin.y, NX_COPY);
    if (beta)
    {
      PScomposite(rect_start.origin.x, rect_start.origin.y,
        rect_start.size.width, rect_start.size.height,
        [bufferBeta gState], rect_now.origin.x
        rect_now.origin.y, NX_SOVER);
    }
    else
    {
```

```
    PSgsave( );
      PStranslate(rect_now.origin.x - rect_start.origin.x,
        rect_now.origin.y - rect_start.origin.y);
      [self drawObject:NULL for:objectId withUcache:YES];
      [self drawControl:NULL for:objectId];
    PSgrestore( );
  }

  /* Flush the drawing so that it's consistent. */
  [window flushWindow];
  NXPing( );

  ...
  }
  ...
  event = [NXApp getNextEvent:NX_MOUSEUPMASK|
        NX_MOUSEDRAGGEDMASK|timermask];

  tracking = (event->type != NX_MOUSEUP);
  }

  [objectId moveAll:&delta];
}


  ...

  [window setEventMask:old_mask];

  return self;
}
```

Taking steps to isolate the changes in an image can reduce the amount of drawing that must be performed, consequently reducing the amount of time spent drawing. In an interactive situation, this effort improves the response time. The difference might not be noticeable when only a few segments are drawn, but it can be quite significant with a large number of complicated paths.

8.7 Conclusions

- The Bézier curve representation used in the PostScript language provides a compact representation while at the same time preserving continuity at the endpoints. This allows a smooth transition between sets of joined lines and curves.

- The Level 2 and Display PostScript extensions provide six operators for determining whether a point or path lies *in* or *on* another path.

- Checking whether the bounding boxes for objects intersect can quickly eliminate many cases for using a more elaborate and expensive hit detection test.

- The flexible imaging model in the PostScript language helps when scaling documents. Changing the mapping from user space to device space is easier and more efficient than changing each point in each graphic to reflect the scale.

CHAPTER 9

Drawing Issues and Scrolling

This chapter focuses on the user path cache and its effect on scrolling. Scrolling is emphasized because it presents a case of repeated drawing of the same paths. When you are scrolling through a document, the display must be synchronized with the actions of the scroll bar, and the response must be immediate. Displaying a complex drawing must be as efficient as possible in order to meet this performance demand.

The Scrolling application is used to demonstrate several drawing issues. It can read in a file that has been processed by Distillery, an application that turns arbitrary PostScript files into a specific "distilled" format. Scrolling reads this format and produces the appropriate graphics structures, which include path, color, line width, line join, and paint type. These structures then appear using PostScript Level 1 operators, user paths, or cached user paths. The times for each method appear in Table 9.1 for comparison.

Figure 9.1 *Scrolling application*

The results appearing in Table 9.1 show that user paths are 25% faster than PostScript Level 1 operators (**moveto, lineto, curveto**, etc.). For example, a drawing with 90 fills and 22 strokes takes .65 seconds with operators versus .5 seconds using user paths. The results also show that while there is a 20% initial overhead cost for the user path cache, the resulting displays are up to two times faster than without the cache.

In certain situations, the results of the user path cache are often unpredictable due to the hit rate of the cache and the complexity of the drawing. In the test drawings, the user path cache approach performed two times faster at 100% scale, but three times better at 400% scale. The reason is the reduced number of paths drawn at 400% scale. The user path cache can be beneficial, but its use must be matched to the type of drawing performed.

Both the Nurse drawing (112 paths) and the Engine drawing (279 paths) show significant benefits with the user path cache. As the number of paths increase, and as the size of the drawing increases, the benefit of the cache begins to diminish. The King Tut drawing contains more than 3000 paths; cached user paths do not perform as well as non-cached user paths.

In addition to information on path construction and performance, this chapter covers several areas related to efficient drawing. These include

- Drawing every path versus only those whose bounding boxes lie in the region to be drawn

- Drawing a complete or preview image versus a wire frame image

- Combining the wire frame image as several large user paths instead of as individual user paths

- Setting the color, line width, and other line settings only when they change instead of for each path

- Drawing in a retained window versus a buffered window

9.1 Scrolling Application

The NeXT Application Kit provides support for drawing and scrolling. The View class provides much of the support for imaging using PostScript language operations. A subclass of View, called ScrollView, is designed specifically for scrolling. A ScrollView contains several subviews: ClipView, a document view, and one or two scrollers (scroll bars).

In the Scrolling application, a specially designed DocView is used. The view in which the main drawing takes place, the DrawingView, becomes a subview of the document view. The DocView positions the DrawingView within the ClipView at the time the DrawingView is scaled.

Several steps occur in an application during scrolling:

1. The portion of the image in the window that remains visible is composited to a new position.

2. The origin of the drawing view is repositioned within the ClipView.

3. The DocView and then the DrawingView are sent **drawSelf::** messages with the newly visible portion of the views passed as one of the rectangle arguments.

The views draw any objects that lie within the rectangles. In the case of the DocView, a border and a drop shadow for the Drawing-View are drawn if the DrawingView is smaller than the window. In the case of the DrawingView, any paths that lie within the visible rectangle are drawn.

4. When the view is finished, the scroll bar is drawn in its new position.

All the events in this sequence are handled automatically by the objects in the NeXT Application Kit except for the drawing in the view. The only thing you must do is include the commands that accomplish this. Figure 9.2 describes the scrolling sequence.

Figure 9.2 *Scrolling sequence*

A mouse event begins the sequence.

1. Any portion still visible is composited to its new location.

2. Only the portion that is new is redrawn.

3. The scroller is redrawn.

End result.

9.2 User Path Cache

The user path cache is a system resource of the PostScript server with a finite limit shared by all applications. Resource sharing isn't a problem because drawing is typically isolated to one application for long periods. However, don't write applications that rely on having images cached. If a single complex image is drawn frequently, such as a dial, the difference in response time between a cache hit and having to recache the image might be large enough to warrant drawing into a bit map and compositing the image onscreen.

Applications take advantage of the cache by placing **ucache** as the first operator in a user path description. The **ucache** operator has no arguments and is followed immediately by the **setbbox** operator.

The interpreter caches an internal representation of a path and uses a checksum of the coordinates and operands as the key to check for a given path. If a path is found in the cache, the interpreter does not need to reinterpret the path description. Example 9.1 shows an ASCII path description of a user path with a **ucache** operator.

Example 9.1 *Sample user path description with **ucache** operator*

```
{
    ucache
    0 0 100 100 setbbox
    0 0 moveto
    0 100 lineto
    100 100 lineto
    100 0 lineto
    closepath
} ufill
```

Note   *Finding a path in the cache can occur across a translated user space. This means that a user path appears as the same key in the cache even if it has been translated to multiple locations within a user space. Caching, though, cannot occur across rotating or scaled user spaces. User paths drawn in a user space transformed by either rotation or scaling are reduced and re-cached when they are first imaged in the new space. Once the image is re-cached, though, a caching hit can occur as before.*

The initial cost incurred for caching a user path is typically 1.2 to 1.5 times that of not caching a user path (which is about the same amount of time as PostScript Level 1 operators). The performance benefit, however, can be up to twice as fast once the paths in a drawing have been cached. Tables 9.1 through 9.3 summarize data for several files. The times are in seconds. The number in parentheses is the initial drawing time for a cached user path.

Table 9.1 *Times for the Nurse drawing*

Number of Paths: 112	Time
Display times in seconds	
Level 1	.650
User Paths	.498
User Paths with Cache	.220 (.600)*

81,919 bytes in user path cache–300,000 byte limit. 112 paths in user path cache–900 path limit.
*Initial setup time.

Table 9.2 *Times for the Caterpillar Engine drawing*

Number of Paths: 466	Time
Display times in seconds	
Level 1	1.250
User Paths	1.060
User Paths with Cache	.662 (1.495)*

112,017 bytes in cache. 279 paths in cache.
*Initial setup time.

Table 9.3 *Times for the King Tut drawing*

Number of Paths: 3114	Time
Display times in seconds	
Level 1	7.719
User Paths	7.128
User Paths with Cache	9.815 (9.829)*

299,898 bytes in cache. 841 paths in cache.
*Initial setup time.

As the numbers show, the performance of the cache is more significant for smaller files. As the number and size of the paths increase, the benefit of the cache lessens until the frequency of hitting the cache reaches zero, and the cost of entry into the cache is incurred for each path each time. As a result, drawings with a large number of paths can experience diminishing results when using the cache.

The point of diminishing returns is dependent on cache size and drawing type. In the initial version of the Display PostScript system, 300 K is the maximum number of bytes allowed in the cache, and 900 is the maximum number of paths. In future versions, however, this number may become configurable by the application program.

The King Tut drawing contains more than 3000 paths. Since the path limit is 900, each drawing of all the paths completely overwrites the contents of the existing cache at least three times, eliminating the chance of caching. Drawing King Tut took more time with the cache than without the cache.

The size of the King Tut drawing is an exception and constitutes one of the worst cases for the number of paths in a drawing. The other files used as examples contain less than 500 paths, and the performance with the cache is very good.

One solution to prevent diminished performance is to limit the number of paths drawn with the cache to the maximum path limit of the cache or some fraction thereof. In the King Tut drawing, limiting the number of paths placed in the cache to 700 showed the normal initial setup cost without the performance hit for subsequent drawings. In fact, the cached user paths performed 10% better than the non-cached version.

Note   *Any application that uses this technique should first obtain the maximum number of paths from **ucachestatus** and then use a percentage of this value instead of hardwiring the number to a certain implementation. This allows the application to take advantage of expanded limits that might be provided by future versions.*

9.3   Drawing Every Path Versus Only Those Necessary

One significant difference in drawing performance in the Scrolling application occurs when only the visible paths are sent to the server. Instead of relying on the DrawingView in the window to clip the image, an application can realize significant performance gains by comparing the dimensions of the drawing area with the bounding box of each path.

Only paths whose bounding box lies within the drawing area are sent to the server. This check, made within the client, reduces sending unnecessary data to the server and improves performance.

This technique has a greater impact when the visible portion of the view is smaller than the dimensions of the entire drawing. An example is the rectangle passed to the **drawSelf:** method as a result of scrolling. These rectangles are typically slivers of the entire drawing. Another example is in an enlarged or scaled view in which only a fraction of the drawing appears. (At 1600% scale, 1/16th of the drawing image is visible.)

In tests with the Caterpillar Engine diagram, drawing all paths versus only those that will be visible took about the same amount of time at 100% scale. Drawing only those visible took 13% less time at 400% scale and 85% less time at 1600% scale.

Figure 9.3 shows the amount of drawing done at each scale and the times for drawing both approaches using non-cached user paths.

Figure 9.3 *Drawing times in seconds for drawing every path (left) versus only those necessary (right)*

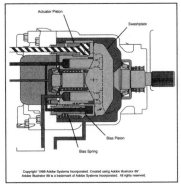
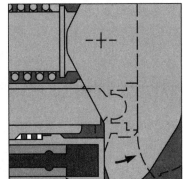
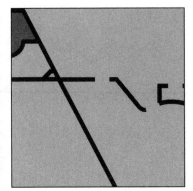

100% scale: 0.985, 0.970   *400% scale: 1.060, 0.820*   *1600% scale: 0.500, 0.136*

The caching of a path occurs before clipping so that any path drawn is placed in the cache regardless of whether it is visible. A large number of paths frequently cross between the visible and the non-visible portions of the drawing and are cached when drawn.

When the drawing is scrolled, these paths are found in the cache and rendered very quickly, although this doesn't mean that you should draw every path in hopes of placing all the paths in the cache. The reduction in client-server messages when drawing only the paths that are necessary outweighs any advantage that might be gained by having paths already in the cache.

9.4 Drawing a Complete Image Versus a Wire Frame

The Scrolling application displays a drawing as either a complete (preview) image or a wire frame model. The complete image incorporates the color, line width, other line settings, and paint type (either a stroke or a fill). The wire frame displays the paths in outline form with each path appearing in a line width equivalent to one pixel. The advantage of the wire frame is that it displays faster and shows the paths more clearly.

Some applications, notably Adobe Illustrator, make extensive use of the wire frame drawing mode. This option has been included in Scrolling for comparison. The color, line width, and other line settings are set at the beginning and not changed; then the paths are constructed and stroked.

In the Scrolling application, the color is set to *NX_BLACK* and the line width to 0.05. (This setting keeps the line width equivalent to one pixel in device space, even at 1600% scale. A setting of 0.15 doesn't do this.) Drawing the complete image of the Nurse takes .5 seconds while drawing the wire frame takes .18 seconds (using non-cached user paths).

Figure 9.4 *Drawing times for complete image versus wire frame image*

Complete image: .5 seconds   *Wire frame image: .18 seconds*

9.5 Combining Paths

Other chapters have pointed out the performance gains of delaying stroking until necessary and of combining user paths into larger user paths. In this application, the performance improvements are more dramatic.

In the PostScript language, paths can consist of a combination of disjoint subpaths. Combining paths with the same color and line width saves on the overhead that each stroke operation requires. The benefit is even more significant when this technique is used in combination with user paths, as shown in Table 9.4.

Table 9.4 *Times for combining paths (wire frame model)*

Method	Level 1	User Paths	User Paths Cached
Display times in seconds			
Individual Paths	1.000	0.717	0.591
Combined into Paths of up to 2500 Points	0.650	0.210	0.100

By using the cache and combining paths, drawing the Caterpillar Engine was reduced from 1 second using PostScript Level 1 operators and stroking after every path to 0.1 seconds by combining paths and using the user path cache. This represents a reduction of 90% in drawing time.

Combining large user paths has some impact when scrolling. If you must draw newly visible paths, they are added to the path description eliminating the possibility of a cache hit. Caching paths individually does not have this problem because each path is a distinct entity in the cache. With combined paths, any added or deleted subpath invalidates the cached representation causing re-caching.

In scrolling situations versus the static display times represented above, the individually cached paths performed slightly better than the collectively cached paths. (With non-cached user paths, it is always better to combine paths.)

The conflicting results show that the technique that best fits an application depends on the type of drawing the application performs. If images are frequently redrawn all at once, then combining and caching user paths can work best. If only parts of the images are drawn, then separate cached user paths might be the best course. It might be necessary to try several alternatives before arriving at the optimal approach.

9.6   Scrolling and the Halftone Phase

Halftoning is the process by which continuous-tone colors are approximated by a pattern of pixels that achieve only a limited number of discrete colors. The halftone functions supported by the PostScript language are based on the use of a halftone screen that tiles the device space starting at the device space origin. This means that the halftone grid is aligned with the point (0,0) in device space regardless of the value for the current transformation matrix. Constant alignment assures that adjacent gray areas are painted in tones having the same phase. Areas that are not in phase typically display a one-pixel vertical or horizontal seam.

On a display, this halftone phase must be more flexible in order to accommodate scrolling operations. A scrolling operation typically involves copying contents of a portion of a window to a different location within the window to reduce the amount of redrawing needed to refresh the window. Copying the portion that will still be visible makes it necessary to draw only areas that are newly exposed, increasing the response in handling scrolling events. To keep the tones in the copied portion and the newly displayed portion in phase, though, the relationship of the halftone grid to the device space must be adjusted with each scroll.

In Display PostScript, the graphics state includes a pair of parameters that define an x and y offset from the device space to a particular point in the halftone cycle. (The halftone grid doesn't have an origin because it is a continuously repeating cycle.) The **currenthalftonephase** and **sethalftonephase** operators allow you to access and modify the halftone phase.

The ClipView class in the Application Kit makes the adjustments to the halftone phase. During a scrolling event, the ScrollView instance sends a message to the **rawScroll:** method in the ClipView instance. This method adjusts the halftone phase, copies the bits, and then sends a display message to its content view to draw the newly exposed portion of the view.

Example 9.2 shows the PostScript language trace that is the result of a **rawScroll:** message. The scroll was a horizontal move 181 points to the right. The end result is that the content view is moved 181 points to the left, the halftone phase is adjusted, and the portion on the right side of the window is redrawn.

Example 9.2 *Halftone phase adjustments made by the Application Kit ClipView object*

PostScript language trace

```
24 execuserobject setgstate
20 28 431 481 rectclip
20 28 translate
-181 0 translate
currenthalftonephase exch -181 add cvi exch 0 add cvi sethalftonephase
362 0 250 481 null 181 0 Copy composite

% Clear the background of the newly exposed portion.
0.666667 setgray
431.5 0.5 180 480 rectfill

% Draw the newly exposed portion of the ClipView.
% In Scrolling, this means the DocView and DrawingView.
1 setgray
431 0 181 481 rectfill
...
```

The ClipView class manages the halftone phase in scrolling events so that, for the most part, you don't have to be aware of its existence. The pattern emulations in PostScript Level 1 use the **currenthalftonephase** operator to keep the pattern tiling in phase but, otherwise, the halftone phase is not much of an issue for the application developer.

9.7 Selectively Setting Graphics State Parameters

Another improvement to better drawing performance is to change only the graphics state parameters that are different from the current state. In the PostScript language, most of the graphics state elements remain the same after a painting operation; the current point and path are the only ones that do not. As a result, setting the current gray when it is already set is an unnecessary operation.

In the Scrolling application, one of the options is to either selectively set the parameter settings (that is, only when they change) or explicitly set the parameter settings for each path. In most of the files used for timing tests, selectively setting the graphics state parameters produced a 10% to 15% improvement.

Examples 9.3 and 9.4 show PostScript language traces for drawing the lips of the nurse in the Nurse drawing. In the first example, the graphics state parameters are explicitly set for each path. In the second, they are set only when they change. Although the color changes most of the time in the drawing, the other line attributes such as the line join and line cap remain the same. Since the current graphics state (except for the path) is retained after a stroke or fill, these operations are unnecessary.

Example 9.3 *Graphics state parameters set for each path*

PostScript language trace

```
0 setlinejoin 0 setlinecap 4 setlinewidth 10 setmiterlimit
0 setgray
<path>
fill
0 setlinejoin 0 setlinecap 4 setlinewidth 10 setmiterlimit
0.322 setgray
<path>
fill
0 setlinejoin 0 setlinecap 4 setlinewidth 10 setmiterlimit
0 setgray
<path>
fill
0 setlinejoin 0 setlinecap 4 setlinewidth 10 setmiterlimit
1 setgray
<path>
fill
0 setlinejoin 0 setlinecap 4 setlinewidth 10 setmiterlimit
1 setgray
<path>
fill
0 setlinejoin 0 setlinecap 4 setlinewidth 10 setmiterlimit
1 setgray
<path>
fill
```

Example 9.4 *Graphics state parameters set only when they change*

PostScript language trace

```
4 setlinewidth
0 setgray
<path>
fill
0.322 setgray
<path>
fill
0 setgray
```

```
<path>
fill
1 setgray
<path>
fill
<path>
fill
<path>
fill
```

Although the difference between display times for the two code segments in Examples 9.3 and 9.4 is only 3 to 4 milliseconds, this difference can become greater during the display of a complex graphic. Drawing King Tut by explicitly setting each parameter for each path took 7.5 seconds. Drawing the same image while setting only the parameters that changed took 6.4 seconds.

Selectively setting the parameters is a matter of keeping a structure of the current parameters and checking it before drawing each graphic. Only set parameters that are different from the current ones; the new parameters are then reflected in the current parameter structure.

9.8 Retained Versus Buffered Windows

The windows in the NeXT Application Kit can have three types of backing: nonretained, retained, and buffered. In this section, we examine using retained and buffered windows in the Scrolling application.

With a *retained* window, the drawing is done onscreen. With a *buffered* window, the drawing is performed in an offscreen buffer, then flushed to the screen when complete. The latter is preferred because the drawing is not seen and no flicker is visible. This is recommended because it gives a consistent visual appearance. In complex drawings, however, the delay can be several seconds, and you have no visual feedback. In scrolling situations, no visual reference keys are available to guide you.

In these situations, it is preferable to see the drawing performed onscreen rather than wait until the drawing is complete. Version 2.0 of NeXTstep allows windows to toggle between buffered and retained. You might want to flip the setting from buffered to retained before extensive drawing in order to show the drawing; you can change the setting back to buffered at the completion of the drawing.

9.9 Conclusions

- The user path cache is beneficial for many types of drawing. Paths found in the cache can be rendered up to three times faster than those not drawn with the cache. The cost for drawing a path for the first time with the cache approaches up to 1.5 times the normal cost for drawing without the cache.

- Infrequently drawn paths and graphics that are unusually large and complex do not show any benefit when drawn using the user path cache. As the complexity of the drawing increases, the benefit of the cache decreases until each path incurs the setup cost every time it is drawn.

- Drawing only those paths that will appear in the drawing region is an important step in the drawing process.

- Set graphics state parameters only when the change provides a slight display savings for each path. This can add up to a significant savings in large drawings.

- Using buffered windows for the drawing windows but switching to retained mode for extensive drawing provides an agreeable interface while at the same time allowing for visual feedback at critical moments.

CHAPTER **10**

Patterns

This chapter, together with the Pattern application, looks at techniques for rendering patterns efficiently as well as the tiling and positioning issues specific to a Display PostScript environment.

When the **fill, stroke**, and **show** operators paint areas of the page, they apply the current color to the areas uniformly. However, you might want to paint an area with a repeating figure or *pattern*.

Figure 10.1 *Pattern application*

Painting with a pattern *(tiling)* means replicating a small, graphical figure (a *pattern cell*) at fixed intervals in x and y. Pattern cells are described by arbitrary PostScript language procedures. They can include filled and stroked areas, text, sampled images, or a combination of these elements. The formal definition and implementation of patterns is a PostScript

175

Level 2 feature. The pattern specification in Level 2 provides a well-defined format as well as special operators and caches to make and display patterns quickly and easily.

It's possible to achieve an emulation of patterns in Level 1. This requires clipping the path to be painted and then tiling the pattern cells through the area. This chapter uses the Pattern application to explore three ways to draw patterns using Level 1 operators. The four pattern cells shown in Figure 10.2 can be tiled through various text and graphic objects using these approaches. Times for each appear in Table 10.1

The recommended approach is to turn the pattern cell into a Type 3 font and take advantage of the font cache. Each separately colored layer is made a character, and each character is tiled through the area to be painted. Only the first instance of a character is rendered, with subsequent instances coming from the font cache. This greatly improves the pattern display speed.

Another approach is to draw each pattern cell individually. This method becomes expensive in terms of performance as the number and the complexity of the pattern cells increase. The third way is to draw the cell in an offscreen buffer and then composite through the clipped region. This approach has a number of problems, the foremost being the difficulty of implementing it.

Another technique that helps drawing performance is to increase the number of images per pattern cell. This increases the size of the cell, reducing the number of cells that must be tiled through a region. The Pattern application expands a pattern cell from 1 image per cell to 4, 9, and 16 images per cell.

In addition to performance, another issue is consistent tiling. Because pattern cells are placed next to each other, even slight variations in position can produce visible effects. A one-pixel difference in the placement of a character is not as noticeable because of the amount of white space involved.

In a Display PostScript environment, tiling variations and placement issues are magnified more than when printing. Pixel resolutions of displays are much lower than in printers, so even a one-pixel difference is noticed more readily.

More detailed information about patterns can be found in the *PostScript Language Reference Manual, Second Edition* and in Technical Note #5112, "Emulation of the **makepattern** and **setpattern** Operators."

10.1 Patterns

The appearance of a pattern cell is defined by an arbitrary PostScript language procedure. It can include graphical elements such as filled areas, text, and sampled images. The shape of a pattern cell doesn't have to be rectangular. Patterns can be used to create various graphical textures, such as weaves, brick walls, and similar geometric tilings.

Figure 10.2 shows four patterns: circle star, weave, octagon, and brick. The pattern cells appear in the top row. The bottom row shows simple graphic tilings with the cells.

Figure 10.2 *Pattern cells and graphics for circle star, weave, octagon, and brick*

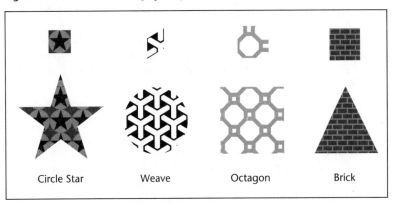

Circle Star   Weave   Octagon   Brick

10.2 Patterns in PostScript Level 2

Painting with a pattern in Level 2 is a four-step procedure.

1. *Describe the prototype pattern* by creating a pattern dictionary that contains information about the pattern. A crucial element of the dictionary is the **PaintProc**, a PostScript language procedure that can be executed to paint a single pattern cell.

2. *Instantiate the pattern*. The **makepattern** operator copies a prototype pattern dictionary and produces an instance of the pattern that is locked to current device space. In other words, the size of the pattern cell and the phase of the tiling in device space are determined by the CTM at the time **makepattern** is executed. The pattern is unaffected by subsequent changes to the CTM or to other graphics state parameters.

3. *Select the pattern as the current color.* A special color space, **Pattern**, has color values that are pattern dictionaries instead of the numeric color values used with other color spaces. The **setcolorspace** and **setcolor** operators set the color space and color value separately; the convenience operator **setpattern** installs a pattern as the current color in a single step.

4. *Invoke painting operators,* such as **fill, stroke, imagemask,** or **show.** All areas that normally are painted with a uniform color are instead tiled with the pattern cell. To accomplish this, the PostScript interpreter calls the pattern dictionary's **PaintProc** (with the graphics state altered) to obtain the pattern cell. It then paints this cell on the current page as many times as necessary. To optimize execution, the interpreter maintains a cache of recently used pattern cells.

Example 10.1 shows the code for painting a rectangular area with a pattern. The pattern is contained in a dictionary called Weave. It is assumed to have been defined in the interpreter previous to this code segment.

Example 10.1 *Pattern invocation under Level 2*

```
/pattern1 Weave [2.59808 1.5 0 -3.0 0 0] makepattern def

%Set the pattern and paint a region.
pattern1 setpattern
10 10 50 50 rectfill
```

10.3   Patterns in PostScript Level 1

Tiling with patterns in PostScript Level 1 can frequently take a long time. A pattern cell can be a relatively complex graphic, and rendering the graphic multiple times through a clipped region in a Level 1 device is a highly intensive operation. Studying the issue of efficiently tiling patterns in Level 1 devices has shown that one approach offers both a reasonable implementation and reasonable performance. This approach turns pattern descriptions into a Type 3 font, redefines the painting procedures to clip the area to be painted, and then repeatedly shows the pattern cell through the clipped area.

Using the Type 3 font provides the performance benefits of the font cache, and the redefinition of the painting procedures provides a relatively seamless integration into the PostScript Level 2 implementation of patterns. A comparison using the Type 3 font versus two other display techniques is found in section 10.4.1. A complete description of this approach is in Technical Note #5112, "Emulation of the **makepattern** and **setpattern** Operators," and an implementation can be found in the source code of the Pattern application. The following paragraphs provide an outline of this approach.

The **makepattern** operator in Level 2 takes a pattern dictionary and matrix that modifies the pattern space to scale, rotate, translate, and skew the pattern. The emulation of **makepattern** takes the pattern dictionary, adds the entries needed for a Type 3 font (**FontType**, **FontBBox**, **FontMatrix**, **Encoding**, and **BuildChar**, among others), then executes a **definefont** leaving the newly created font on the operand stack. (The **makepattern** operator in Level 2 leaves a pattern on the stack; the emulation leaves a font.)

The **setpattern** operator in Level 2 takes a pattern created by **makepattern** as its argument. The **setpattern** emulation takes a font created by the **makepattern** emulation. The **setpattern** emulation stores it as the current pattern, and then redefines the painting and text showing operators. When invoked, the redefined operators clip the current path and then tile the current pattern through the region.

The process under Level 1 appears in Example 10.2. Note that the **makepattern** and **setpattern** emulations are not named *makepattern* and *setpattern*. Instead they are named **PATmp** and **PATsp**. Convention holds that only emulations that are complete replacements can use the same name. Since the emulations are not complete replacements, they don't use the same name.

Example 10.2 *Pattern emulation under Level 1*

```
%Define the PatternDict dictionary.
/PatternDict
  35 dict begin

  % Procedures for handling patterns defined here.
  ...

  currentdict
  end
def

% Define the pattern in the Userdict dictionary.
PatternDict begin
  userdict /pattern1 Weave [2.59808 1.5 0 -3.0 0 0] PATmp put
end

%Set the pattern and paint a region.
```

```
PatternDict begin
  pattern PATsp
    10 10 50 50 rectfill
  PATusp
end
```

In the emulation in PostScript Level 1, the pattern must be unset after it is finished. This is not necessary for Level 2. With the Level 1 emulations, the painting operators must be redefined to their previous values, the color must return to its value before the pattern (patterns can modify the current color), and the pattern handling dictionary must be taken off the dictionary stack. The **PATusp** together with the **end** performs this cleanup.

The example below shows the redefinition for the **fill** operator. This redefinition occurs with the **PATsp** procedure. The **PATusp** replaces the previous definition. The **PATdraw** is a PostScript language procedure that is part of the emulation package. It performs two steps: it calculates the information for the tiling (starting position, number of rows, and columns), and then uses this information to perform the actual tiling.

```
/fill {/clip load PATdraw newpath} bind def
```

10.4 Patterns under Display PostScript (Using Level 1 Emulations)

The following sections explores some of the issues with displaying patterns in the Display PostScript system. The first two sections involve performance and implementation strategies while the last three sections explore issues that are either exclusive or at least more pertinent to painting with patterns on a display than in a print environment.

The display approaches and the issues associated with them are based on the PostScript Level 1 strategy for emulating patterns. Once the Level 2 operators are incorporated into the Display PostScript system, painting with patterns on the display is a matter of using the Level 2 pattern operators. Even after this happens, though, the Level 1 display approaches and the issues raised are still important. The former because they are needed for supporting Level 1 devices and the latter because many of the same issues arise in PostScript Level 2.

10.4.1 Display Approaches

The three approaches outlined in the following sections (font, drawing, and compositing) rely on the emulation of **makepattern** and **setpattern** as well as the redefinition of the painting operators. Although this introduces a fair amount of PostScript language code, it has the advantage of making painting with a pattern similar to painting with a color.

The alternative is to have different code paths in the client application for painting with a color and painting with a pattern. Each time a new graphic is added, the logic to determine whether to paint with a color or pattern must be included. It is much simpler to rely on the redefinitions placed on the dictionary stack in the server than on maintaining a separate code path in the client. Either redefining the operators in the server or using separate code paths produces the same results, but the first approach is more transparent.

Table 10.1 *Times for imaging approaches*

Pattern	(No. of Layers)	Font	Drawing	Composite
Times in milliseconds. 9-image pattern cell used.				
Circle Star	(3)	315	11230	135
Octagon	(1)	115	2220	105
Brick	(2)	200	3120	90
Weave*	(2)	282	19414	1500
Skewed pattern cell.				

Font Approach

The recommended approach for displaying patterns in Level 1 is to turn them into Type 3 fonts. This approach takes advantage of font cache to increase the performance of the pattern display. Instead of rendering each pattern cell, only the first instance of each layer is rendered. Subsequent instances are displayed from the images stored in the font cache. (Large pattern cells can exceed the maximum size of the font cache. When this happens, each instance must be imaged every time instead of being taken from the cache.)

Drawing Approach

Another way to paint with patterns is to explicitly draw each pattern cell. This is not recommended because it is not as efficient as a Type 3 font. The difference is greater in a printer because the increased resolution increases the time it takes to render a drawing. Since each cell is rendered every time with this approach, it takes many times longer than the font approach.

Compositing Approach

Compositing a pattern cell might seem like a reasonable approach to tiling, but it is discouraged for two reasons:

- It can't be used for printing. Having separate code paths for display and printing increases the complexity of pattern handling. The performance is not significantly greater than turning the pattern into a font and in some cases, especially with nonlinear pattern spaces, the performance can be much worse.

- The level of difficulty involved with this display is significant. Trying to image a pattern cell into an offscreen window or NXImage object is not a trivial task because of the pattern locking to the device space. Added to this is the difficulty in tiling the composited image into the clipped region.

10.4.2 Cell Size

The size of the pattern cell can make a significant difference in drawing speed. Pattern cells typically have one image per cell. Expanding the pattern cell to contain multiple images increases the size of the cell, reducing the number of cells needed to tile through an area.

In the Pattern application, the cell size ranges from 1 image per cell to 4, 9, and 16 images per cell. Performance doubles with the increase from one to four images per cell. The increase for the next steps are not as great but are still pronounced.

The size of the pattern cell should be smaller than the maximum size of a character in the font cache. (The font cache for printers might be lower than the font cache in a Display PostScript system. A 3 x 3 pattern cell for similarly sized patterns seems to be the upper limit for the smallest font cache found in printers.) If it grows too large, the benefits of the font cache are lost. This means that each cell must be rendered each time it is drawn. Table 10.2 shows the times for the range of cell sizes.

Note   *The 3 x 3 recommendation is based on a fingernail-sized pattern cell. Large pattern cells might not show any benefits from expansion.*

The increase in cell size can be done at the time the pattern is defined or used. The most appropriate time is when the pattern is defined. The options are more limited for applications that use patterns defined in other applications. While it is possible to expand the pattern cell, it might be difficult in terms of programming to decide when and how far to do so.

Table 10.2 *Times for different cell sizes*

Pattern	1	4	9	16
Times in milliseconds. Displayed as a Type 3 font.				
Circle Star	553	374	315	300
Octagon	173	140	115	118
Brick	273	198	200	186
Weave*	538	387	282	285
Skewed pattern cell.				

10.4.3   Tiling

The lower resolution of displays versus printers makes pattern tiling and placement much more of an issue in a display environment. Two items are important here: The appearance of the pattern on the display and the consistency of the pattern between the display and the printer.

The Pattern definition in Level 2 contains an entry labeled **TilingType** that controls the adjustments made to the pattern cell to fit it to device space. The choices are

- *TilingType 1, constant spacing.* Pattern cells are spaced consistently by a multiple of a device pixel. The pattern might be distorted slightly by making small adjustments to the horizontal and vertical spacing and the matrix for the pattern.

- *TilingType 2, no distortion.* The pattern cell is not distorted, but the spacing between pattern cells can vary by as much as one device pixel in both x and y dimensions when the pattern is painted.

- *TilingType 3, constant spacing and faster tiling.* This is similar to **TilingType 1**, but with additional distortion of the pattern cell, which enables a more efficient implementation.

When using a pattern of **TilingType** 2, the spacing can vary by up to one pixel. Since displays typically have lower resolutions than printers, this difference can be noticed more easily in a display. Figure 10.3 shows two images of the same pattern. The image on the left is a screen capture and the image on the right is a printed version. The one-pixel difference created by a **TilingType** 2 pattern leaves a white band in the middle of the screen image, but the band is hardly noticeable in the printed image.

Figure 10.3 *TilingType 2*

Screen capture   Printed version

Although the white band might seem unacceptable, the tiling is consistent between the display and the printed page. The pattern cells fall at the same places in the painted region. For example, the cuts in the pattern cells along the edges are at the same points for both images. Since some users might want to position pattern cells explicitly within a clipped region, it might be in the interest of the application to preserve the relationship between the display and the printed page. Patterns with **TilingTypes** of 1 and 3 don't display any breaks because the pattern is distorted slightly to fit it to device space. Because of this, the patterns might tile slightly differently between the display and the printer. For most patterns, it is barely noticeable.

10.4.4 Locking

The default behavior in Level 2 and the Level 1 emulations is to lock a pattern to the current device space at the time of the **makepattern**. This freezes the tiling, meaning that the same tiling occurs regardless of subsequent changes in the CTM.

Locking to Window

In the NeXT Application Kit, documents typically are placed in a View object, which is contained in a window. Locking a pattern to the current device space at the time of the **makepattern** locks the pattern into the relationship between the window and the view. (The window is the device. This means that the tiling is based on the window, not the view.)

If the relationship between the window and the view changes, the placement of the pattern within the painted region can change. The point where the pattern tiling starts is no longer the same because the view now occupies a different position in the window. This condition can be caused by something as simple as resizing the window. Another effect when freezing the tiling is that the size of the pattern cell remains constant regardless of the scale of the document.

Locking to View

One way around the locking of the pattern to window space is to lock the pattern to the view. This has the effect of always tiling the pattern cell from the same point in the view. Even if the view is repositioned within the window, the pattern cells fall in the same places relative to the view.

In the Level 1 emulations in the Pattern application, this effect is accomplished by adding another dictionary on top of the PatternDict with operators that explicitly adjust the user space to reflect the location of the view within the window. This dictionary and the procedures used to accomplish this are too involved to cover here. They can be found in the source file, *PSWpatterns.psw,* for the Pattern application.

In short, the procedures keep track of the matrix for the view and use the translation components of the matrix to adjust the pattern space. In this case, only the translation components are used, so the size of the pattern cells do not change with the scale of the document.

Figure 10.4 *Locking to View*

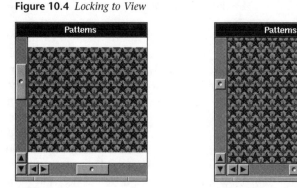

100% scale   *400% scale*

In the PostScript Level 2 implementation of patterns, this adjustment must be done differently. The pattern machinery prevents access to the pattern space once a pattern has been created with **makepattern**. As a result, the only solution is to remake the pattern whenever the positioning of the view changes in relation to the window. Although this is not a transparent solution, with proper isolation of these events, it is possible to minimize the amount of effort required to remake the patterns.

Locking to View—Reflecting the Document Scale

In the previous case, the translation components of the view matrix alone were used to adjust the pattern space. If the entire matrix is used, the scale of the document is figured into the adjustment to the pattern space. This has the effect of enlarging and reducing the pattern cell to match the scale of the document.

Figure 10.5 *Locking to View—reflecting scale*

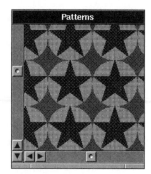

100% scale   *400% scale*

The Pattern application uses a dictionary similar to the one used in the previous section to adjust the pattern space at the time of tiling. The dictionary is also in the file *PSWpatterns.psw*. To achieve the same locking effect in Level 2, the same adjustment must be made whenever the scale of the view changes, and whenever the position of the view changes in relation to the window.

10.5 Scrolling

The issue of locking to the device has implications when scrolling using the Level 1 emulations. When the pattern is locked to the window, any scrolling of a view within the window is not taken into account. The tiling falls at the same position within the window regardless of the position of the view. As a result, the drawing regions created by scrolling events have misaligned patterns. This does not occur when the pattern is locked to a view because the tiling of the pattern is based on the matrix for the view regardless of its relationship with the window. (This also doesn't happen in PostScript Level 2 because changes to the halftone phase are reflected in the tiling of patterns existing before the change.)

To calculate where the pattern cells should tile when locking a pattern to a window, use the current halftone phase as an indication of how much to adjust the tiling. The **currenthalftonephase** operator provides the relationship between the halftone grid and the device space. Transforming this relationship with the **idtransform** operator provides the amount of translation needed in the current user space to align the tiling with the previous tiling.

The procedure in Example 10.4 is used in the emulation when calculating the starting position and number of rows and columns for tiling. It is needed only in a display environment, so it is defined conditionally based on the existence of the **currenthalftonephase** operator. (The **currenthalftonephase** operator exists in the Display PostScript system but not in PostScript Level 2.)

Example 10.3 *Pattern adjustment for scrolling*

```
% PATthtp - translate to current halftonephase
/currenthalftonephase where
{
  pop
  /PATthtp { % -
    currenthalftonephase% dx dy
    idtransform% x y
    translate% -
  } bind def
} { /PATthtp { } def } ifelse
```

10.6   Conclusions

- Level 2 provides a formal definition and implementation of patterns. The definition is embodied within a dictionary. The implementation for tiling a path with a pattern is much the same as painting with a color.

- Patterns can be emulated for devices that do not support Level 2 implementations by turning patterns into Type 3 fonts and tiling them through the clipped region with the **show** operator.

- The three tiling types in the pattern definition prescribe different tiling behavior. The tiling differences are more pronounced on a low resolution display than on higher resolution printers.

- Patterns are locked to the current device when they are instantiated. The current device in a display environment is the window. This can affect the tiling of the pattern through a document when the document moves within the window.

CHAPTER 11

Text Handling Issues

The NeXT Application Kit together with several of the NeXTstep functions provide a significant amount of high-level text-handling support. Rather than duplicate the existing documentation, this chapter concentrates on text management and display issues at the PostScript language level.

The Text application has been created to highlight these topics. It displays two paragraphs of static lines that appear in a single font at several point sizes: Times-Roman at 10, 11, and 12 points. You can leave the text left- or full-justified, kerned, spaced apart (tracked), shown with the screen font or outline font, displayed using **xshow**, **rmoveto**, and **show** pairings, or displayed in the best combination of **show** variations **ashow, widthshow**, and **awidthshow**). In addition, the page can be imaged with or without the font cache as well as rotated, reduced, and enlarged.

Figure 11.1 *Text application*

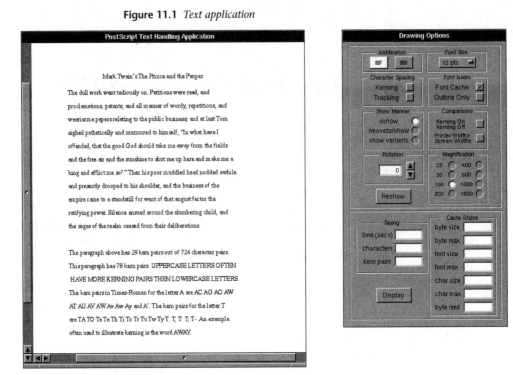

The structures and the methods used in the application are not intended to provide a model for text-handling applications. They are used for displaying a set of static lines with no editing or line breaking. The intention of the application is to highlight the PostScript language portion of text handling, not the application level.

More information is available on these topics from the Adobe Developers' Association. The *PostScript Language Program Design* manual covers a number of text- and font-handling topics, while two technical notes deal exclusively with the Adobe Font Metrics (AFM) files and generic text handling: "Adobe Font Metrics File Specification" (LPS5004) and Technical Note #5118, "Overview of the Generic Text Interface."

11.1 Justification, Pair Kerning, and Tracking

Displaying text properly is not simply a matter of taking each line of text and sending it as a string argument for the **show** operator. There are other issues such as justification, pair kerning, and tracking. Each of these items overrides the default character spacings of the text. All three are important to the appearance of text, making them important to anyone who develops text applications.

11.1.1 Justification

Justification refers to the alignment of lines in a text block. The common types of justification are *left, right, center,* and *full.* Left-justification refers to lines that are aligned on the left and run *ragged* on the right. Right-justification refers to the opposite; the lines are aligned on the right and run ragged on the left. Center-justification refers to lines that are centered within the left and right margins and run ragged on both left and right edges. Full-justification refers to lines that are aligned on both the left and right edges. This is achieved by adding additional spacing between the words (and sometimes characters) in each line until the line length is reached.

Figure 11.2 *Justification styles*

This line of text is left-justified, which means it is aligned on the left and runs ragged on the right.	This line of text is right-justified, which means it is aligned on the right and runs ragged on the left.	This line of text is center-justified, which means both the left and right edges run ragged.	This line of text is full-justified, which means both the left and right edges are aligned.
Left-justification	*Right-justification*	*Center-justification*	*Full-justification*

11.1.2 Pair Kerning

When a line of text is imaged with **show**, the width and a default spacing of a character are used to determine where it lies in relation to the preceding character. Since individual characters within a font can vary in size and shape, certain combinations of letters can produce unappealing groupings when the normal spacings are used.

In most cases, too much space appears between the combinations. This gap is often the result of the edges of the characters receding away from each other, as in the case of the letters *W* and *A*, or the edges appearing at a different height, as is the case of the letters *T* and *e*. To overcome the visual disparity, different spacings between the characters can be used to create a more appealing separation. Modifying the intercharacter spacing for pairs is called *kerning*.

Typesetters and graphic designers go to great lengths to achieve proper positioning of characters in the materials they produce. Almost any application that handles text should provide some level of kerning. In most cases, this means simply displaying kerned text. More sophisticated text handling applications might allow manual adjustment of the character spacing or finer spacing control.

Figure 11.3 shows the canonical case used to illustrate kerning. The example on the left is without kerning and the example on the right is with kerning. The differences in the character spacings are apparent. The edges of the characters in the word *AWAY* recede from each other creating large gaps between the letters. In the first case, no adjustments are made. In the second, the characters are moved more closely together (kerned) to compensate for the receding edges.

Figure 11.3 *Kerning*

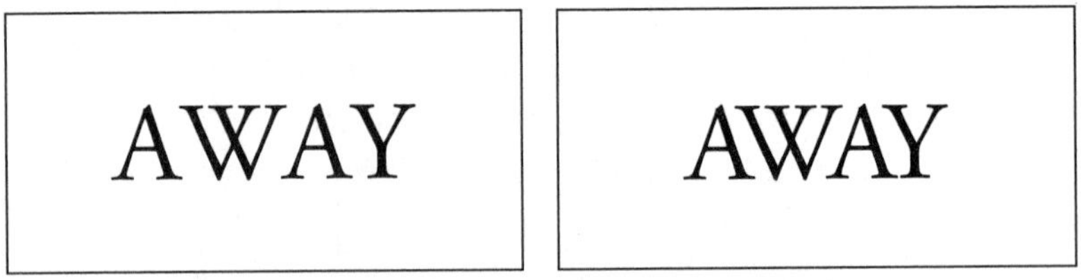

Without kerning   *With kerning*

In Figure 11.4, no individual adjustments are necessary because the combinations of character shapes do not produce any noticeable gaps or spaces. (Kerning is a subjective decision, but in this case kerning does not appear to be necessary.)

Figure 11.4 *No kerning*

The most common approach to kerning in a computer environment, and the one that requires the least computation, is *pair kerning*. A kerning pair is a sequence of two letters with spacing different from the default. In the word *AWAY*, the kerning pairs are *AW, WA,* and *AY*. In the word *ABCD*, there are no kerning pairs.

Each kerning pair specifies a certain distance to adjust the position of the second character. In the case of the *A* and *W* pair, *W* is moved to the left of its default position by 1.08 points for a 12-point font.

The number of kerning pairs for a font is typically set by the font designer, although applications have been written to allow you to modify the kerning tables. For most common uses, the tables supplied with the font are adequate. People in high-end publishing and other related areas, though, often use customized kerning tables.

The number of kerning pairs found in a font varies between fonts. Typically about 4% to 8% of the possible character combinations are marked as kerning pairs. Most fonts share a common set of kerning pairs since many are centered around several key characters, including *A, T, V, W, Y,* and *r*.

Kerning pairs can and often do include punctuation symbols, numbers, and other characters besides letters. The Times-Roman font has 282 kerning pairs listed in its AFM file, Helvetica has 250 kerning pairs, and Adobe Garamond Regular has 602 kerning pairs.

11.1.3 Tracking

Tracking refers to adding a uniform amount of space between each character in a piece of text. The amount of space can be either negative or positive. A common use of tracking is in display type where an increased amount of spacing creates an appealing effect. The bottom line in Figure 11.5 illustrates tracking.

Figure 11.5 *Tracking*

11.2 Adobe Font Metric (AFM) Files

Adobe Font Metric (AFM) files are available for all Adobe Type 1 fonts and provide general characteristics about the font, as well as specific characteristics about each character in the font. An AFM file is ASCII text and contains character widths, bounding boxes, and kerning pairs and other font information. Many applications read the files and place the information in arrays or other data structures suitable for efficient processing. The location of AFM files is system dependent. The NeXT system places them in the Font directories within the various library directories. Other systems place them in different folders or directories.

One of the features of the Font object in the NeXT Application Kit is that it parses the AFM files automatically. Character widths and pair kerning information can be accessed with a few table lookups.

Example 11.1 is an excerpt from the AFM file for the Times-Roman font. The initial portion contains general information about the font. The character metrics section, **CharMetrics**, begins with **StartCharMetrics** followed by the number of lines in the section. The lines after this contain the encoding number, width, name, and bounding box for each character found in the font. The encoding is prefaced by **C**, the width by **WX**, the name by **N**, and the bounding box by **B**. The end of the section is marked by **EndCharMetrics**.

The kerning pairs follow the character metrics. Only the pairs for *A* appear in this example. The number on each line following the **KPX** and the two characters indicate the amount to move the second character relative to its normal position. This value is based on a 1000-point font coordinate system, so the value must be divided by 1000 and multiplied by the current font scale. Only a few of the two-letter combinations for *A* have an entry. No entry means that no kerning pair is defined.

Example 11.1 *Adobe font metrics (AFM) file for Times-Roman*

```
StartFontMetrics 2.0
Comment Copyright (c) 1985, 1987, 1989, 1990 Adobe Systems Incorporated.
All Rights Reserved.
Comment Creation Date: Tue Mar 20 12:15:44 1990
Comment UniqueID 28416
Comment VMusage 30487 37379
FontName Times-Roman
FullName Times Roman
FamilyName Times
Weight Roman
```

ItalicAngle 0
IsFixedPitch false
FontBBox -168 -218 1000 898
UnderlinePosition -100
UnderlineThickness 50
Version 001.007
Notice Copyright (c) 1985, 1987, 1989, 1990, 1991 Adobe Systems
Incorporated. All Rights Reserved. Times is a trademark of Linotype AG and/or its
subsidiaries.
EncodingScheme AdobeStandardEncoding
CapHeight 662
XHeight 450
Ascender 683
Descender -217
StartCharMetrics 228
C 32 ; WX 250 ; N space ; B 0 0 0 0 ;
C 33 ; WX 333 ; N exclam ; B 130 -9 238 676 ;
C 34 ; WX 408 ; N quotedbl ; B 77 431 331 676 ;
C 35 ; WX 500 ; N numbersign ; B 5 0 496 662 ;
...
C 65 ; WX 722 ; N A ; B 15 0 706 674 ;
C 66 ; WX 667 ; N B ; B 17 0 593 662 ;
C 67 ; WX 667 ; N C ; B 28 -14 633 676 ;
C 68 ; WX 722 ; N D ; B 16 0 685 662 ;
...
EndCharMetrics
StartKernData
StartKernPairs 283

KPX A y -92
KPX A w -92
KPX A v -74
KPX A u 0
KPX A quoteright -111
KPX A quotedblright 0
KPX A p 0
KPX A Y -105
KPX A W -90
KPX A V -135
KPX A U -55
KPX A T -111
KPX A Q -55
KPX A O -55
KPX A G -40
KPX A C -40
...
EndKernPairs
EndKernData
StartComposites 58

```
CC Aacute 2 ; PCC A 0 0 ; PCC acute 195 212 ;
CC Acircumflex 2 ; PCC A 0 0 ; PCC circumflex 195 212 ;
CC Adieresis 2 ; PCC A 0 0 ; PCC dieresis 195 212 ;
CC Agrave 2 ; PCC A 0 0 ; PCC grave 195 212 ;
CC Aring 2 ; PCC A 0 0 ; PCC ring 185 187 ;
CC Atilde 2 ; PCC A 0 0 ; PCC tilde 195 212 ;
...
EndComposites
EndFontMetrics
```

Composite characters (characters made up of characters already existing in the font program) are marked by the composite pair entries that follow the kerning pair entries. Refer to the AFM specification file for more information on this topic.

11.2.1 Font Metrics with PostScript Language Operators

For optimum processing efficiency, font metric information should not be obtained through PostScript language operations. Although the width of a string can be obtained through **stringwidth** and the bounding box through **charpath pathbbox**, these types of operations are not as efficient as reading the data from the AFM files. The client-server round trip and the interpreter cycles needed to process the requests are extremely wasteful when compared to array lookups. In most cases, it makes sense to use the information contained in the AFM files.

11.2.2 Font Object and NXFontMetrics Structure

The Font object in the NeXT Application Kit parses the AFM files and places the AFM information into a data structure that can be accessed by other objects. In the Text application, the kerning information is obtained from the font by messaging the font instance with the **metrics** method. A kerning pair lookup is then performed for each character pair when setting the text.

The text in the Text application is drawn one line at a time. The text string and an array to hold the kerning values are passed to a procedure to obtain the kerning and spacing information. This procedure zeros the array and places the appropriate kerning adjustment at the proper index in the array. (If **xshow** is used to display the characters, the width of each character also is included.)

The *NXFontMetrics* structure obtained from the font is fairly complex, containing more than ten pointers to various arrays. Three arrays are used in this application: the encoding array, *NXCharMetric* structure, and *NXKernPair* or *NXKernXPair* structures.

The structure and procedure in Example 11.2 show the lookup that occurs for each character pair. First, the encoding values for the two characters in each pair are obtained from the encoding array using the character codes as indexes. Next, the index and number of kerning pair entries in the kerning array are obtained from the *NXCharMetrics* entry for the first character. These values are then used to search for a match between the second encoding value and the *secondCharIndex* field in the kerning pair array. If a match is found the value is returned.

The *kerns* entry in the *NXFontMetrics* structures references either an array of *NXKernPair* structures or an array of *NXKernXPair* structures. The *hasXYKerns* field indicates the type of array. If *hasXYKerns* is *YES* then use the *NXKernPair* structure to access the kerning information; otherwise use the *NXKernXPair* structure.

The parsing routines that fill the *NXFontMetrics* array premultiply the kerning values in the AFM files by 0.001, so the value in the kerning pair array only needs to be multiplied by the font point size.

Note   *The kerning values for screen fonts already contain the absolute values for the particular font size, so they don't need to be scaled.*

Example 11.2 *NXFont Metric structures (defined in appkit/afm.h)*

C language code

```
typedef struct {                        /* per character info */
    short charCode;                     /* character code, -1 if unencoded */
    unsigned char numKernPairs;         /* pairs starting with this char */
    unsigned char reserved;
    float xWidth;                       /* width in X of this character */
    int name;                           /* name - an index into stringTable */
    float bbox[4];                      /* character bbox */
    int kernPairIndex;                  /* index into NXFontMetrics.kerns array */
} NXCharMetrics;


typedef struct {                        /* elements of the kern pair array */
    int secondCharIndex;                /* index into NXFontMetrics.charMetrics */
    float dx;                           /* displacement relative to first char */
    float dy;
} NXKernPair;
```

```
typedef struct {                        /* elements of the kern X pair array */
    int secondCharIndex;                /* index into NXFontMetrics.charMetrics */
    float dx;                           /* X displacement relative to first char */
                                        /* Y displacement is implicitly 0 for these */

} NXKernXPair;

typedef struct _NXFontMetrics {
    char *formatVersion;                /* version of afm file format */
    char *name;                         /* name of font for findfont */
    char *fullName;                     /* full name of font */
    char *familyName;                   /* "font family" name */
    float *widths;                      /* character widths in x */
    ...
    char hasXYKerns;                    /*Do any of the kern pairs have nonzero dy?*/
    ...
    short *encoding;                    /* 256 offsets into charMetrics */
    ...
    NXCharMetrics  *charMetrics;        /* array of NXCharMetrics */
    int  numCharMetrics;                /* num elements */
    ...
    union {
      NXKernPair  *kernPairs;           /* array of NXKernPairs */
      NXKernXPair  *kernXPairs;         /* array of NXKernXPairs */
    } kerns;
    int numKernPairs;                   /* num elements */
    ...
} NXFontMetrics;
```

Example 11.3 *Access routine for kerning information (DrawingView object)*

```
/*
 * Look up the kern pairs for the first character and see if
 * there is an entry for the second character. Returns the
 * value to kern if any.
 */
static NXCoord getkernvalue(NXFontMetrics *metrics, unsigned char char1,
unsigned char char2)
{
  int   enc1, enc2,
        i, kindex, klen;

  NXCoord value = 0.0;

  enc1 = metrics->encoding[char1];
  enc2 = metrics->encoding[char2];
  if (enc1 < metrics->numCharMetrics &&
        enc2 < metrics->numCharMetrics)
  {
    kindex = metrics->charMetrics[enc1].kernPairIndex;
    klen = metrics->charMetrics[enc1].numKernPairs;
```

```
        if (kindex+klen < metrics->numKernPairs)
        {
          for (i = kindex; i < kindex + klen; i++)
          {
            if (metrics->hasXYKerns)
            {
              if (enc2 == metrics->kerns.kernPairs[i].secondCharIndex)
              {
                value = metrics->kerns.kernPairs[i].dx;
                break;
              }
            }
            else
            {
              if (enc2 == metrics->kerns.kernXPairs[i].secondCharIndex)
              {
                value = metrics->kerns.kernXPairs[i].dx;
                break;
              }
            }
          }
        }
      }

      return value;
}
```

11.3 Approaches to Displaying Text (Text Application)

The Text application compares the performance of three approaches to displaying text:

- The Display PostScript operator **xshow**

- Combinations of **rmoveto/show** operations

- A mixture of **show, ashow, widthshow**, and **awidthshow** operators to best meet the requirements of the text block

A Display PostScript application that allows for kerning or justification or makes any similar adjustments to the spacing between characters should use the **xshow** operator for displaying text on the screen. Although **show** is faster when no kerning, tracking, or justification are used, the performance of **show** degrades significantly when kerning, tracking, justification, or similar features are added. The **xshow** operator is a more efficient and consistent way to display text in all cases.

Since **xshow** is not compatible with PostScript Level 1 printers, a different approach is needed for printing. An **xshow** emulation that replaces the **xshow** with a series of **rmoveto/show** operations is one possibility. The print package supplied by NeXT for printing to Level 1 devices supplies such an emulation. However, with this emulation each character uses a separate **rmoveto/show** operation, performing in a similar manner to when tracking is used with the **rmoveto/show** approach. A comparison of the times in Table 11.1 shows that this is a poor approach.

A better approach is to use combinations of **show, ashow, widthshow,** and **awidthshow** operators to minimize the amount of data sent and the number of operators performed. This is not as easy as creating a PostScript language procedure to emulate **xshow** since it requires a separate code path for printing, but the performance difference (about 500%—480 ms versus 2380 ms in the text case in Table 11.1) seems to outweigh the additional effort.

Table 11.1 *Times for displaying text*

Method	Plain	Kerning	Kerning Justification	Kerning Justification Tracking
Times in milliseconds for 1130 characters				
xshow[1]	225	260	260	265
rmoveto/show	110	360	650	2380
show variants[2]	110	400	460	480

[1]*Use for display.*
[2]*Use for printing.*

11.3.1 xshow

The **xshow** operator takes a text string and either a number array or a number string. The numbers represent the x displacement of each character relative to the starting position of the preceding character. This means that the width of the preceding character has to be figured in with any additional spacing. The first entry in the array is extracted after the first character has been positioned so that the first number represents the displacement between the first and second characters.

Each line in the Text application is displayed by filling an array with the spacing information, then performing a **PSmoveto( )** and a **PSxshow( )**. Example 11.4 shows the PostScript language trace. (There are no spacing adjustments from the default in this case, but each case—kerning, justification, and tracking—would look the same except for different numbers.)

Example 11.4 *Example using* *xshow*

PostScript language trace

```
130 200 moveto
(The dull work went tediously on. Petitions were read, and) [7.332 6 5.328 3 6 6
3.336 3.336 3 8.664 6 3.996 6 3 8.664 5.328 6 3.336 3 3.336 5.328 6 3.336 6 6
4.668 3.336 6 3 6 6 3 3 6.672 5.328 3.336 3.336 3.336 3.336 6 6 4.668 3 8.664
5.328 3.996 5.328 3 3.996 5.328 5.328 6 3 3 5.328 6 6] xshow
(proclamations, patents, and all manner of wordy, repetitious, and) [6 3.996 6
5.328 3.336 5.328 9.336 5.328 3.336 3.336 6 6 4.668 3 3 6 5.328 3.336 5.328
6 3.336 4.668 3 3 5.328 6 6 3 5.328 3.336 3.336 3 9.336 5.328 6 6 5.328 3.996
3 6 3.996 3 8.664 6 3.996 6 6 3 3 3.996 5.328 6 5.328 3.336 3.336 3.336 3.336
6 6 4.668 3 3 5.328 6 6] xshow
```

11.3.2   rmoveto/show

When no changes are made to the default character spacing, the **show** operator performs better than **xshow**. When the text is kerned but not justified or tracked, the **rmoveto/show** method performs not as well but not significantly worse. Only 3% to 8% of the character pairs in text typically need kerning, so the other character pairs use the standard spacings. Only a relatively small number of additional operators are introduced when kerning, as the trace in Example 11.5 shows.

Example 11.5 *Kerning using* *rmoveto* *and* *show*

PostScript language trace

```
130 200 moveto
(The dull w) show
-0.12 0 rmoveto (ork went tediously on. Petitions were read, and) show
130 225 moveto
(proclamations, patents, and all manner of w) show
-0.12 0 rmoveto (ordy) show
-0.78 0 rmoveto (, repetitious, and) show
```

When full-justification is added, the number of additional operators increases so that, at the least, an **rmoveto/show** operation is needed for each word. When tracking is added, an **rmoveto/show** is needed for each character. The difference in times between these cases indicates that this is not a good solution for either display or printing. Smaller samples of the trace in Examples 11.6 and 11.7 show the additional data and operators needed for the two worst-case scenarios.

Example 11.6 *Kerning and full-justification using* **rmoveto** *and* **show**

PostScript language trace

```
130 200 moveto
(The ) show
5.832 0 rmoveto (dull ) show
5.832 0 rmoveto (w) show
-0.12 0 rmoveto (ork ) show
5.832 0 rmoveto (went ) show
5.832 0 rmoveto (tediously ) show
5.832 0 rmoveto (on. ) show
5.832 0 rmoveto (Petitions ) show
5.832 0 rmoveto (were ) show
5.832 0 rmoveto (read, ) show
5.832 0 rmoveto (and) show
    ...
```

Example 11.7 *Kerning, full-justification, and tracking using* **rmoveto** *and* **show**

PostScript language trace

```
130 200 moveto
(T) show
2 0 rmoveto (h) show
2 0 rmoveto (e) show
2 0 rmoveto ( ) show
9.832001 0 rmoveto (d) show
2 0 rmoveto (u) show
2 0 rmoveto (l) show
2 0 rmoveto (l) show
2 0 rmoveto ( ) show
9.832001 0 rmoveto (w) show
1.88 0 rmoveto (o) show
2 0 rmoveto (r) show
2 0 rmoveto (k) show
2 0 rmoveto ( ) show
9.832001 0 rmoveto (w) show
2 0 rmoveto (e) show
2 0 rmoveto (n) show
2 0 rmoveto (t) show
2 0 rmoveto ( ) show
    ...
```

11.3.3 show Variants

The PostScript language has several variations of the **show** operator. Among these are **ashow, widthshow,** and **awidthshow.** Used separately or intermixed, they can adequately handle the demands made by kerning, justification, and tracking.

- **ashow** adds a uniform amount of spacing between each character in the string.

- **widthshow** adds spacing after a specific character (the space character, for example).

- **awidthshow** does both, adding uniform spacing and additional spacing after a specific character.

The Text application employs a subset of the framework found in the Generic Text Interface prepared by the Adobe Developers' Association. Refer to Technical Note # 5118, "Overview of the Generic Text Interface," for a complete description.

The Generic Text Interface provides a series of low-level routines that fit between the line-breaking and editing algorithms and the printing machinery. It assumes the actual layout of the text has already taken place. It specifies a structure for placing information about the display of a single line and determines which display method or methods are appropriate for the data.

In the Text application, the line breaks are statically defined, but the other editing characteristics such as kerning, justification, or tracking can be turned on or off through buttons in the interface. Support routines fill up the structure for each line and send the structure to the Generic Text Interface text display routine. This routine walks through the structure, sending the data and the appropriate **show** variation.

Examples 11.8 through 11.11 are an output of this approach for each of the test cases.

Example 11.8 *No spacing adjustments made from the default*

PostScript language trace

```
130 200 moveto
(The dull work went tediously on. Petitions were read, and) show
130 225 moveto
(proclamations, patents, and all manner of wordy, repetitious, and) show
```

Figure 11.6 *Printed text for the traces in Examples 11.8 through 11.11*

The dull work went tediously on. Petitions were read, and
proclamations, patents, and all manner of wordy, repetitious, and
Plain

The dull work went tediously on. Petitions were read, and
proclamations, patents, and all manner of wordy, repetitious, and
Kerning

The dull work went tediously on. Petitions were read, and
proclamations, patents, and all manner of wordy, repetitious, and
Kerning, justification

The   dull   work   went   tediously   on.   Petitions   were   read,   and
proclamations,   patents,   and   all   manner   of   wordy,   repetitious,   and
Kerning, justification, tracking

Example 11.9 *Kerning using **show** variants (same as Example 11.5)*

PostScript language trace

```
130 200 moveto
(The dull w) show
-0.12 0 rmoveto
(ork went tediously on. Petitions were read, and) show
130 225 moveto
(proclamations, patents, and all manner of w) show
-0.12 0 rmoveto
(ordy) show
-0.78 0 rmoveto
(, repetitious, and) show
```

Example 11.10 *Kerning and full-justification*

PostScript language trace

```
130 200 moveto
5.832 0 32 (The dull w) widthshow
-0.12 0 rmoveto
5.832 0 32 (ork went tediously on. Petitions were read, and) widthshow
130 225 moveto
2.3685 0 32 (proclamations, patents, and all manner of w) widthshow
-0.12 0 rmoveto
```

```
2.3685 0 32 (ordy) widthshow
-0.78 0 rmoveto
2.3685 0 32 (, repetitious, and) widthshow
```

Example 11.11 *Kerning, full-justification, and tracking using **show** variants*

PostScript language trace

```
130 200 moveto
7.832 0 32 2 0 (The dull w) awidthshow
-0.12 0 rmoveto
7.832 0 32 2 0 (ork went tediously on. Petitions were read, and) awidthshow
130 225 moveto
2.6185 0 32 2 0 (proclamations, patents, and all manner of w) awidthshow
-0.12 0 rmoveto
2.6185 0 32 2 0 (ordy) awidthshow
-0.78 0 rmoveto
2.6185 0 32 2 0 (, repetitious, and) awidthshow
```

11.3.4   Conclusions to Displaying Text

The traces in the previous examples provide a corollary to the timings. In other words, the amount of data and the number of operators used in an operation provide an indication of the efficiency of the operation. The operation with the smallest amount of data and the fewest operators is probably the fastest.

The simplest approach to preparing the PostScript data and operators is easier to comprehend and maintain than an approach that requires special cases handling. Achieving the optimum level of efficiency by adding greater complexity is only warranted when matched with significant gains in performance.

The **xshow** approach provides a high degree of both efficiency and simplicity. It has a fair amount of data but a minimum number of operators. More importantly, the **xshow** approach allows for a simple and general way to set text. The traces for each of the drawing cases are the same except for different numbers. Whenever possible, use this approach.

Note   *The amount of data is not as much of an issue in a Display PostScript environment because of the increased bandwidth of the system. The number of operators, though, is still an important factor in any implementation.*

The **xshow** operator shouldn't be used for printing to a Level 1 printer. An emulation is available, but it requires a **moveto** and **show** operation *for each character.* Use the **show** variant approach whenever a significant amount of text is displayed. Even though it is more complex than the **rmoveto/show** approach, the gains in performance appear to outweigh the loss in simplicity.

11.4   Screen Fonts

Outline fonts have a number of advantages over screen fonts consisting of bitmap characters. They are infinitely scalable making a continuous range of point sizes available, even fractional sizes. They also take up less disk space. Unlike bitmapped fonts where different bitmaps are needed for each size, only one outline font description is needed for all sizes. The PostScript font machinery scales the outline to fit the point size you want.

At small point sizes, though, outline fonts can sometimes present a legibility problem. Even though the algorithms for displaying type at small point sizes have improved greatly, hand-tuned bit maps still provide the best visual representation for small sizes. Screen fonts can be used in the Display PostScript system, and they are provided with either the system software by the OEM or a font by the font manufacturer.

The Display PostScript system uses screen fonts, as long as they are installed in the proper place, wherever the size matches the size of the outline font. The system provides some variability for substituting close approximations and rotated bitmaps, but some systems do not support these substitutions. The NeXT implementation supports close approximations but not rotated bitmaps.

In the case of Times-Roman, for example, a 12-point screen font is substituted for a 12-point outline font and a 10-point screen font is substituted for a 10-point outline font. For an 11-point font, the system substitutes a 10-point screen font but uses an 11-point character width. Screen font character glyphs are substituted but not character widths. The widths from the outline font still determine the character spacing.

Figure 11.7 shows the enlarged screen captures of 10-, 11-, and 12-point type represented with screen fonts.

Figure 11.7 *Screen font screen capture*

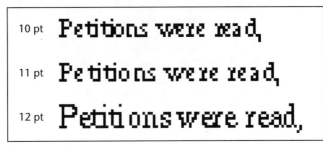

Enlarged 200%

Four entries in the top level of the dictionary for each font specify the substitution behavior: **BitmapWidths**, **ExactSize**, **InBetweenSize**, and **TransformedChar**. In the NeXT system, the default behavior is to substitute the exact size screen font or the closest match (within a certain threshold). When the coordinate system is skewed or rotated, no substitution occurs, and the outline font is used. Refer to the *PostScript Language Reference Manual, Second Edition* for more information on these entries and their values.

The Text application can override the default behavior and use the outline font at all times by creating a copy of the font and setting the four entries to turn off any screen font substitution, although this is probably not a common need in any application. The wrap in Example 11.12 shows how this is done. The name of the font to copy and the name of the new font are passed as arguments. The wrap copies the font omitting any **FID** or **UniqueID** entry during the copy and then defines the font under the new name. When used, it is set with the **selectfont** operator.

Example 11.12 *Redefining font to use outline font at all times*

PostScript language code

```
/*
 * Reencode the font, add BitmapWidths, ExactSize, InBetweenSize and
 * TransformedChar entries set to 0 to force the use of outline fonts at all times.
 */
defineps PSWCopyFont(char *F1; char *F2)
  /F1 findfont dup begin
  dup length 4 add dict begin
    {
      1 index /FID ne
      2 index /UniqueID ne and
      { def } {pop pop} ifelse
    } forall
```

```
/FontName /F2 def

/BitmapWidths false def
/ExactSize 0 def
/InBetweenSize 0 def
/TransformedChar 0 def

/F2 currentdict definefont pop
end
end
endps
```

Figure 11.8 shows the screen captures of the same sample in 10-, 11-, and 12-point type with an outline font instead of a screen font.

Figure 11.8 *Outline font screen capture*

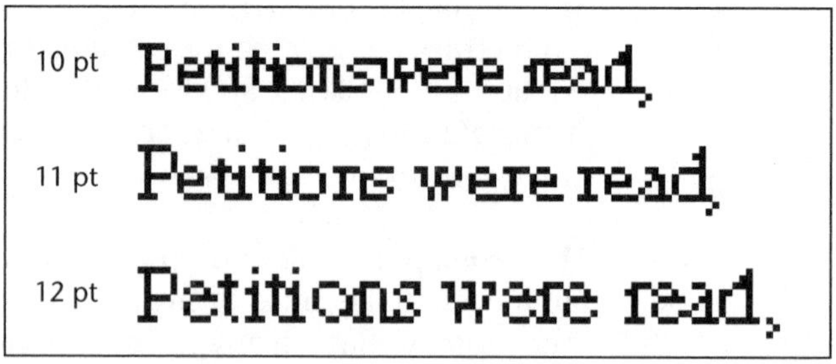

Enlarged 200%

The screen captures for the outline font show that they are legible even at small point sizes. This indicates the level of sophistication the font rendering algorithms have achieved. At the same time, ambiguities and inconsistent weightings appear (most noticeably in the serifs). These irregularities are magnified when seen on a screen showing a greater number of characters. Screen fonts, because they are hand-tuned, can often provide a more consistent and readable image. Until screen resolution improves, screen fonts are likely to be an important part of text display.

11.5   Screen and Printer Widths

One concern with using outline fonts at small point sizes (besides the loss in legibility) is the loss in consistency between the character widths. Differences in placement can have a significant impact on how a word looks. In some cases, the difference can make one word appear as two words or two words appear as one. This is an artifact of low screen resolution on the display that won't appear on the printed page, but it can make reading or editing text difficult on the screen.

The use of screen widths in these situations reduces the amount of variation between letters, resulting in a more readable display. The screen widths, like the screen glyphs, have the advantage of being tuned for the display. In the case of the NeXT MegaPixel Display, the screen widths are integer values that match the default device space.

Sending a message to an existing font object with the **screenFont** method returns the screen font's font object (if it exists). The *NXFontMetrics* structure obtained from this object contains the screen widths for the font at the existing size.

When screen fonts are used, the application should use the screen fonts for displaying the text, but use printer fonts for calculating the line breaks since the printer widths are used when printing. The difference can be distributed between the word breaks, which has the effect of preserving the location of the line breaks.

Figure 11.9 shows a sentence from the Text application. The top line uses the screen widths, and the bottom line uses the printer widths. The screen widths space the characters more uniformly for the display, but if they were used for printing, the character spacing would be off, showing large gaps between the letters in the words. This situation is shown in Figure 11.10.

Figure 11.9 *Screen capture using screen and printer widths*

Screen	The dull work went tediously on. Petitions were read, and
Printer	The dull work went tediously on. Petitions were read, and

Figure 11.10 *Printed sample using screen and printer widths*

Screen	The dull work went tediously on. Petitions were read, and
Printer	The dull work went tediously on. Petitions were read, and

11.6   Font Cache

The font cache is a system resource that stores character descriptions as masks. Large masks are stored in a compressed format. When a character is displayed, the cache is checked; if a matching mask is found, it is used instead of rendering a new character. The time it takes to display a set of characters with the cache can be up to 1000 times faster than without the cache.

The font cache rarely needs adjustment. The Text application only disables the font cache to show its benefit. For the most part, the settings of the font cache should not be changed.

Table 11.2 *Times for font cache performance*

Method	Time
Display times in milliseconds for 1130 characters	
With Font Cache	229
Without Font Cache	25352

11.7   Conclusions

- Justification, pair kerning, and tracking are three cases in which the default character spacing must be overridden to display the text.

- The most common approach to kerning in a computer environment is to use kerning pairs provided with the font or created by an application. These pairs indicate to the characters where the space between them should change and how much it should change.

- Adobe Font Metric (AFM) files provide general information about a font as well as specific information about each character, such as the widths, bounding boxes, and kerning pairs. The Font class in the Application Kit parses these files and places the information into a structure that can be accessed quickly.

- The **xshow, yshow**, and **xyshow** operators are preferred to the **show** operator for text display because they allow flexible spacing between characters.

- The Display PostScript system supports several modes of screen font substitution strategies. The NeXTstep implementation substitutes a screen font if the screen font size and the requested size match exactly or are a close approximation.

CHAPTER 12

Importing and Exporting Graphics Files

The NeXT Application Kit and the Display PostScript system provide support for importing and exporting EPS and TIFF (tag image file format) files into and out of applications. Imported EPS files can be imaged directly to the screen instead of relying on a preview image.

Figure 12.1 *Main drawing window for Import application*

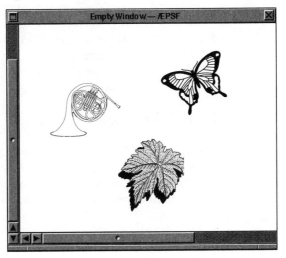

The encapsulated PostScript file format (EPS) describes a standard format for importing and exporting PostScript language files in all computer system environments. The TIFF file format specifies a standard format for bitmap images on many platforms. These formats enable you to import graphics produced with one application into another application.

For example, specifying a common ground between the *exporter* (the application producing the file) and the *importer* (the application including the file) allows a chart in a spreadsheet program to be incorporated into a publication prepared with a page layout program.

Another example is importing a logo designed in a graphics illustration program and placing it within an image drawn with another illustration program. Most of the illustrations in this book are examples of imported files.

Including and exporting EPS and TIFF files should be a standard feature in most graphics and desktop publishing applications as well as in many other applications. The Import application has been developed as a guide to incorporating graphics files into an application in a Display PostScript environment.

The NeXT Application Kit and the Display PostScript system provide many of the capabilities needed to import EPS and TIFF files and view the files on the screen. The Import application and this chapter take this process a step further by showing the process within an application and by incorporating other capabilities not provided for in Version 2.0 of the Application Kit. (The term *file* is used two ways in this chapter: to refer to a file containing an EPS or a TIFF graphic and to refer to the graphic picture described by the file.)

The features of the application are

- Placing an imported file in a page description. The recommended steps for placing an EPS or TIFF file in a page description are to translate, rotate, and scale the file. In addition, EPS files need a second translation along with a few other steps.

- Representing the position of an imported file. A boundary rectangle and a rotation instance variable are used to represent the position of an EPS file within a document. The rectangle holds the origin and size of the graphic in the document, and the rotation variable holds the amount of rotation of the file. (The rotation is relative to the lower left corner of the graphic.)

- Offscreen buffering of imaged files. An NXImage object holds the most recent image of the imported file. A new image is drawn whenever the graphic is resized or rotated or whenever the scale of the document changes. (Redrawing the graphic is not necessary if it is moved within the document because the offscreen image does not change.)

Using an offscreen image eliminates redrawing the graphic with each scroll or move. When a scroll or move occurs, the image stored in the NXImage object is composited into the document window.

- Error response and recovery for imported EPS files. EPS files are imaged into a separate DPS context provided by the NXEPSImageRep object. Using the separate context protects the application's context from errors that might be in an imported file. If an error occurs when imaging a file, an error message appears, and the error is logged to the console. Without the shielding, errors in an EPS file might affect the application, causing potentially fatal errors.

- Parsing EPS files. Parsing EPS files and extracting relevant information is an important part of importing EPS files. Routines provided in the Import application have been written so that they can be extended as future parsing requirements dictate. The NXEPSImageRep class parses EPS files, but it only validates the file as an EPS file, gets the bounding box, and parses the fonts in the %%DocumentFonts: comment.

  The fonts are not matched to the system fonts nor are other resources extracted. The parsing routines supplied in the Import application retrieve the resource information, check the availability within the system, and display a panel when some resources cannot be located. The resources checked in the routines include the fonts, files, procedure sets, forms, and patterns.

- Exporting as EPS or TIFF. Exporting a page or portion of the page as an EPS file means directing the PostScript page description to a stream context instead of to the window server. Use the View object method **copyPSCodeInside:to:** for this. The method takes a rectangle and a stream and directs the PostScript imaging to the stream. Exporting as a TIFF means first imaging the portion of the document into a buffer and then converting the raster image to the TIFF format. Objects and routines in the Application Kit are available to perform the bulk of the conversion.

- Saving as EPS with or without a preview. The encapsulated PostScript file format specification lists several options for incorporating a preview image along with the PostScript code. One of these preview images, encapsulated PostScript interchange format (EPSI), is featured in the Import application. Although not needed with a Display PostScript system, the preview can be a great help in a non-Display PostScript system.

In addition to these features, the Import application introduces several user interface techniques that provide more complete interaction with imported files. These techniques include rotation; constraining to original aspect, original size, and original ratio menu options; and *click to drop* and *click and drag* placement interfaces. These are not required nor are they meant to establish a standard interface for imported files. They are provided as examples of basic capabilities that are possible when importing files into an application.

12.1   EPS Files

An EPS file is a single-page PostScript language program that describes an illustration. It is similar to other PostScript language page descriptions but it has a few restrictions that allow the file to be imported into an application and still behave in a predictable and expected manner. The format is limited to one page because importing a multi-page description into a document raises a number of issues. Page independence and device independence are required so that the file appears the same structurally regardless of the placement on the page or the output device.

Every EPS file should contain two components in addition to the actual PostScript language page description. Represented as PostScript language comments, one identifies the file as an EPS file and the other describes the bounding box of the file. The bounding box is used by importing applications to place the graphic and to provide you with a visual aspect of the size of the graphic.

Other comments and components are optional but are included to provide expanded capabilities and error checking. One of the more common components is a *preview image*. Although not required by the EPS specification, the preview image is encouraged in environments that do not have access to the Display PostScript system and cannot image the files onscreen. A preview image is not necessary in a Display PostScript environment because the file can be imaged on the screen. It is useful on non-DPS systems and has become an expected part of EPS files in such systems.

The types or formats for the preview images often differ from system to system simply because different systems support different imaging capabilities. A PICT representation is the more common type of preview image for the Macintosh® environment while a TIFF representation is more common in the DOS world and GIF is more common in the UNIX world.

Other optional comments include the types of fonts or colors used or needed in the description and the names of files included in the description. Some of these are covered in the following sections. The complete description of the EPS format can be found in Appendix H of the *PostScript Language Reference Manual, Second Edition*.

12.2 TIFF Files

The tag image file format (TIFF) is one standard for representing bitmap images. Applications can import and export TIFF files as long as the application can read and write the correct format and render the image on the display. Functions and classes in the Application Kit help with formatting issues while the Display PostScript system handles imaging issues. The Import application uses a subclass of the NXBitmapImageRep class to manage the conversion of the TIFF format to a machine-readable format and to display the image at the correct size, scale, and rotation.

The coordinate mapping between user space and device space in the PostScript imaging model plays a large role in the display of images. The bitmap image in a TIFF file does not need to conform to bit-to-pixel mapping. The transformation matrix maps the bits in the image to the appropriate pixel or pixels, so that images do not have to scale by a number divisible by two. Images can be variably and nonuniformly scaled leaving mapping to device space to the interpreter.

Figure 12.2 *Mapping image data to device space*

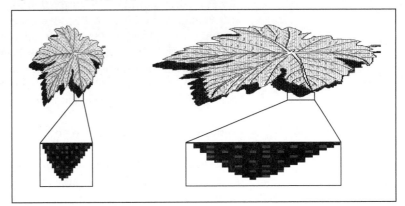

12.3   Placing an EPS or TIFF File in a Page Description

In the Import application, you can position, scale, and rotate imported files within documents. The interfaces in applications that allow these capabilities are often very complex from a programming standpoint. Once the placement, angle, and size has been determined, though, the steps for placing the file in a page description are straightforward and apply when writing a file to the screen or to a printer. These steps assume a nonflipped coordinate system (default orientation, positive values at the top) and rotation relative to the lower left corner of the imported file.

Perform the following steps when placing an imported file at a specific location on a page:

1. Translate to where the lower left corner will appear.

2. Rotate the desired number of degrees.

3. Scale the coordinate system to match the new dimensions.

These steps position the lower left corner of the page of the imported file at the selected position in the document. In a TIFF file, this is all that is required.

Positioning an EPS file requires additional steps. As with a TIFF file, an EPS file has a width and height dimension. In addition, though, it has an origin. An EPS file with a bounding box comment such as %%BoundingBox: 20 20 80 80 means that the lower left corner of the graphic is at (20, 20) and the upper right corner of the graphic is at (80, 80). (The width and height are the difference in the x and y values.) Without additional steps to compensate for the movement away from the origin, an imported file would be out of position by the distance between (0, 0) and the lower left corner of the bounding box.

Perform the following steps to position the file correctly:

1. Translate the coordinate space in the opposite direction to counter-act the offset from the origin. (Take the negative of the values of the lower left corner.)

2. Place a clipping path around the EPS file using the dimensions from the bounding box as the frame for the clip. The clipping path prevents any marks drawn by the EPS file from appearing outside the bounding box of the imported file.

Note *An application can also provide a user interface option for allowing an arbitrary path to be used as the clipping path.*

Figure 12.3 *Placing an imported file within a page description*

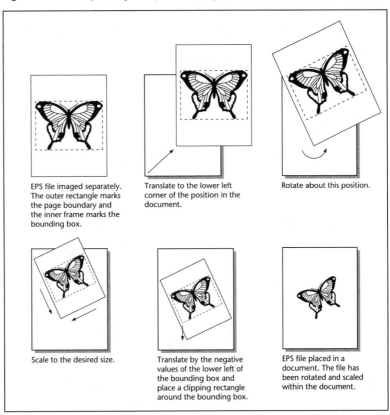

EPS file imaged separately. The outer rectangle marks the page boundary and the inner frame marks the bounding box.

Translate to the lower left corner of the position in the document.

Rotate about this position.

Scale to the desired size.

Translate by the negative values of the lower left of the bounding box and place a clipping rectangle around the bounding box.

EPS file placed in a document. The file has been rotated and scaled within the document.

Another important consideration when including an EPS file in a document is to protect the state of the operand and dictionary stacks and to initialize the graphics state for the EPS file before imaging the file. The NXEPSImageRep handles this preparation and provides a method, **prepareGState**, for overriding the initialization portion.

Returning the operand and dictionary stacks to their states before the import is important because subsequent operations might rely on values or dictionaries placed on the stack. Items left on these stacks by an EPS file can cause problems for these operations. Initializing the graphics state is important because the imported file might not initialize it. If the current color was left as white before the import, but the imported file assumed it was black, then parts or all of the file would appear as white.

The PostScript language trace in Example 12.1 shows steps for a TIFF image and Example 12.2 show steps for an EPS file. The initial file position is the same, but the EPS files require additional steps. Appendix H, "Encapsulated PostScript File Format—Version 3.0," in the *PostScript Language Reference Manual, Second Edition* provides the full text of this positioning and preparation steps for EPS files.

Example 12.1 *Positioning a TIFF file*

PostScript language trace

```
131 225 translate
0 rotate
18.6875 18.6875 scale
%%BeginDocument: /Local Library/Art/Import.tiff
... TIFF file written here ...
%%EndDocument
```

Example 12.2 *Positioning an EPS file*

PostScript language trace

```
142 276 translate
25 rotate
0.893548 0.893548 scale
0 0 260 310 rectclip
-95 -145 translate

/__NXEPSSave save def
/showpage { } def
0 setgray 0 setlinecap 1 setlinewidth
0 setlinejoin 10 setmiterlimit [ ] 0 setdash newpath count
/__NXEPSOpCount exch def
/__NXEPSDictCount countdictstack def
%%BeginDocument: /Local Library/Art/Rooster.eps
... EPS file written here ...
%%EndDocument
```

```
count __NXEPSOpCount sub {pop} repeat
countdictstack __NXEPSDictCount sub {end} repeat
__NXEPSSave restore
```

12.4 Representing the Position of Imported Files

The position of a file within a page can be represented several ways. The approach taken in the Import application uses two variables to retain the position, scale, and rotation of an imported file. (Some of the variables in the NXEPSImageRep and NXBitmapImageRep are also used for positioning and scaling.) These variables appear as instance variables in the GraphicImport object, which is used by the Import application to handle imported files. Each imported file is represented by an instance of the GraphicImport class.

The *bounds* rectangle holds the position and size of the file within the current document. The *rotation* instance *variable* holds the amount of rotation of the file in radians. (The trigonometry functions in UNIX C library routines use radians and the trigonometry functions in PostScript language routines use degrees, so the radian value needs to be converted to degrees before it is sent to the server.)

The rotation occurs about the lower left corner of the *bounds* rectangle. The scale of the graphic is represented by the relationship between the widths and heights of the *bounds* rectangle and the original bounding box of the file. The bounding box of an EPS file is an instance variable in the NXEPSImageRep class, and the size of a TIFF file is an instance variable in the NXBitmapImageRep class.

When the file is imaged, the *bounds* rectangle provides the information for the first translate, the *rotation* provides the information for the rotate, and the ratio between the *bounds* and the original bounding box or size dimensions provides the scale factor. The original bounding box provides values for the last translate and clipping values for the file.

Example 12.3 *Representing the position of imported files (GraphicImport.m)*

C language code

```
/*
 * The image variable holds the NXImage (the offscreen buffer of
 * the file). The imagerep variable holds the NXEPSImageRepSub
 * or NXBitmapImageRepSub. This class retains the original
 * dimensions of the file as an instance variable. The rotation
 * variable stores the rotation of the file and the bounds holds
 * the position and dimensions of the file in the document.
 * (The dimensions are in unrotated space.)
 */
@interface GraphicImport:Object
{
    ...
    id      image,
            imagerep;

    float   rotation;

    NXRect bounds;
    ...
}
@end
```

The interface issues for positioning an imported file within a document are more complicated and varied than the actual placement in a page description. Some of the issues are covered in section 12.11, "User Interface Issues," in this chapter. Other details can be obtained from the source code of the application.

12.5 Error Response and Recovery for EPS Files

An application has no control over the contents of an included EPS file, so it cannot ensure that the file won't contain errors. In a non-Display PostScript environment, errors in imported EPS files are not catastrophic. The page might not print or might appear different than anticipated, but it won't affect the operation of the application.

In a Display PostScript environment, however, the situation is more serious. PostScript language errors can cause unpredictable side effects within a context if an error occurs. In the application context, the operation of the application is at risk. As a result, an application must protect its context from errors contained in EPS files.

Note *A context can be thought of as a virtual printer. It has its own set of stacks, input/output facilities, and memory space. Each application typically has its own context to control drawing and window events. The Application object within the NeXT Application Kit manages much of the overhead associated with creating, managing, and destroying the application context.*

One way to protect against errors is to use the **save** and **restore** operators in connection with the *NX_DURING*, *NX_HANDLER*, and *NX_ENDHANDLER* macros. This is satisfactory, but it is not nearly as robust as needed.

The Import application takes the approach a step further by imaging EPS files with the NXEPSImageRep object, taking advantage of the separate context provided by this object. When the NXEPSImageRep is sent a **draw** or **drawIn:** message, it captures the current gstate, which includes the current device (a window in this case) and CTM, and installs it as the current gstate in another context.

Errors within the EPS file affect the other context and not the application context. The return value of the **draw** and **drawIn:** methods indicates the success of the drawing operation. In the Import application, an alert panel appears if this value indicates any errors. (The NXEPSImageRep automatically writes the PostScript errors to the console.)

12.6 Offscreen Buffering of Imaged Files

EPS and TIFF files can be of any length or complexity. Some can image almost instantly while others can take several seconds or more. (Some of the test files used with the Import application take from two to eight seconds to image in our timings.) NXImage objects are used in the Import application to reduce the number of times a file must be imaged. These images are composited onto the drawing view of the document when needed. This allows for more responsive scrolling and moving of files within the document.

A file is imaged into a NXImage when the file is first imported, the size changes (either by grabbing and dragging a control point or by selecting the Original Size or Original Ratio menu items), the rotation changes, or the scale of the document is enlarged or reduced. When you drag a control point, only a gray outline and the control points appear. (Imaging an imported file after each mouse drag is impractical.) Once you release the mouse button, the imported file is drawn to fit into the gray outline.

Because the imported file is imaged in an offscreen buffer, the drawing cannot be seen onscreen. In the Import application, a gray box appears with the string **imaging file...** displayed in the center. Once the drawing is complete, the offscreen buffer is composited into the document window.

Imported files are reimaged whenever you zoom in or out of the document. Although scaling the bitmaps is possible, it is much simpler and cleaner to reimage the file into a different sized buffer. Reimaging the file takes advantage of the halftoning and other features of the interpreter to provide the best representation of the file at the selected size, scale, and rotation. If the buffer size becomes too large, the file is imaged directly into the drawing view of the document.

The Import application sets the maximum size of the buffer at 1.5 times the screen size. Not employing an upper limit might result in disk thrashing when the size of the files exceeds the available RAM size. Scrolling and moving are significantly slower when imported files are imaged directly into the drawing view because the entire file has to be reimaged for each refresh.

The Import application employs a preference option that turns off the imaging of imported files, illustrated in Figure 12.4. When this option is set to not image the files, a gray box appears in place of the imaged file. This option is helpful when editing documents with a large number of imported files where visual inspection of the files is not important. (This book is an example.)

Figure 12.4 *Example of imaging turned off*

12.7   Main Drawing Routine for the GraphicImport Object

In the Import application, each imported EPS and TIFF file is represented by a GraphicImport object. One instance variable in this class is an id to an NXImage object. Another instance variable is an id to a subclass of NXEPSImageRepSub or NXBitmapImageRep. The NXImage object handles buffering the image, while the NXEPSImageRepSub or NXBitmapImageRep object handles the imaging of the file. These are important components of the drawing process.

Additional issues become apparent when trying to provide a responsive and complete drawing environment. These involve knowing when to draw the file or composite from the buffer, knowing when to image the file or a gray box, and knowing when to draw into the NXImage or the drawing view directly. Interface issues include displaying a gray box when imaging and displaying an error panel when errors occur.

Example 12.4 is the drawing routine for the GraphicImport object. The types of drawing involve drawing the frame of the file (the optimal response when resizing or rotating), drawing a gray box, drawing for printing, copying cases, and drawing to the display.

A dirty flag indicates when the image must be redrawn. The flag is marked dirty whenever the size or rotation changes. The relationship between the size of the NXImage and the combination of the scale and the dimensions of the file also factor into the decision of whether to redraw the image.

Example 12.4 *Drawing routine (GraphicImport object)*

C language code

```
- drawObject:(NXRect *) r  withFlags:(int) flags  inView:view
{
  BOOL    useImage;

  float      scale;

  NXRect  rect, frame;

  if (!r || IntersectsRotatedRect (r, &bounds, rotation))
  {
    if (flags & REDRAWFLAG)
    {
      scale = [[view  superview]  scale];
      PSgsave( );
      PSWTranslateRotate (bounds.origin.x, bounds.origin.y,
```

```
                            rotation * ANGLE);
        PSWSetLine (1.0/scale, NX_LTGRAY);
        PSrectstroke(0.0, 0.0, bounds.size.width, bounds.size.height);
        PSgrestore( );
    }
    else if (gflags.unimageable || ![NXApp imagingFlag])
    {
        /* Draw a gray box if the file is not to be imaged. */
        [self drawBoxforRect:r imaging:NO];
        gflags.new = NO;
    }
    else if (NXDrawingStatus == NX_PRINTING ||
                NXDrawingStatus == NX_COPYING)
    {
        [imagerep drawIn:&bounds with:(rotation*180/M_PI)];
    }
    else
    {
        useImage = YES;

        /* Get the frame of the epsf file. */
        RotateRectBounds (&frame, &bounds, &bounds.origin, rotation);
        scale = [[view superview] scale];

        /*
         * Size the cache.Use the NXImage if the size is less than
         * a predetermined size.
         */
        [image getSize:&rect.size];
        if (frame.size.width*scale != rect.size.width ||
          frame.size.height*scale != rect.size.height)
        {
            gflags.dirty = YES;
            rect.size.width = frame.size.width * scale;
            rect.size.height = frame.size.height * scale;
            if (rect.size.width < IMAGE_MAX &&
                    rect.size.height < IMAGE_MAX)
            {
                [image setSize:&rect.size];
                [image getSize:&rect.size];
            }
            else
                useImage = NO;
        }

        if (gflags.dirty)
        {
            /*
             * Draw the gray box that tells the user the file
```

```
* is being imaged.
*/
[view lockFocus];
[self drawBoxforRect:r imaging:YES];
[view unlockFocus];
[[view window] flushWindow];
NXPing( );

/*
* Setup the drawing so that it goes into an NXImage.
* Some prep work needs to be done to set the
* position.
*/
if (useImage)
{
  rect.origin.x = rect.origin.y = 0;
  [image lockFocus];
  PSsetalpha(0.0);
  PSsetgray(NX_WHITE);
  NXRectFill(&rect);
  PSsetalpha(1.0);

  PSscale(scale, scale);
  PStranslate(-frame.origin.x, -frame.origin.y);
}

/*
* Draw the file into a subclass of NXEPSImageRep.
* Take the rotation into account.
*/
gflags.error = ![imagerep drawIn:&bounds
    with:(rotation*180/M_PI)];

if (useImage)
  [image unlockFocus];

/*
* Display an error panel if one occurs. If it is
* a newly imported file, it will not be
* imported. If it is an existing file, it
* will be marked as unimageable.
*/
if (gflags.error)
{
  gflags.unimageable = YES;
  [self displayError];
  if (!gflags.new)
    [self drawBoxforRect:r imaging:NO];
}
```

```
    }

    /*
    * Composite the buffer to the currently focused view.
    */
    if (useImage && !gflags.error)
    {
      rect.origin.x = rect.origin.y = 0;
      rect.size.width = frame.size.width * scale;
      rect.size.height = frame.size.height * scale;
      [image  composite:NX_SOVER  fromRect:&rect
          toPoint:&frame.origin];
    }

    gflags.new = NO;
    gflags.dirty = NO;
  }
}

  return self;
}
```

12.8   Parsing an EPS File

When importing EPS files, the importing application must parse the file
and extract important characteristics from within the file. The most
important aspects of parsing are to validate the file as a legal EPS file and
to obtain the bounding box of the file.

A valid EPS file is marked by a %!PS-Adobe-a.a EPSF-b.b comment as
the first line in the file where the *a*'s correspond to the version of the
Document Structuring Conventions, and the *b*'s correspond to the
version of the EPS file format specification. The parsing routines in
the Import application look for this comment as an indication of a
valid file.

The versions of the DSC and EPS comments are not as important at this
level of import. Print managers, color separators, and other types of
applications might be more concerned about the version numbers.
The version numbers provide information about the types of comments
and capabilities you can expect.

The bounding box comment can appear at the beginning or end of the file. If it is not present, the importing application should issue an error message and terminate the import. The format of the comment is

%%BoundingBox: *llx lly urx ury*

The first two numbers are the coordinates of the lower left of the image and the last two are the coordinates of the upper right of the image. (These dimensions are not the same as the origin and size dimensions in the NeXT rectangle structure.)

Although these comments are the most important, others carry significant weight when trying to handle imported files in a complete sense. Knowing which resources (files, fonts, procedure sets, forms, and patterns) are in an imported file is important for several reasons:

- Unavailable resources can be flagged and their absence relayed to you. Finding that fonts used in the file are not in the system or that included files or procedure sets can't be found, allows the application to substitute fonts or prompt for the location of the missing resources. The panel in Figure 12.5 lists the unavailable resources.

Figure 12.5 *Panel listing unavailable resources*

Resources included in the document with a %%Include... comment can be located and incorporated into the document. The Import application expands any files that contain a %%IncludeFile: comment by writing a temporary file containing the expanded PostScript code. The file listed in the comment is written into the temporary file (instead of the %%IncludeFile: command). The temporary file is then used for display and printing. (Use the original file for saving.)

- Certain resources might need to be skipped when parsing. This mainly applies to included files (EPS files contained within the EPS file). When parsing a file, it is important to know where the file begins and ends so that the parser can skip through and not process any comments. (The %%BeginDocument and %%EndDocument comments indicate an included file.) Otherwise, comments within a nested file might cause a conflict with the comments for the document. The bounding box comment in a nested file is one example where a conflict could occur.

- Resources in the imported EPS file must be propagated to the document comments. This practice provides complete information about the document to print managers, color separators, and other similar applications.

Note   *Removing multiple copies of procedure set definitions is possible once the importing application knows the procedure sets and where they lie. Importing two Adobe Illustrator files imports two separate copies of the procedure sets. Propagating the procedure sets to the beginning of the document and eliminating multiple sets reduces the size of the document. The savings increases with each subsequent inclusion of an Illustrator file. Imported procedure sets are not handled this way in the Import application, but applications that make extensive use of imported files might want to consider this.*

The parsing routines in the Import application check for a proper EPS file header, obtain the bounding box and the list of resources used in the file, and skip through any nested files. The structure and routines of the parser are written so that they can be extended to handle additional parsing requirements. Source code for the routines is not included in this document because of the length.

The code in Example 12.5 shows an excerpt from an EPS file. The areas in bold indicate the comments recognized and processed by the parsing routines in the Import application.

Example 12.5 *Parsed comments in sample EPS file*

```
%!PS-Adobe-2.0 EPSF-1.2
%%Creator: Adobe Illustrator 88(TM) 1.9.3
%%For: (Joe Green) (Adobe Systems Incorporated)
%%Title: (SampleFile.eps)
%%CreationDate: (5/18/90) (15:13)
%%DocumentFonts: Times-Roman Caslon
%%DocumentNeededFonts: Times-Roman Caslon
%%DocumentProcSets: Adobe_packedarray 1 0
%%DocumentSuppliedProcSets: Adobe_packedarray 1 0
```

```
%%DocumentProcSets: Adobe_cmykcolor 2 0
%%DocumentSuppliedProcSets: Adobe_cmykcolor 2 0
%%DocumentProcSets: Adobe_cshow 3 0
%%DocumentSuppliedProcSets: Adobe_cshow 3 0
%%DocumentProcSets: Adobe_customcolor 4 0
%%DocumentSuppliedProcSets: Adobe_customcolor 4 0
%%DocumentProcSets: Adobe_Illustrator881 5 0
%%DocumentSuppliedProcSets: Adobe_Illustrator881 5 0
%%ColorUsage: Black&White
%%DocumentProcessColors: Black
%%BoundingBox:117 54 436 675
%%TemplateBox:276 376 276 376
%%TileBox:-552 730 0 1460
%%DocumentPreview: None
%%EndComments

... The rest of the prolog and the procedure set definitions would be here ...

%%EndProlog

... Some of the script of the document would be here ...

%%BeginDocument: EmbeddedFile.eps
%!PS-Adobe-2.0 EPSF-1.2
%%DocumentFonts: Times-Roman
%%BoundingBox:0 0 612 792
%%EndComments
%%EndProlog

... The script of the embedded file would be here ...

%%EndDocument

... The rest of the script of the document would be here ...

%%Trailer
```

Note   *TIFF images must also be parsed, but the NXBitmapImageRep class handles this, requiring no additional intervention or capabilities.*

12.9   Exported EPS and TIFF Files

Exporting a page or a portion of a page in a document as an EPS file involves redirecting the PostScript page description from the window server to a stream or file. The View class method **copyPSCodeInside:to:** takes a rectangle and stream, sets up a stream context, then sends a message to **drawSelf::** to draw the portion needed. This method also sends a message to the methods that insert the PostScript language comments needed for a correct EPS file (!PS-Adobe... and %%BoundingBox...). The code in Example 12.7 shows the steps.

Exporting a portion of the document as a TIFF means first imaging a page or portion of a page into an offscreen window or NXImage object, turning the raster image into the TIFF format, and writing the TIFF to a stream. The Application Kit has objects and routines designed for this purpose. The Draw application of the */NextDeveloper/Examples* directory in the NeXT file system is a good source for information on this process.

12.10   Including Preview Data in EPS Files

Preview data in an EPS file is not needed in a Display PostScript environment because the PostScript in the file can be executed directly and displayed on the screen. Computers that don't use the Display PostScript system as their imaging model, however, don't have the same advantage. For a visual key to the contents of the file, some form of preview data must be provided with the EPS file.

The Import application exports one type of preview: the encapsulated PostScript interchange (EPSI) format. This format consists of an EPS file with a hex data preview image appearing as comments in the header. The hex data is enclosed within a %%BeginPreview and a %%EndPreview comment nesting. Example 12.6 shows the EPSI format.

Example 12.6 *Sample EPS files with EPSI preview image*

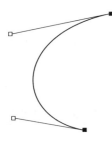

PostScript language code

```
%!PS-Adobe-2.0 EPSF-1.2
%%Title: /simple.eps
%%BoundingBox: 102 536 126 559
%%EndComments

%%BeginPreview: 24 23 1 23
% 000000
% 000000
% 000000
% 000000
% 000000
% 000000
% 000000
% 000000
% 000000
% 000000
% 000000
```

```
% 0007c0
% 007c00
% 079000
% 002000
% 004000
% 002000
% 007800
% 001e00
% 000100
% 000000
% 000000
% 000000
%%EndPreview

%%EndProlog
...

%%Trailer
...
```

A raster image of the file is necessary for any type of preview image. The Import application images the file into an NXImage with a two-bit-per-pixel depth. An NXBitmapImageRep is created from the NXImage by initializing the NXBitmapImageRep with an **initFromData: fromRect:**. This method reads the data from the currently focused view and places it in an instance variable in an NXBitmapImageRep object. The two-bit-per-pixel data in the NXBitmapImageRep is reduced to a one-bit image and printed as a hex comment at the appropriate point in the printing process.

The image data starts at the top left and continues to the right and down. In other words, the top of the image should be at the beginning of the data and the bottom of the image at the end.

The code used to obtain the image data as well as the top-level routines for writing preview lines as hex comments appear in Example 12.7. The *imageId* variable is an instance variable, since it is accessed within methods with no formal connection to each other. The **writeEpsfPreview** procedure reduces the two-bit-per-pixel image to one bit and writes it as a comment to the correct Display PostScript context.

Example 12.7 *Exporting an EPS file (Document.m)*

C language code

```
/*
 * Writes out the document in EPS format. Messaged by a
 * menu item.
 */
- saveTo:sender
{
  id    savepanel;

  NXStream*stream;

  savepanel = [[SaveAsPanel  new]  setSaveTo];
  if ([savepanel runModal])
  {
    stream = NXOpenMemory(NULL, 0, NX_WRITEONLY);
    if (stream)
    {
      [drawingviewId writePSToStream:stream];
      NXSaveToFile(stream, [savepanel  filename]);
      NXCloseMemory(stream, NX_FREEBUFFER);
    }
    else
      Notify("Save Error", "Cannot open a stream to the file.");
  }

  return self;
}
```

Example 12.8 *Exporting an EPS file (DrawingView.m)*

C language code

```
@interface DrawingView:View
{
  id           imageId,
  ...
}
@end

@implementation DrawingView
...

/*
 * This method copies the PostScript code for the graphics and
 * writes it to the stream passed in. Includes the preview image
 * when appropriate. Creates an NXImage with a two bit per pixel
 * depth and then draws the graphics into it. An NXBitmapImage is
 * created from that image. The NXBitmapImage is then used
```

```
    * during the printing routines to provide the hex preview data.
    */
- writePSToStream:(NXStream *) stream
{
  id    nximageId, templist;

  NXRectbbox;

  if (stream)
  {
    imageId = NULL
    nximageId = NULL
    templist = graphiclistId;
    graphiclistId = selectedlistId;
    [graphiclistId  getBounds:&bbox];
    if ([[SaveAsPanel  new]  format] == SAVE_EPSPREVIEW)
    {
      nximageId = [[NXImage  alloc]  initSize:&bbox.size];
      [nximageId  useCacheWithDepth:NX_TwoBitGrayDepth];
      if ([nximageId  lockFocus])
      {
        PStranslate(-bbox.origin.x, -bbox.origin.y);
        PSsetgray(NX_WHITE);
        NXRectFill(&bbox);
        [graphiclistId  drawObject:&bbox  withFlags:NOFLAGS
            inView:self];

        imageId = [[NXBitmapImageRep  alloc]  initData:NULL
            fromRect:&bbox];
        [nximageId  unlockFocus];
      }
    }

    [self copyPSCodeInside:&bbox to:stream];

    selectedlistId = graphiclistId;
    graphiclistId = templist;
    [nximageId  free];
    [imageId  free];
    imageId = NULL;
  }

  return self;
}

/*
* Add the preview image data if requested.
*/
- endHeaderComments
```

```
{
  DPSContextctxt;

  if (NXDrawingStatus == NX_COPYING)
  {
    ctxt = DPSGetCurrentContext( );
    DPSPrintf(ctxt, "%%%%EndComments\n\n");
    ...
    if (imageId && [[SaveAsPanel  new]  format] == SAVE_EPSPREVIEW)
      WriteEpsfPreview(imageId);
  }
  else
    [super  endHeaderComments];

  return self;
}
@end
```

12.11   User Interface Issues

This section shows some basic interface techniques for manipulating
imported files. The items addressed include full range rotation, constraining to original aspect, *click to drop* and *click and drag* placement
interfaces, and original size and original ratio menu options. These are
not meant to establish a user interface standard for importing EPS and
TIFF files, but rather to illustrate basic techniques that are common to
importing applications.

12.11.1   Rotation

Rotating an imported file is not as common as moving and resizing, but
it is as simple to perform within the PostScript language. The steps are
to translate, rotate, and then scale. (Scaling before the rotation will skew
the axes if the scale is not proportional.)

The difficulty is not in the low-level routines but in the interface. Determining whether a mouse click is near a control point or inside a rotated
rectangle requires more than an intersecting rectangle check. One alternative is to keep the exact location of the control points. When a check
is made, the control points can be tested, with the path formed by the
four corners.

An easier way is to keep the rectangle as if not rotated. The rotation is
recorded in a separate variable as the amount about the origin of the
rectangle. When a hit detection check is made, instead of rotating the

control point, the mouse point is rotated. This is done in the negative direction about the origin of the rectangle. The negative rotation on the mouse point has the same effect as a positive rotation on the rectangle.

The new coordinates can then be tested on the control points and rectangle using the rectangle intersection routine. Figure 12.6 shows how this technique works. The example assumes a nonflipped coordinate system and the lower left corner of the rectangle as the center of rotation.

The mouse down point and the rotated rectangle are dotted, while the solid rectangle is retained as an instance variable along with the rotation. The black point is the mouse point after the negative rotation although the orientation of the mouse point is the same. Even though the orientation of the rectangles is different, the amount of latitude that is built into the hit detection check makes this difference insignificant.

Figure 12.6 *Rotating mouse point to make hit detection check*

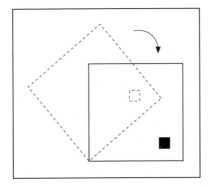

Another area where more effort is required is in keeping track of the enclosing frame for a rotated rectangle. An application must know the frame of the rectangle to determine whether or not to draw the graphic. Again, a separate variable can hold the frame. As in the previous case, this information is obtained only when needed.

A procedure in the Import application takes a rectangle rotated about a point at a given angle and calculates the enclosing frame. Figure 12.7 illustrates the concept. The black rectangle is the rotated rectangle and the gray rectangle is its bounding box in nonrotated space.

Figure 12.7 *Frame enclosing rotated rectangle*

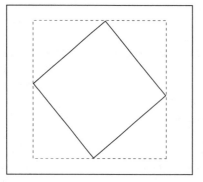

The important aspects of the framework used in the Import application are

- To establish a center of rotation; in this case it is the lower left corner of the file. Other possible locations include the center, the upper left corner, or any arbitrary point you choose.

- To negatively rotate any point used in calculations and to positively rotate any point returned from the GraphicImport object. The negative rotation counteracts the rotation of the file while the positive rotation reflects the true coordinates to external objects.

12.11.2   Constraining to Original Aspect Ratio

When resizing imported files, you should be given the opportunity to preserve the ratio between the width and the height. Resizing a file without keeping the same ratio of the dimensions provides interesting special effects, but usually you want to preserve the original ratio.

In the Import application, the file is constrained to the original aspect in two instances. The first is when you import the file with the click and drag interface. With this method you select the file to import, click the mouse where the upper left corner of the file should go, and then drag out a rectangle for the file. When you release, the file is imaged to fit into the rectangle.

When you drag out this rectangle initially, the ratio of the width versus the height reflects the ratio of the original bounding box. Subsequent resizes are not constrained to these dimensions except when you hold down the shift key during a resize. In these instances, the rectangle drawn reflects the current ratio between the width and the height, which might be different from the original ratio.

12.11.3 Original Ratio Menu Option

In connection with the option to constrain when resizing, is an option to return the file to its original aspect ratio once it is placed in the file. This is useful when you have changed the dimensions of the imported file nonproportionally. An Original Ratio menu item appears in the Edit menu in the Import application. This returns the selected EPS and TIFF files to their original ratios. The file uses the smallest dimension as a guide to calculate the size of the other dimension. This fits the newly proportioned file into the previous bounding box.

Figure 12.8 *Return to original ratio option*

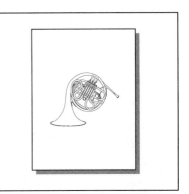

EPS file scaled nonproportionally   *After original ratio option is applied*

12.11.4 Original Size Menu Option

Related to the Original Ratio option is an Original Size menu option, which appears in the Edit menu. This feature returns the imported file to its original width and height. The upper left corner of the new bounds remains in the same spot as the previous bounds.

12.11.5 Placement Interfaces

The problem of how to initially position an imported file within a document arises in any application that imports files. Several interfaces are available. You begin by selecting the file from an open or import panel. After this, the three most common interfaces differ:

- One images the file at its original dimensions and places it in either the center of the document or within a selected mask or frame.

- Another produces an icon and waits for you to mouse down at a location in the document. The file is imaged at its original width and height with some location of the file positioned at the mouse-down point. In the Import application, this *click to drop* interface positions the upper left corner of the imported file at the mouse-down location. Other applications might use other places as reference points.

  Related to this interface is the ability to drag file icons from the NeXT Workspace Manager into application documents. Instead of a mouse-down, though, the placement is initiated by a mouse-up. (The Application Kit provides some support for this feature, but the developer must integrate this capability into the application.)

- The third produces an icon and waits for a mouse-down. Instead of acting immediately, this interface marks the mouse-down and tracks the mouse until you release the mouse button, the whole time drawing the rectangle between the original mouse-down and the current mouse position. This *click and drag* interface enables you to immediately resize the file and position it without having to image it first at full size.

Note *The second and third interfaces can be combined. If you release the mouse without dragging, you get the original size. If you drag and then release, you get a scaled image.*

12.12 Conclusions

- The NeXT Application Kit and the Display PostScript system provide much of the support for importing and exporting EPS and TIFF files.

- Imaging EPS and TIFF files into NXImage objects eliminates having to reimage the files with each scroll or movement of the file. The file can be composited to its position in the document whenever it is needed.

- The NXEPSImageRep class uses a separate Display PostScript context to image EPS files. Using this context shields the application context from errors that might be present in an imported EPS file.

- Parsing EPS files and extracting bounding box and resource information is an important part of importing EPS files.

CHAPTER 13

Binary Encoding Formats

The Display PostScript system and PostScript Level 2 specify two language encodings in addition to the standard ASCII encoding. These encodings, *binary token* and *binary object sequence*, represent PostScript objects (numbers, operators, strings, etc.) as one or more 8-bit binary representations instead of the standard 7-bit ASCII object encodings. Refer to the *PostScript Language Reference Manual, Second Edition* and the *Display PostScript System Reference Binder* for the encoding specifications and more detailed information.

The purpose of this chapter is to introduce the formats, supply timing studies and file size comparisons for the encoding formats, and provide guidance for using them in a Display PostScript application.

The binary encoding formats can improve performance over an ASCII representation to some degree, but the amount varies according to several factors including the bandwidth of the communications channel and the type of PostScript objects contained in the data stream.

The binary token format encodes numbers and operators in a more compact format. The amount of reduction varies with the contents of the file. Graphics files (files with many numbers and operators) shrink much more than text files. The sizes of example files in this chapter were reduced by about half using the binary token encoding. This is the best-case reduction since these are strictly graphics files containing minimal text. The performance improvement is largely the result of reduced traffic over the communications channel. The lower the bandwidth of the communications channel, the better the performance improvement.

The binary object sequence is different in that it encodes sequences of objects, creating a representation that is close to the internal representation used in the interpreter. Creating this representation beforehand eliminates the need for the scanner to do it during the interpretation. The file size of a binary object sequence is often larger than its ASCII counterpart, but this is offset by increased processing efficiency.

All three encodings can be intermixed within any PostScript language program. PostScript Level 1 devices, though, do not support these new encodings: Binary token and binary object sequence encodings result in run-time errors when sent to a Level 1 printer.

Level 2 devices support these encodings, enabling you to send the formats as long as the communications channel can handle 8-bit codings. (Some channels only accommodate 7-bit data; 8-bit data causes transmission problems. See Technical Note #5081, "Adobe Binary Communications Protocol," for encoding 8-bit data over serial and parallel channels.)

The performance benefits of the binary encodings are more important from a system viewpoint than an application standpoint. You can be more productive writing efficient PostScript language code than altering the encoding format. User paths, the show operators (**xshow**, **yshow**, and **xyshow**), and the rectangle operators (**rectfill**, **rectstroke**, and **rectclip**) can greatly increase performance over Level 1 approaches. Make the PostScript language operations in an application as efficient as possible before addressing language encodings.

Note   *Binary encodings for PostScript language objects are an essential part of the Display PostScript system but are commonly transparent to the user and the developer. As PostScript Level 2 printers become more widespread, these encodings will find more acceptance as a mainstream representation. Until then, their use outside of the system-level framework should be examined carefully.*

13.1   Binary Token

The binary token encoding format represents PostScript language elements using fewer characters than an ASCII representation. Each object is represented by a token describing the type of data followed by the actual data. Numbers, for example, are represented with several formats ranging in size from two bytes to six bytes. Operators are represented with two bytes. In addition, the spaces separating each object are removed. If a binary token file is expanded to use the ASCII encodings, the structure of the file appears identical. (This is not the case for binary object sequence encoding.)

Table 13.1 lists the binary token formats for encoding numbers. Each has a token type and the number of additional characters necessary for the data. A number represented in ASCII can vary according to the size and precision: A single-digit number such as *1* takes one character whereas the largest integer value allowed in the PostScript language (*+2,247,483,648*) takes 14. The binary number encodings use the same size for a particular number type regardless of the value of the number.

Table 13.1 *Binary token number encodings*

Number Type	Token	Additional Characters
8-bit integer	136	1
16-bit integer	134	2
32-bit integer	132	4
16/32-bit fixed	137	3 or 5
32-bit real	138	4

Representing strings in a binary token format is different from ASCII, but it does not generate any space savings. As a result, text files (made up of strings and **show** operators) will not be reduced as much as graphics files (made up of numbers and path construction operators). The binary token encoding format can be helpful when the communications bandwidth is limited or storage space for PostScript language data is a concern.

13.2 Binary Object Sequence

The binary object sequence encoding represents a sequence of one or more PostScript objects as a single syntactic entity. Although this format can take up more space than an ASCII representation, it can be produced and interpreted very efficiently. This format is suitable for the Display PostScript system because bandwidth is not as great an issue as performance. In a display environment, the communications channel is often large so that increased interpreter performance is realized with minimal communications channel impact.

The binary object sequence format represents each object as eight successive bytes. Simple objects such as operators and numbers are represented with the eight bytes. Composite objects such as strings, arrays, and procedures include a reference to another part of the sequence where the value resides. This well-defined structure can be described easily using the data types found in computer languages such as C and Pascal.

The nature of the format makes it possible to form a binary object sequence of arbitrary PostScript code with fixed locations where specific values can be inserted at a later point. The pswrap translator uses this capability by creating a C function with a partially formed binary object sequence declared as a static structure within the function. When the function is called, the arguments passed in are inserted into their locations in the binary object sequence, then the sequence is sent to the server.

13.3 Timing Studies and File Size Comparisons

Timing studies and file comparisons are listed in Tables 13.2 and 13.3 for two different images. One image has an ASCII file size of 100 K and the other is about 660 K. Both images contain numbers, path construction operators, and graphics state operators. No text, math, or control operations are included, so the display times do not represent an exact performance measure. In addition, the times measure the cost of *execution*, and not the cost of *formatting* the data.

Four different formats are featured: ASCII, ASCII with abbreviated operator names, binary object sequence, and binary token.

The binary token encoding formats show a 15% or greater performance gain over the ASCII encodings. They also reduce the file size by about 50% while the file size for the binary object sequence format ranges from either slightly less to about 10% more than the ASCII file size. The abbreviated ASCII reduces the size by about 15%. Some of the difference in the display time for the binary token format is associated with the smaller file size.

Table 13.2 *Times for the Caterpillar Engine drawing*

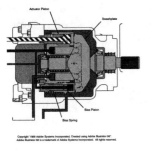

File Type	Time	% Diff.	Size	% Diff.
	Times in seconds. Size in kilobytes.			
ASCII	1.123	—	96.1	—
ASCII abbrev.	1.098	2.2%	77.5	19.3%
Binary Object Seq.	1.045	6.9%	106.0	(10.3%)
Binary Token	.893	20.4%	49.1	48.9%

Table 13.3 *Times for the King Tut drawing*

File Type	Time	% Diff.	Size	% Diff.
	Times in seconds. Size in kilobytes.			
ASCII	6.9	—	635	—
ASCII abbrev.	6.7	2.8%	532	16.2%
Binary Object Seq.	6.4	7.2%	617	2.8%
Binary Token	5.4	21.7%	284	55.2%

The abbreviated ASCII replaces the PostScript language operator names with abbreviations. The most commonly used are to replace **moveto** with **m** and **lineto** with **l**. This is recommended for most cases in which operator names appear frequently.

13.4 Uses in a Display PostScript Application

The binary object sequence is used extensively within any Display PostScript application through the use of the Client Library routines and the pswrap utility. A call to a single operator or wrap sends a binary object sequence to the server.

In addition, the pswrap translator provides a *numstring* data type that enables you to pass PostScript operands as numeric elements in a normal C number array. The pswrap translator generates code that converts them at run time to the encoded number string representations.

A few less apparent uses for the binary encodings are possible within an application, but careful thought should be given before using them extensively. Limitations when printing to Level 1 devices and communicating over 7-bit communications lines are considerations when determining suitability.

Binary token encoding might be useful, for example, for storing help screens or other PostScript language files intended for display. In both cases, the space savings is appreciable for large amounts of data. At the same time, other types of representations might provide similar benefits: Two examples are to store help information in a Rich Text format (RTF) or EPS files in ASCII with shortened operator names.

If binary encodings are used outside the framework of the Client Library, take advantage of system level routines and utilities to perform the conversion between formats wherever possible. As an example, the NeXT implementation of the Display PostScript system supports the creation of stream contexts for any of the encoding formats. Using the **DPSCreateStreamContext( )** procedure, a stream context can be created with a particular encoding type. The three encoding values permitted are *dps_ascii*, *dps_binObjSeq*, and *dps_encodedTokens*. Any PostScript language code sent to that context is written to the stream in the specified encoding.

Example 13.1 shows a sample of creating a stream context with a particular encoding, setting the context, and then drawing to it by sending a message to the **drawSelf::** method.

Example 13.1 *Creating a stream context with a specific encoding*

```
static const DPSNameEncoding  nameEncoding[4] = {dps_strings, dps_strings,
    dps_indexed, dps_indexed};

static const DPSProgramEncoding  programEncoding[4] = {dps_ascii, dps_ascii,
    dps_binObjSeq, dps_encodedTokens};

/*
 *Saves the file in the format specified.
 */
- saveFile:sender
{
  NXStream *stream;

  DPSContext newContext, oldContext;

  oldContext = DPSGetCurrentContext( );
  ...stream = NXOpenMemory(NULL, 0, NX_WRITEONLY);
```

```
    if (stream)
    {
      newContext = DPSCreateStreamContext(stream, 0,
        programEncoding[format], nameEncoding[format], NULL);
      DPSSetContext(newContext);

      ...
      [self  drawSelf:&bounds  :1];
      ...

      NXSaveToFile(stream, tempBuf);
      NXCloseMemory(stream, NX_FREEBUFFER);

      DPSSetContext(oldContext);
      DPSDestroyContext(newContext);
    }
    ...

    return self;
}
```

13.5 Conclusions

- Replacing common PostScript language operators with abbreviating names can reduce the size of a PostScript file by up to 15%.

- The binary token format encodes numbers and operators in a more compact format. The organization and structure of the data stream remains unchanged from the ASCII representation.

- The binary object sequence format encodes sequences of PostScript language objects creating a representation that is close to the internal representation used in the interpreter. The file size is often larger than the ASCII counterpart, but it can be produced and interpreted very efficiently.

- The benefits from the binary encoding formats are more valuable from a system standpoint than from an application standpoint. Application developers can be more productive by making the PostScript language operations in an application more efficient than they can by altering the encoding format.

CHAPTER 14

Printing Issues

The Display PostScript system provides a single imaging model for both the printer and the display. Other systems rely on a driver to translate the screen imaging model to the PostScript language or require that each application write a driver to convert its internal data structures into the PostScript language. The Display PostScript system consolidates this effort, making it relatively straightforward to create PostScript language page descriptions that are supported by all PostScript devices.

Despite the unified imaging model, some printing issues still arise. This chapter focuses on a few of them. One is producing page descriptions that are compatible with PostScript Level 1. Every application should produce PostScript Level 1 compatible page descriptions as a minimum requirement.

Another highlight of this chapter is a description of the printing architecture of the Application Kit. The two objects that figure predominantly are the PrintInfo object and the View object. The PrintInfo object contains information concerning the page layout and the print job while the View object contains methods that manage the different components of the document structuring conventions (DSC): header, procedure definitions, document setup, pages, and document trailer. These methods can be overridden to add or modify comments or PostScript language code segments in the page description.

This chapter touches on just a few of the document structuring conventions. The complete description can be found in Appendix G of the *PostScript Language Reference Manual, Second Edition*.

14.1   Level 1 Compatible Page Descriptions

The Display PostScript system has many features that are not found in Level 1 of the PostScript language. Some have been designed with an interactive environment in mind and should not be made a part of a page description. Others are performance optimizations such as user paths and rectangle operations that directly address imaging issues.

Many of these operations are used in the imaging aspects of Display PostScript applications, making it important to convert them to a format that is compatible with Level 1 devices. This can be as simple as providing an operator that emulates the language extension using Level 1 operators. You define this emulation in a procedure set in the script of the page description and, whenever the operator is invoked, the emulation is used. In other cases, the application might send different operators to the server depending on whether the application is drawing on a display, printing to a device, or saving to a file.

The following sections outline some of the more common operations using Display PostScript extensions and the compatibility issues that arise with each. Many of the operations can be emulated, at least partially, with Level 1 operators. The emulations are taken from the NeXT Print Package that is by default placed in the prolog by the View class. Not all forms of the extensions are emulated; you should be aware of the limitations of each.

For example, the encoded number strings are not supported by the emulations. Some of the extensions take this encoding format as an argument. In these cases, you must convert the operations to forms that are supported or create emulations that address these formats. Some Display PostScript features, such as stroke adjustment, do not have an emulation in the NeXT Print Package. A later section in this chapter, "Including a Procedure Set in the Prolog," explains how to include a stroke adjust emulation in the prolog of a page description

Appendix D, "Compatibility Strategies," of the *PostScript Language Reference Manual, Second Edition* contains a detailed description of compatibility strategies and emulation guidelines. The general rule for emulations is to install only operators that are not currently defined in the interpreter. Check the availability of each operator in the prolog of the page description. If the operator already exists, the emulation should not be defined. The procedures in Example 14.1 use the **where** operator to determine whether the operator currently exists in the interpreter. The emulation is only defined if **where** returns *false*. When **where** returns *true*, the emulation is popped off the stack.

Example 14.1 *Conditionally defining emulations (the second binds the definition)*

/__NXdef{1 index where {pop pop pop}{def}ifelse} bind def

/__NXbdef{1 index where {pop pop pop}{bind def} ifelse } bind def

14.1.1 User Paths

User paths can be emulated relatively easily, but the NeXTstep function **DPSDoUserPath( )** provides several advantages that make it a preferred way to construct user paths. One advantage is that it converts the numbers into a binary encoded string, which is more efficient to interpret. The other is that it produces the correct form of output for the current device. If the drawing is sent to the display, the user path operands and operators are sent to the server; if the drawing is sent to a print stream, the Level 1 path construction and rendering operators are used; substituting the correct format occurs automatically.

The PostScript trace in Example 14.2 is for a random path rendered with the **DPSDoUserPath( )** function. The first part of the example is a user path that is sent to the display; the second is a user path that is sent to a print context. **DPSDoUserPath( )** handles the conversion from the user path format of the original to the PostScript Level 1 path construction operators.

Example 14.2 *Sample trace of DPSDoUserPath( )*

PostScript language trace (sent to window server)

```
[<9530000e42b5e6664360f33343ff86664420833343ff8000442080000000000
0c3d08000c3d20000000000000000000000043d0800043d2000000000000>
<0001040404040a>] ustroke
```

PostScript language trace (written to stream context)

```
gsave
newpath
systemdict
begin
511 642 moveto
0 -417 rlineto
-420 0 rlineto
0 417 rlineto
420 0 rlineto
closepath
end
stroke
grestore
```

The **DPSDoUserPath( )** function does not address path limits. This responsibility lies with the developer. Path limits in the Display PostScript system are larger than those on most Level 1 printers and, for the most part, are not an issue on the display.

Note   *The user path examples in this book set an upper limit of 2500 points on stroked paths primarily because of transmission limits in the Client Library. When a path threatens to exceed this limit, the path is stroked and path construction begins again. This works for discontinuous stroked paths, but a different strategy is necessary for handling continuous paths.*

*One strategy is to stroke the path constructed, and move back one segment and continue anew. A **closepath** operation, though, must be preceded with an explicit **lineto** from the last point in the path to the first point in the path. Otherwise, the **closepath** closes to the wrong point.*

The typical path limit in a Level 1 device is 1500 points. This limit is for all active paths, which include the current path, clip path, and paths saved by **save** and **gsave**. Applications containing path descriptions that might exceed this limit must develop a strategy for breaking the paths into more manageable segments. The actual strategy depends on the nature of the application.

Note   *Some path construction operators, such as **strokepath**, need particular attention. The **strokepath** operator converts a path into an outline that can then be filled. The resulting paths can be displayed in a Display PostScript system without regard to size. Many of these paths, however, exceed the typical Level 1 path. For this reason, consider the use of **strokepath** carefully.*

14.1.2   Rectangles

The rectangle operations in the Display PostScript system provide a clean and efficient interface to the common operation of stroking or filling rectangles. These operations can be emulated easily without any significant loss in efficiency. The NeXT Print Package provides the emulation in Example 14.3 for the singular rectangle and number array cases. The encoded number string does not have an emulation, so applications that use encoded number strings must develop their own emulation for this number format.

Example 14.3 *Emulations for the rectangle operators*

```
/__NXRectPath{4 2 roll moveto 1 index 0 rlineto
  0 exch rlineto neg 0 rlineto closepath}__NXbdef

/__NXProcessRectArgs{
```

```
1 index type /arraytype eq{
  exch 0 4 2 index length 1 sub{
    dup 3 add 1 exch{1 index exch get exch}for
    5 1 roll 5 index exec
  }for pop pop
}{exec}ifelse
}__NXbdef

/rectfill{gsave newpath {__NXRectPath fill} __NXProcessRectArgs
grestore}__NXbdef

/rectclip{newpath {__NXRectPath} __NXProcessRectArgs clip newpath}__NXbdef

/rectstroke{
  gsave newpath dup type /arraytype eq{dup length 6 eq}{false}ifelse{
    {gsave __NXRectPath null concat stroke grestore}
    dup length array cvx copy dup 2 4 -1 roll put __NXProcessRectArgs
  }{{__NXRectPath stroke} __NXProcessRectArgs}ifelse grestore
}__NXbdef
```

The emulations in Example 14.3 work for individual rectangles with
negative widths and heights, but the effects of the nonzero winding
number are unpredictable when drawing multiple rectangles that have
negative widths or heights. An emulation can be created that will work
for these cases, but flexibility is added at the expense of performance.

14.1.3   xyshow, xshow, yshow

The **xyshow, xshow**, and **yshow** operators are emulated much like the
rectangle operators. However, the performance is much worse with the
emulations than an approach that uses **show, ashow, widthshow**, and
awidthshow. The emulation for **xyshow, xshow**, and **yshow** in the
NeXT Print Package appear in Example 14.4.

Example 14.4 *Emulations for the **xyshow, xshow**, and **yshow** operators*

```
/xyshow{
  0 1 3 index length 1 sub{
    currentpoint 4 index 3 index 1 getinterval show
    3 index 3 index 2 mul 1 add get add exch
    3 index 3 index 2 mul get add exch moveto pop
  }for pop pop
}__NXbdef

/xshow{
  0 1 3 index length 1 sub{
    currentpoint 4 index 3 index 1 getinterval show
    exch 3 index 3 index get add exch moveto pop
```

```
    }for pop pop
}__NXbdef

/yshow{
    0 1 3 index length 1 sub{
      currentpoint 4 index 3 index 1 getinterval show
      3 index 3 index get add moveto pop
    }for pop pop
}__NXbdef
```

These emulations result in the execution of a **moveto** and a **show** operation for each character. The cost of doing this for a small amount of text is not appreciable, but for a full page of text it can be prohibitive.

The performance is much better when combinations of **show, ashow, widthshow**, and **awidthshow** are used. Applications that format large amounts of text might want to distinguish between displaying to the screen and displaying to a printer, and use the appropriate approach for a given device. Chapter 11, "Text Handling Issues," provides more detail on this approach and on the performance difference between emulations and using **show** and its variant operators.

14.1.4   User Objects

A user object is an integer identifier of a PostScript language object stored in the server. User objects allow you to refer to objects in the server using integer keys rather than name keys. User objects, for the most part, are used primarily for windows and views and usually are not made a part of a page description.

The NeXT print driver provides an emulation that consists of an expanding array. The array holds the object, with the index of the array serving as the object identifier. This emulation adds little overhead. The only caveat is that the user objects must be defined in the page description prior to their use. Inserting the user object definitions in the document setup section of the page description satisfies this requirement.

Example 14.5 *Emulation of user objects*

```
/UserObjects 10 array __NXdef
/defineuserobject{
    exch dup 1 add dup UserObjects length gt{
      array dup 0 UserObjects putinterval
      /UserObjects exch def
    }{pop}ifelse UserObjects exch 3 -1 roll put
}__NXbdef
```

```
/undefineuserobject{UserObjects exch null put} __NXbdef
```

```
/execuserobject{UserObjects exch get exec} __NXbdef
```

User objects are more a convenience feature than a performance optimization. Short operator names provide the same advantages that user objects provide. User objects are generally not recommended for page descriptions unless they are used in the display engine of the application, making it necessary to include them in the page description in order to support these references.

14.1.5 Graphics States

A graphics state object is an internal data type in the Display PostScript system. The advantage of a graphics state is that it allows indiscriminate switching between arbitrary states. This is more appropriate in a window environment than in a page description.

Graphics state objects are also more difficult to emulate than any of the other operators. The line width, color, and other graphics state parameters can be stored in an array, but other components, such as the clip path and current path, are more difficult to manage. Because of this, their use in a page description is discouraged.

14.1.6 Limits

PostScript Level 1 printers have limitations not present in Level 2. When developing applications that might have to work with Level 1 as well as Level 2 printers, there are several system limitations you should know. These include how Level 1 devices manage memory, the allowable number of points along a user path, the size of the operand stack, and the level of successive **save** operations.

Limits are important when going from the Display PostScript system to Level 1 interpreters. Level 2 of the PostScript language removes many of these restrictions, but they still must be considered for supporting the installed base of Level 1 printers. The following is a list of some of the limits for a typical Level 1 interpreter. A complete list and descriptions can be found in Appendix B of the *PostScript Language Reference Manual, Second Edition*.

Memory	The Display PostScript system uses a more sophisticated approach to handle the less structured memory demands of a display environment including automatic virtual memory reclamation, popularly know as "garbage collection." This feature automatically reclaims memory of composite objects no longer accessible by a PostScript language program, which means they do not appear on any of the stacks or as elements of other composite objects.

Level 1 PostScript interpreters use a much simpler approach. Memory consumed by composite objects is only reclaimed when the **restore** operator is invoked. The memory reverts to the state it was in at the time of the matching **save**. This is important because instances in which memory is reclaimed automatically in the Display PostScript system might not have memory reclaimed in Level 1 PostScript interpreters. A program that endlessly consumes VM and never executes **save** and **restore** eventually encounters a **VMerror** if executed by a PostScript interpreter that does not have garbage collection.

Encapsulating pages with a **save** and **restore** and using the recommended approaches for downloading fonts and including EPS files is usually sufficient to avoid **VMerrors**. Some applications, though, might need additional **save** and **restore** nestings depending on the type of PostScript language operations invoked and the amount of data used in the page descriptions.

Operand Stack	In Level 1, the maximum size of the operand stack (the number of the elements that can be on the stack at any one time) is 500. Most PostScript language programs typically do not approach this number, but some types of operations can momentarily fill up the stack unexpectedly. For example, the **aload** operator takes an array and successively pushes the elements of the array onto the stack. An emulation that uses **aload** instead of **getinterval** to access operands in an array can run into **stackoverflow** errors when using large arrays.

Paths	The path limit in Level 1 for all active path descriptions (including the clip path and paths saved by **save** and **gsave**) is 1500 points. You should be aware of this and take steps to avoid overrunning this limit.

save and **gsave**	The typical limits on **save** and **gsave** levels in Level 1 PostScript interpreter implementations are 15 and 31, respectively. (Each **save** performs an implicit **gsave**.) For most PostScript language programs these limits are not a problem. But since the View class writes out some portions of the page descriptions, be aware of the limit and take steps to reduce the number of **save**s and **gsave**s if they begin to approach the Level 1 limits.

14.2 Writing to a Context

The Client Library has three procedures that are designed for writing to a context: **DPSPrintf( )**, **DPSWritePostScript( )**, and **DPSWriteData( )**. All three provide a convenient way to send PostScript data, operators, and comments to the server without going through single operator calls or custom wraps. The invocations appear in Example 14.6.

Example 14.6 *Procedures for writing to a context*

```
void DPSPrintf(DPSContext context, const char *fmt, ...)
void DPSWritePostScript(DPSContext context, const void *buf,
    unsigned int count)
void DPSWriteData(DPSContext context, const void *buf,
    unsigned int count)
```

The **DPSPrintf( )** procedure is similar to **printf**, the standard C library routine. It formats arguments into ASCII text and writes this text to the context. Small PostScript language programs or text data can be sent in this manner, but the most common use of **DPSPrintf( )** is to write PostScript comments. Single operator calls and wraps do not support writing comments as readily. Example 14.7 writes a formatted PostScript comment to the current context.

Example 14.7 *Sample DPSPrint( ) invocation*

```
const char*aTitle;

DPSContextctxt;

ctxt = DPSGetCurrentContext( );
aTitle = "SampleTitle";
DPSPrintf(ctxt, "%%%%Title: %s\n", aTitle);
```

Depending on the implementation and whether it permits a context to change encoding types, **DPSWritePostScript( )** can be used, for example, to convert encodings from binary object sequences to ASCII text. If the implementation doesn't allow changes, it sends PostScript to the server without changing the form.

The **DPSWriteData( )** procedure can be used to send any type of data to a context and to avoid the automatic conversion of **DPSWritePostScript( )**. For example, use **DPSWriteData( )** to send hexadecimal image data. Example 14.8 uses **DPSWritePostScript( )** to write the procedure set initialization statement to the current context.

Example 14.8 *Sample **DPSWritePostScript( )** invocation*

```
const static char EpsfProcSetInit[ ] = "EPSF_Illustrator_abbrev /initialize get
exec\n";

void  WriteEpsfProcSetInit ( )
{
  DPSWritePostScript(DPSGetCurrentContext( ), EpsfProcSetInit,
    strlen(EpsfProcSetInit));
}
```

14.3   Application Kit Objects

The PrintInfo and View classes of the Application Kit are the primary
objects used to control printing in the applications built under the
Application Kit framework.

14.3.1   PrintInfo Class

The PrintInfo class is a holding place for page dimension and print job
information. It obtains this data from the PageLayout and Print panels.
Access this information through methods in the PrintInfo class instead
of through the panels.

The information retained in the PrintInfo class about the page layout
includes the dimensions of the page, the margins, and the orientation.
The information about the print job includes the order, the page range,
and the number of copies. In addition, the name and type of the printer
can be obtained.

A partial list of methods you can use to retrieve these variables appears
in Example 14.9. An example of how this information is used is
included in the description of the View class printing methods in the
section 14.3.2, "View Class."

Example 14.9 *Partial list of PrintInfo methods*

```
- (const NXRect *) paperRect;
- getMarginLeft:(NXCoord *)leftMargin
    right:(NXCoord *)rightMargin
    top:(NXCoord *)topMargin
    bottom:(NXCoord *)bottomMargin;
- (char)orientation;

- (char)pageOrder;
- (int)firstPage;
- (int)lastPage;
```

```
- (int)copies;

- (const char *)printerName;
- (const char *)printerType;
```

Note   *Use **printerType** in conjunction with PostScript printer description files*
(PPDs). Avoid logic that tries to handle each printer type separately (such as
a switch statement that keys off the type of printer). Use the type to get the
PPD file, which in turn should be used to control special portions of the printing
process. The printer support architecture is likely to change from NeXTstep
Version 2.0 to 3.0. Keep this in mind if you are designing code to support
different printer types.

Multiple PrintInfo Objects

The Application class has, by default, a single PrintInfo object. This
has the effect of constraining all the documents of the application to
a single page dimension. Many applications such as graphic design
and page layout programs want greater flexibility across documents.
This is done by giving each document its own PrintInfo object and
installing it as the application's PrintInfo object whenever the document
is the current document (the key window). The Draw program in the
/NextDeveloper/Examples directory in the NeXT file system uses this
technique. The code in Example 14.10 summarizes the process.

Example 14.10 *Using multiple PrintInfo objects*

```
@interface DrawDocument : Object
{

    id printInfo;                          /* The print information for the GraphicView */
                                           /*  defined as an instance variable.*/
    ...
}
@end

@implementation:DrawDocument
/*
 *Switch the Application's PrintInfo to the document's
 *when the document window becomes the main window.
 */
- windowDidBecomeMain:sender
{
  [NXApp setPrintInfo:printInfo];
  ...

  return self;
```

```
    }

    /*
    *Set the Application's PrintInfo to NULL when the document
    *is closed.
    */
    - windowWillClose:sender
    {
        ...
        [NXApp setPrintInfo:nil];

        return self;
    }
    @end
```

14.3.2   View Class

The View class performs several steps that help make the construction
of a page description transparent to the developer. The developer most
often is concerned only with writing out the PostScript language
instructions to draw the pages of the document. Because the imaging
model for the screen and printer are the same, the instructions, for
the most part, are the same. Once the display portion is written, the
printing can be added with very little work. The print process begins by
sending a message to either **printPSCode:** or **faxPSCode:**. The steps that
the View class performs include

- Determining the pagination

- Redirecting all the PostScript output from the Window Server to a
  spool file or printer

- Writing the NeXT Print Package into the prolog

- Writing document structuring convention comments

- Repeatedly sending a message to the View to draw pages

- Closing the spool file or communication channel to the printer

- Reestablishing the Window Server context as the current context

At the minimum level, subclasses need to place the drawing portion
of the application in the **drawSelf::** method. The print architecture
repeatedly sends messages to **drawSelf::** with rectangles that describe

particular pages. The drawing instructions can include many common Display PostScript extensions because the emulations in the NeXT Print Package handle the ones most likely to appear in a page description.

Many applications, however, will want to perform some part of the print process (such as determining pagination) using their own print drivers or writing their own DSC comments. The printing methods in the View class can be overridden to add to or change this functionality.

A description of the print context and pagination process is found in the NeXT Application Kit documentation. The sections that follow focus primarily on the structure of a PostScript language document and how to override the methods that insert the DSC comments. These examples serve as an introduction to the document structuring conventions.

Document Structuring Conventions

A page description is organized into two sections: a prolog and a script. The prolog contains application-dependent definitions and has two subsections: a header and procedure definitions (procedure sets). The script describes the pages using the definitions defined in the prolog and embodies three main categories: document setup, pages, and document trailer.

The prolog typically remains the same across documents within an application. (The comments for the title, date, and number of pages change, but the order of the comments and the procedure set definitions typically remain the same.) The comments and procedure sets are stored somewhere accessible to the application and incorporated as a standard preface for each document. The script is usually generated automatically by an application and reflects the contents of the data structures for the particular document at the time of printing.

The PostScript language comments in Example 14.11 mark the structure of a conforming document. If a section is present that corresponds to a comment, that comment must be used to mark the section. All comments except the page comments appear once for each file. The page comments, %%Page:, %%BeginPageSetup, %%EndPageSetup, and %%PageTrailer, appear once for each page.

Example 14.11 *Partial list of document structuring convention comments*

```
%!PS-Adobe-3.0
%%Pages:
%%EndComments
%%BeginProlog
%%EndProlog
%%BeginSetup
%%EndSetup
%%Page:
%%BeginPageSetup
%%EndPageSetup
%%PageTrailer
%%Trailer
%%EOF
```

The document structuring conventions help ensure that documents are device independent and allow documents to communicate their structure and requirements to document managers without affecting the imaging of the document.

Printing Methods of the View Class

A close match occurs between the document structuring convention sections and the printing methods of the View class. Example 14.12 lists the methods that control these sections.

Example 14.12 *Partial list of the printing methods in the View object*

```
- beginprologBBox:creationDate:createdBy:
    fonts:forWhom:pages:title:
- endHeaderComments
- endProlog
- beginSetup
- endSetup
- beginPage:label:bBox:fonts:
- addToPageSetup
- endPageSetup
- endPage
- beginTrailer
- endTrailer
```

Including a Procedure Set in the Prolog

The code segment in Example 14.13 illustrates the process of installing a custom procedure set. The routines establish dictionaries in the prolog and place the appropriate dictionary on the dictionary stack in the document setup of the page description. The procedure set in the example emulates the stroke adjustment capability found in the Display PostScript system and in Level 2 of the language. The procedures emulate the absolute path construction operators (for example, **moveto, lineto, curveto**) as well as the relative operators (for example, **rmoveto, rlineto, rcurveto**) to adjust the positions of the paths in order to produce lines of uniform pixel width. Chapter 3, "The Coordinate System," contains more information on the stroke adjustment process.

A simpler version that only emulates the absolute operators can be used, depending on the operators an application chooses to implement. Emulation of the relative path operators incurs the cost of having to maintain some location context from operator to operator.

Performing a relative move from an altered location, rather than from the originally specified location, can result in landing in a pixel different from the one indicated by the path. Performing a series of relative path operations, without correcting the location differences caused by rounding, results in a noticeable accumulated error. The **savelocation** procedure stores the absolute location to eliminate any accumulated error.

The rule with emulations is to install them if the desired features do not already exist on the target interpreter. If you know the level of the interpreter in advance, the procedure sets for that level can be sent. Otherwise, the generic procedure set must be sent with conditionals provided to install procedures only as necessary at the time of interpretation. (The **save** and **restore** operators in the procedure set reclaim memory taken up by the unimplemented portions of the procedure set.)

Note *The Level 1 emulations contain two dictionaries, GRdict and SAdict. The first is for no stroke adjustment and the second is for stroke adjustment. If an application always uses stroke adjustment, GRdict is unnecessary and the GRdict entry in GRinit can be changed to SAdict.*

Example 14.13 *Including a procedure set in the prolog*

```
/*
 * This array contains the stroke adjust procedure set.
 */
const static char Adobe_SpecialGraphicsRel_L2DPS [ ] =
"
/Level2|DPS /setstrokeadjust where {pop true} {false} ifelse def

Level2|DPS  not {save} if
Level2|DPS {
%%BeginResource: procset Adobe_SpecialGraphicsRel_L2DPS 1.0 0
 /m /moveto load def
 /l /lineto load def
 /c /curveto load def
 /rm /rmoveto load def
 /rl /rlineto load def
 /rc /rcurveto load def
 /GRinit { } def
 /SA /setstrokeadjust load def
%%EndResource
} if
Level2|DPS  not {restore} if

Level2|DPS {save} if
Level2|DPS not {
%%BeginResource: procset Adobe_SpecialGraphicsRel_L1 1.0 0
 /GRdict 8 dict def
 GRdict begin
 /m /moveto load def
 /l /lineto load def
 /c /curveto load def
 /rm /rmoveto load def
 /rl /rlineto load def
 /rc /rcurveto load def
 /sa { % true, false   sa   - setstrokeadjust
   {mark countdictstack 2 sub
    {currentdict GRdict eq
    {SAdict begin exit} {currentdict end} ifelse} repeat
    counttomark {begin} repeat pop}
   {mark countdictstack 2 sub
    {currentdict SAdict eq
    {end exit} {currentdict end} ifelse} repeat
    counttomark {begin} repeat pop
    } ifelse
   } bind def
 end  % GRdict


 /GRinit {  % put GRdict on dictionary stack under userdict
```

```
    countdictstack array dictstack cleardictstack
    dup 0 GRdict put {begin} forall
} bind def

/SAdict 9 dict def
SAdict begin
  % snap user space location to device space pixel
  /snaptopixel  { % x y   snaptopixel   sx sy
    transform
    .25 sub round .25 add exch
    .25 sub round .25 add exch
    itransform
  } bind def

  % save absolute user space location for next relative operator
  /savelocation { % x y   savelocation   x y
    2 copy /uy exch def /ux exch def
  } bind def
  /m { % x y   m   -   moveto
    savelocation  snaptopixel moveto
  } bind def
  /l { % x y   l   -   lineto
    savelocation  snaptopixel lineto
  } bind def
  /c { % x1 y1 x2 y2 x3 y3   CT   -   curveto
    savelocation   snaptopixel curveto
  } bind def        % note control points are not snapped
  /rm { % dx dy   RM   -   rmoveto
    exch ux add  exch uy add % convert dx dy to user space absolute
    savelocation  snaptopixel  moveto
  } bind def
  /rl { % dx dy   RL   -   rlineto
    exch ux add  exch uy add
    savelocation  snaptopixel  lineto
  } bind def

  /rc { % x1 y1 x2 y2 x3 y3   RC   -   rcurveto
    3 { 6 1 roll ux add  6 1 roll uy add } repeat
    savelocation  snaptopixel  curveto
  } bind def   % note control points are not snapped

  /__NXRectPath { % x y w h   Rt -   rectangle
    4 -2 roll m % bottom left hand corner
    dtransform round exch round exch idtransform  % round h and w
    dup 0 exch rlineto  % to upper left
    exch 0 rlineto  % to upper right
    neg 0 exch rlineto  % to lower right
    closepath
  } bind def
```

```
end  % SAdict
%%EndResource
} if
Level2IDPS {restore} if\n";
. . .

/*
* Write the procedure set in the prolog.
*/
- endHeaderComments
{
  DPSContext ctxt;

  ctxt = DPSGetCurrentContext( );
  DPSPrintf(ctxt, "%%%%EndComments\n\n");

  DPSWritePostScript(ctxt, Adobe_SpecialGraphicsRel_L2DPS
      strlen(Adobe_SpecialGraphicsRel_L2DPS));

  return self;
}

/*  Initialize the procedure set in the Document Setup section. */
- beginSetup
{
  DPSContext ctxt;

  ctxt = DPSGetCurrentContext( );
  DPSPrintf(ctxt, "%%%%BeginSetup\n");
  DPSPrintf(ctxt, "GRinit\n");

  return self;
}
```

The procedure set is stored as an initialized character array, not defined as a wrap. Placing a procedure set in a wrap and sending the wrap to write the procedure set to the print context has several disadvantages:

- PostScript language comments in the wraps are not written to the print context.

- The executable code for the wrap consumes much more space than a simple ASCII representation.

- The code is not necessarily more efficient than sending the ASCII from a file or an initialized array using **DPSWritePostScript( )** or **DPSWriteData( )**.

An alternative to storing the procedure set as an initialized array in the application is to use a file that is accessible to the application.

The printing methods of the View class can be subclassed for a variety of reasons besides including a custom procedure set. The Import application in Chapter 12 not only includes a custom procedure set (an abbreviated version of one of the Illustrator procedure sets) but also writes out a preview image when creating an EPS file. This image is embedded within comments in the prolog of the page description. As in Example 14.13, the **endHeaderComments** method is subclassed to perform both these operations.

14.4   Conclusions

- Every application that prints should produce Level 1 compatible page descriptions as a minimum requirement.

- Most Level 2 and Display PostScript system operators can be emulated with Level 1 compatible procedures. In some cases, however, an emulation is not as efficient as using a separate approach to Level 1 and Level 2 devices. Displaying text is one such case.

- The View and PrintInfo classes in the Application Kit are the primary objects used in the printing process.

- **DPSPrintf( )**, **DPSWritePostScript( )**, and **DPSWriteData( )** are useful procedures for sending PostScript comments, files, and prologs to the server or to a stream context. Placing these items in wraps is discouraged.

Client Library

This appendix provides descriptions of Client Library procedures and conventions. These constitute the programming interface to the Display PostScript system.

Note   *This is the January 23, 1990 edition of "Client Library" taken from the "Display PostScript System Reference Binder."*

A.1 System-Specific Documentation

The term *system specific* refers to areas of the Client Library implementation that are customized to fit a machine and operating system environment. This appendix describes aspects of the Client Library that are common to all Display PostScript system implementations.

Notes and comments alert you to system-specific issues. For more information about system-specific aspects of your Client Library implementation, see the documentation provided by your Display PostScript system vendor.

A.2 The Client Library

The Client Library is your link to the Display PostScript system, which makes the imaging power of the PostScript interpreter available for displays as well as for printing devices. An application program can display text and images on the screen by calling Client Library procedures. These procedures are written with a C language interface. They generate PostScript language code and send it to the interpreter in the Display PostScript server for execution. This is illustrated in Figure A.1.

Figure A.1 *The Client Library link to the Display PostScript server*

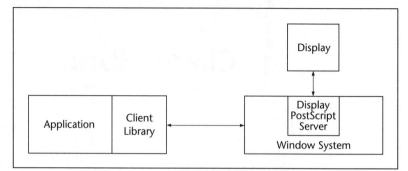

You can customize and optimize applications by writing PostScript language programs. The pswrap translator produces application-defined PostScript language programs with C-callable interfaces.

Note   *The terms input and output apply to the execution context in the PostScript interpreter, not to the application. An application "sends input" to a context and "receives output" from a context. This usage prevents ambiguity that might exist since input with respect to the context is output with respect to the application and vice versa.*

A.3   Overview of the Client Library

The Client Library is a collection of procedures that provide an application program with access to the PostScript interpreter. It includes procedures for creating, communicating with, and destroying PostScript execution contexts. A context consists of all the information (or state) needed by the PostScript interpreter to execute a PostScript language program. In the Client Library interface, each context is represented by a *DPSContextRec* data structure pointed to by a *DPSContext* handle. PostScript execution contexts are described in section 7.1, "Multiple Execution Contexts," of the *PostScript Language Reference Manual, Second Edition.*

It might appear that Client Library procedures directly produce graphical output on the display. In fact, these procedures generate PostScript language statements and transmit them to the PostScript interpreter for execution. The PostScript interpreter then produces graphical output that is displayed by device-specific procedures in the Display PostScript system. In this way, the Client Library makes the full power of the PostScript interpreter and imaging model available to a C language program.

The recommended way of sending PostScript language code to the interpreter is to call wrapped procedures generated by the pswrap translator. For simple operations, you can send PostScript language fragments to the interpreter by calling single-operator procedures, each the equivalent of a single PostScript operator.

It is also possible to send PostScript language programs as ASCII text, for example to a laser printer with a PostScript interpreter. This can be used for development and debugging or for displaying PostScript language code imported by the application, for instance, from an EPS file.

A.3.1   Phases of an Application

The following describes a typical application program, written in C, using the Client Library in the different phases of its operation:

1. *Initialization*. The application establishes communication with the Display PostScript system. It then calls Client Library procedures to create a context for executing PostScript language programs. It also performs other window-system-specific initialization. Higher-level facilities, such as toolkits, perform initialization automatically.

2. *Execution*. Once an application is initialized, it displays text and graphics by sending PostScript language programs to the interpreter. These programs can be of any complexity from a single-operator procedure to a program that previews full-color illustrations. The Client Library sends the programs to the PostScript interpreter and handles the results received from the interpreter.

3. *Termination*. When the application is ready to terminate, it calls Client Library procedures to destroy its contexts, free their resources, and end the communications session.

A.3.2   Header Files

The Client Library procedures that an application can call are defined in C header files, also called *include* or *interface* files. The Client Library interface represented by these header files can be extended in an implementation, and the extensions are compatible with the definitions given in this appendix. There are four Client Library-defined header files and one or more system-specific header files.

- *dpsclient.h* provides support for managing contexts and sending PostScript language programs to the interpreter. It supports applications as well as application toolkits. It is always present.

- *dpsfriends.h* provides support for wrapped procedures created by pswrap, as well as data representations, conversions, and other low-level support for context structures. It is always present.

- *dpsops.h* provides single-operator procedures that require an explicit context parameter. It is optional. At least one single-operator header file must be present; that is, *dpsops.h*, *psops.h*, or both.

- *psops.h* provides the single-operator procedures that implicitly derive their context parameter from the current context. It is optional. At least one single-operator header file must be present; that is, *dpsops.h*, *psops.h*, or both.

- One or more system-specific header files provide support for context creation. These header files can also provide system-specific extensions to the Client Library, such as additional error codes.

A.3.3   Wrapped Procedures

The most efficient way for an application program to send PostScript language code to the interpreter is to use the pswrap translator to produce *wrapped procedures*, that is, PostScript language programs that are callable as C procedures. A wrapped procedure (*wrap* for short) consists of a C language procedure declaration enclosing a PostScript language body. There are several advantages to using wraps:

- Complex PostScript programs can be invoked by a single procedure call, avoiding the overhead of a series of calls to single-operator procedures.

- You can insert C arguments into the PostScript language code at run time instead of having to push the C arguments onto the PostScript operand stack in separate steps.

- Wrapped procedures can efficiently produce custom graphical output by combining operators and other elements of the PostScript language in a variety of ways.

- The PostScript language code sent by a wrapped procedure is interpreted faster than ASCII text.

You prepare a PostScript language program for inclusion in the application by writing a wrap and passing it through the pswrap translator. The output of pswrap is a procedure written entirely in C language. It contains the PostScript language body as data. This has been compiled into a binary object sequence (an efficient binary encoding), with placeholders for arguments to be inserted at execution. The translated wraps can then be compiled and linked into the application program.

When a wrapped procedure is called by the application, the procedure's arguments are substituted for the placeholders in the PostScript language body of the wrap. A wrap that draws a black box is defined in Example A.1.

Example A.1 *Wrap that draws a black box*

```
defineps PSWBlackBox(float x, y)
  gsave
    0 0 0 setrgbcolor
    x y 72 72 rectfill
  grestore
endps
```

pswrap produces a procedure that can be called from a C language program as follows (the values shown are only examples):

```
PSWBlackBox(12.32, -56.78);
```

This procedure replaces the x and y operands of **rectfill** with the corresponding procedure arguments, producing executable PostScript language code:

```
gsave
  0 0 0 setrgbcolor
  12.32 -56.78 72 72 rectfill
grestore
```

All wrapped procedures work the same way as Example A.1. The arguments of the C language procedure must correspond in number and type to the operands expected by the PostScript operators in the body of the wrap. For instance, a procedure argument declared to be of type *float* corresponds to a PostScript real object; an argument of type *char* corresponds to a PostScript string object; and so on.

The nominal outcome of calling a wrapped procedure is the transmission of PostScript language code to the interpreter for execution, normally resulting in display output. The Client Library can also provide the means, on a system-specific basis, to divert transmission to another destination, such as a printer or a text file.

A.4 Basic Client Library Facilities

This section introduces the concepts you need to write a simple application program for the Display PostScript system, including: creating a context, sending code and data to a context, and destroying a context.

A.4.1 Contexts and Context Data Structures

An application creates, manages, and destroys one or more contexts. A typical application creates a single context in a single private VM (space). It then sends PostScript language code to the context to display text, graphics, and scanned images on the screen.

The context is represented by a record of type *DPSContextRec*. A handle to this record (a pointer of type *DPSContext*) is passed explicitly or implicitly with every Client Library procedure call. In essence, the *DPSContext* handle is the context.

A context can be thought of as a destination to which PostScript language code is sent. The destination is set when the context is created. In most cases, the code draws graphics in a window or specifies how a page is printed. Other destinations include a file (for execution at a later time) or the standard output; multiple destinations are allowed. The execution by the interpreter of PostScript language code sent to a context can be immediate or deferred, depending on the context creation procedure called and on the setting of *DPSContextRec* variables.

A.4.2 System-Specific Context Creation

The system-specific interface contains, at minimum, procedures for creating the *DPSContextRec* record for the implementation of the Client Library. It also provides support for extensions to the Client Library interface such as additional error codes.

Every context is associated with a system-specific object such as a window or a file. The context is created by calling a procedure in the system-specific interface. Once the context has been created, however, a set of standard Client Library operations can be applied to it. These operations, including context destruction, are defined in the standard header file *dpsclient.h*. (See section A.8, "dpsclient.h Header File," for more information.)

A.4.3 Current Context

The current context is the one that was specified by the last call to **DPSSetContext( )**. If the application has only one context, call **DPSSetContext( )** at the time the application is initialized. If the application manages more than one context, it must set the current context when necessary.

Many Client Library procedures do not require the application to specify a context; they assume the current context. This is true of all single-operator procedures defined in *psops.h* as well as any wrapped procedures that were defined to use the current context implicitly.

An application can find out which is the current context by calling **DPSGetCurrentContext( )**.

A.4.4 Sending Code and Data to a Context

Once the context has been created, the application can send PostScript language code to it by calling procedures such as

- Wraps (custom wrapped procedures) developed for the application

- Single-operator procedures defined in *dpsops.h* and *psops.h*

- The **DPSPrintf( )**, **DPSWritePostScript( )**, and **DPSWriteData( )** Client Library procedures provided for writing to a context

A wrapped procedure is a PostScript language program encoded as a binary object sequence. These are described in section A.10.4, "Binary Object Sequences," and in section 3.12.2 of the *PostScript Language Reference Manual, Second Edition.* Creating wrapped procedures is discussed in Appendix B, "pswrap."

Once the PostScript language program has been embedded in the body of a wrap by using the pswrap translator, it can be called like any other C procedure. Wraps are the most efficient way to specify any PostScript language program as a C-callable procedure.

The following list contains six examples of sending code and data to a context.

- Consider a wrap that draws a small colored circle around the point where the mouse was clicked, given an RGB color and the x, y coordinate returned by a mouse-click event. The exact PostScript language implementation is left for you as an exercise, but the C declaration of the wrap might look like this:

```
extern void PSWDrawSmallCircle(/*
  DPSContext ctxt; int x, y; float r, g, b)*/;
```

An application might call this procedure as part of the code that handles mouse clicks. Suppose the struct *event* contains the *x, y* coordinate. To draw a bright green circle around the spot, call the wrapped procedure with the following arguments:

```
PSWDrawSmallCircle(ctxt, event.x, event.y, 0.0, 1.0, 0.0);
```

- If a wrap returns values, the procedure that calls it must pass pointers to the variables into which the values will be stored. Consider a wrap that, given a font name, tells whether the font is in the **SharedFontDirectory**. Define the wrap as follows:

```
defineps PSWFontLoaded(
  DPSContext ctxt; char *fontName| boolean *found)
```

The corresponding C declaration is

```
extern void PSWFontLoaded(
DPSContext ctxt; char *fontName; int *found);
```

Note that Booleans are of the C type *int*. Call the wrapped procedure by providing a pointer to a variable of type *int* as follows:

```
int fontFound;
PSWFontLoaded(ctxt, "Courier", &fontFound);
```

Wraps are the most efficient way to specify any PostScript language program as a C-callable procedure.

- Occasionally, a small PostScript language program (one operator) is needed. In this case, a single-operator procedure is appropriate. For example, to get the current gray level, provide a pointer to a *float*, and call the single-operator procedure equivalent of the PostScript **currentgray** operator, use the following lines:

```
float gray;
DPScurrentgray(ctxt, &gray);
```

  See section A.9.4, "psops.h Procedure Declarations," for a complete list of single-operator procedure declarations.

- **DPSPrintf( )** is one of the Client Library facilities provided for writing PostScript language code directly to a context. **DPSPrintf( )** is similar to the standard C library routine **printf( )**. It formats arguments into ASCII text and writes this text to the context. Small PostScript language programs or text data can be sent this way. The following example sends formatted text to the **show** operator to represent an author's byline:

```
struct {
    int x, y;         /* location on page for byline */
    char *titleString;      /* title of document */
    char *authorsName;      /* name of author */
    } byline;

DPSPrintf(ctxt, "%d %d moveto (%s by %s) show\n",
    byline.x,
    byline.y,
    byline.titleString,
    byline.authorsName);
```

  The x, y coordinate is formatted in place of the two %d field specifiers, the title replaces the first %s, followed by the word by. The author's name replaces the second %s.

Warning   *When you use **DPSPrintf( )**, leave white space (newline with \n, or just a space) at the end of the format string if the string ends with an operator. PostScript language code written to a context appears as a continuous stream. Thus, consecutive calls to **DPSPrintf( )** appear as if all the text were sent at once. For example, suppose the following calls were made:*

```
DPSPrintf(ctxt, "gsave");
DPSPrintf(ctxt, "stroke");
DPSPrintf(ctxt, "grestore");
```

*The context receives a single string **gsavestrokegrestore**, with all the operators run together. Of course, this might be useful for constructing a long string that isn't part of a program, but when sending operators to be executed, add white space to the end of each format string. For example:*

```
DPSPrintf(ctxt, "gsave\n");
```

- The **DPSWritePostScript( )** procedure is provided for writing PostScript language code of any encoding to a context. If **DPSChangeEncoding( )** is provided by the system-specific interface, use **DPSWritePostScript( )** to convert a binary-encoded PostScript language program into another binary form (for instance, binary object sequences to binary-encoded tokens) or into ASCII text. Send code for immediate execution by the interpreter as binary object sequences. Send code that's intended to be read by a human as ASCII text.

Warning   *Although PostScript language of any encoding can be written to a context, unexpected results can occur when intermixing code of different encodings. This is particularly important when ASCII encoding is mixed with binary encoding. (See section 3.12, "Binary Encoding Details," of the "PostScript Language Reference Manual, Second Edition" for a discussion of encodings.)*

The following code, which looks correct, might fail with a syntax error in the interpreter, depending on the contents of the buffer:

```
while (/* more buffers to send */) {
  count = GetBuffer(file, buffer);
  DPSWritePostScript(ctxt, buffer, count);
  MyWrap(ctxt);
}
```

***GetBuffer( )** reads a PostScript language program in the ASCII encoding from a file. The call to **MyWrap( )** generates a binary object sequence. If the program in the buffer passed to **DPSWritePostScript( )** is complete, with no partial tokens, **MyWrap( )** works correctly. If, however, the end of the buffer contains a partial token, mov, and the next buffer starts with eto, the binary object sequence representing **MyWrap( )** is inserted immediately after the partial token, resulting in a syntax error.*

*This applies to all procedures that send code or data to a context, including the Client Library procedures **DPSPrintf( )**, **DPSWritePostScript( )**, **DPSWriteData( )**, and **DPSWaitContext( )**.*

- To send any type of data to a context (such as hexadecimal image data) or to avoid the automatic conversion behavior built into **DPSWritePostScript( )**, use **DPSWriteData( )**.

The following example reads hexadecimal image data line by line from a file and sends the data to a context:

```
while (!feof(fp)) {
    fgets(buf, BUFSIZE, fp);
    DPSWriteData(ctxt, buf, strlen(buf));
}
```

A.4.5   Spaces

A context is created in a space. The space is either shared with a previously created context or is created when a new context is created. Multiple contexts in the same space share all data. Coordination is required to ensure that they don't interfere with each other. Contexts in different spaces can operate more or less independently and still share data by using shared VM. See the discussion of VM and spaces in the *PostScript Language Reference Manual, Second Edition*.

Destroying a space automatically destroys all of the contexts within it. **DPSDestroySpace( )** calls **DPSDestroyContext( )** for each context in the space.

The parameters that define a space are contained in a record of type *DPSSpaceRec*.

A.4.6   Interrupts

An application might need to interrupt a PostScript language program running in the PostScript interpreter. Call **DPSInterruptContext( )** for this. (Although this procedure returns immediately, an indeterminate amount of time can pass before execution is actually interrupted.)

An interrupt request causes the context to execute an **interrupt** error. Since the implementation of this error can be changed by the application, the results of requesting an interrupt cannot be defined here. The default behavior is that the **stop** operator executes.

A.4.7   Destroying Contexts

An application should destroy all the contexts it creates when they are no longer needed by calling **DPSDestroyContext( )** or **DPSDestroySpace( )**. Destroying a context does not destroy the space it occupies, but destroying a space destroys all of its contexts.

The PostScript interpreter detects when an application terminates abnormally and destroys any spaces and contexts that the application has created.

A.5   Handling Output from the Context

Output is information returned from the PostScript interpreter to the application. In the Display PostScript system, three kinds of output are possible:

- Output parameters (results) from wrapped procedures

- ASCII text written by the context (for example, by the **print** operator)

- Errors

Each kind of output is handled by a separate mechanism in the Client Library. Handling text and errors is discussed in the remainder of this section.

Note   *You might not get text and error output when you expect it.*

*For example, a wrap that generates text to be sent to the application (for instance, with the **print** operator) might return before the application receives the text. Unless the application and the interpreter are synchronized, the text might not appear until some other Client Library procedure or wrap is called. This is due to delays in the communications channel or in scheduling execution of the context in the PostScript interpreter.*

These delays are an important consideration for handling errors, since notification of the error can be received by the application long after the code that caused the error was sent.

A.5.1 Callback Procedures

You must specify callback procedures to handle text and errors. A callback procedure is code provided by an application and called by a system function.

A text handler is a callback procedure that handles text output from the context. It is specified in the *textProc* field of the *DPSContextRec*. A system-specific default text handler might be provided.

An error handler is a callback procedure that handles errors arising when the context is passed as a parameter to any Client Library procedure or wrap. It is specified in the *errorProc* field of the *DPSContextRec*. **DPSDefaultErrorProc( )** is the default error handler provided with every Client Library implementation.

Text and error handlers are associated with a context when the context is created, but the **DPSSetTextProc( )** and **DPSSetErrorProc( )** procedures give the application the flexibility to change these handlers at any time.

Using a callback procedure reverses the normal flow of control, which is as follows:

1. An application that is active calls the system to provide services, for example, to get memory or open a file.

2. The application gives up control until the system has provided the service.

3. The system procedure returns control to the application, passing the result of the service that was requested.

In the case of callback procedures, the application wants a custom service provided at a time when it is not in control. It does this as follows:

1. The application notifies the system, often at initialization, of the address of the callback procedure to be invoked when the system recognizes a condition (for example, an error condition).

2. When the error is raised, the system gets control.

3. The system passes control to the error handler specified by the application, thus "calling back" the application.

4. The error handler does processing on behalf of the application.

5. When the error handler completes, it returns to the system.

In the Display PostScript system, the text and error handlers in the Client Library interface are designed to be used this way.

Note   *Client Library procedures and wraps should not be called from within a callback procedure. This protects the application against unintended recursion.*

A.5.2   Text Handlers

A context generates text output with operators such as **print, writestring**, and ==. The application handles text output with a text handler, which is specified in the *textProc* field of the *DPSContextRec*. The text handler is passed a buffer of text and a count of the number of characters in the buffer; what is done with this buffer is up to the application. The text handler might be called several times to handle large amounts of text.

Note that the Client Library gets buffers; it doesn't provide any logical structure for the text and it doesn't indicate (or know) where the text ends.

The text handler can be called as a side effect of calling a wrap, a single-operator procedure, or a Client Library procedure that takes a context. You can't predict when the text handler for a context will be called unless the application is synchronized.

A.5.3   Error Handlers

The *errorProc* field in the *DPSContextRec* contains the address of a callback procedure for handling errors. The error callback procedure is called when there is a PostScript language error or when an error internal to the Client Library, such as use of an invalid context identifier, is encountered. The standard error codes are listed in section A.8.2, "dspclient.h Procedures."

When the interpreter detects a PostScript language error, it invokes the standard **handleerror** procedure to report the error, then forces the context to terminate. The error callback procedure specified in the *DPSContextRec* is called with the *dps_err_ps* error code.

After a PostScript language error, the context becomes invalid; further use causes another error.

A.5.4 Error Recovery Requirements

For many applications, error recovery might not be an issue because an unanticipated PostScript language error or Client Library error represents a bug in the program that will be fixed during development. However, since applications sometimes go into production with undiscovered bugs, provide an error handler that allows the application to exit gracefully.

There are a small number of applications that require error recovery more sophisticated than simply exiting. If an application falls into one of the following categories, it is likely that some form of error recovery will be needed:

- Applications that read and execute PostScript language programs generated by other sources (for example, a previewer application for PostScript language documents generated by a word-processing program). Since the externally provided PostScript language program might have errors, the application must provide error recovery.

- Applications that allow you to enter PostScript language programs. This category is a subset of the previous category.

- Applications that generate PostScript language programs dynamically in response to user requests (for example, a graphics art program that generates an arbitrarily long path description of a graphical object). Since there are system-specific resource limitations on the interpreter, such as memory and disk space, the application should be able to back away from an error caused by exhausting a resource and attempt to acquire new or reclaim used resources.

Error recovery is complicated because both the Client Library and the context can be left in unknown states. For example, the operand stack might have unused objects on it.

In general, if an application needs to intercept and recover from PostScript language errors, keep it simple. For some applications, the best strategy when an error occurs is either to destroy the space and construct a new one with a new context or to restart the application.

A given implementation of the Client Library might provide more sophisticated error recovery facilities. Consult your system-specific documentation. Your system might provide the general purpose exception handling facilities described in section A.12, "Exception Handling," which can be used in conjunction with **DPSDefaultErrorProc( )**.

A.5.5 Backstop Handlers

Backstop handlers handle output when there is no other appropriate handler. The Client Library automatically installs backstop handlers.

Call **DPSGetCurrentTextBackstop( )** to get a pointer to the current backstop text handler. Call **DPSSetTextBackstop( )** to install a new backstop text handler. The text backstop can be used as a default text handler implementation. The definition of what the default text handler does is system specific. For instance, for UNIX systems, it writes the text to *stdout*.

Call **DPSGetCurrentErrorBackstop( )** to get a pointer to the current backstop error handler. Call **DPSSetErrorBackstop( )** to install a new backstop error handler. The backstop error handler processes errors internal to the Client Library, such as a lost server connection. These errors have no specific *DPSContext* handle associated with them and therefore have no error handler.

A.6 Additional Client Library Facilities

This section describes five utilities and support functions for applications in the Client Library.

A.6.1 Chained Contexts

Occasionally it is useful to send the same PostScript language program to several contexts. This is accomplished by chaining the contexts together and sending input to one context in the chain; for example, by calling a wrap with that context.

Two Client Library procedures are provided for managing context chaining:

- **DPSChainContext( )** links a context to a chain.

- **DPSUnchainContext( )** removes a child context from its parent's chain.

One context in the chain is specified as the parent context, the other as the child context. The child context is added to the parent's chain. Subsequently, any input sent to the parent is sent to its child, and the child of the child, and so on. Input sent to a child is not passed to its parent.

A context can appear on only one chain. If the context is already a child on a chain, **DPSChainContext( )** returns a nonzero error code. However, you can chain a child to a context that already has a child.

Note   *A parent context always passes its input to its child context. However, for a chain of more than two contexts, the order in which the contexts on the chain receive the input is not defined. Therefore, an application should not rely on* **DPSChainContext( )** *to create a chain whose contexts process input in a particular order.*

For chained contexts, output is handled differently from input, and text and errors are handled differently from results. If a context on a chain generates text or error output, the output is handled by that context only. Such output is not passed to its child. When a wrap that returns results is called, all of the contexts on the chain get the wrap code (the input), but only the context with which the wrap was called receives the results.

The best way to build a chain is to identify one context as the parent. Call **DPSChainContext( )** to make each additional context the child of that parent. For example, to chain contexts *A*, *B*, *C*, and *D*, choose *A* as the parent and make the following calls to **DPSChainContext( )**:

```
DPSChainContext(A,B);
DPSChainContext(A,C);
DPSChainContext(A,D);
```

Once the chain is built, send input only to the designated parent, *A*.

The most common use of chained contexts is in debugging. A log of PostScript operators executed can be kept by a child context whose purpose is to convert PostScript language programs to ASCII text and write the text to a file. This child is chained to a parent context that sends normal application requests to the interpreter. The parent's calls to wrapped procedures are logged in human-readable form by the child as a debugging audit trail.

Chained contexts can also be used for duplicate displays. An application might want several windows or several different display screens to show the same graphics without having to explicitly call the wrapped procedure in a loop for all of the contexts.

A.6.2   Encoding and Translation

PostScript language code can be sent to a context in three ways:

- As a binary object sequence typically used for immediate execution on behalf of a context

- As binary-encoded tokens typically used for deferred execution from a file

- As ASCII text typically used for debugging, display, or deferred execution from a file

Chapter 13, "Binary Encoding Formats," provides introductory information on the encoding types as well as some file sizes for the different formats. See section 3.12, "Binary Encoding Details," of the *PostScript Language Reference Manual, Second Edition* for the binary encoding formats' complete specifications.

Since the application and the PostScript interpreter can be on different machines, the Client Library automatically ensures that the binary representation of numeric values, including byte order and floating-point format, are correctly interpreted.

Encoding PostScript Language Code

On a system-specific basis, the Client Library supports a variety of conversions to and from the encodings and formats defined for the PostScript language. These are:

- Binary object sequence to binary object sequence, for expanding user name indexes back to their printable names

- Binary object sequence to ASCII encoding, for backward compatibility with printers, interchange, and debugging

- Binary object sequence to binary-encoded tokens, for long-term storage

- Binary-encoded tokens to ASCII, for backward compatibility and interchange

DPSProgramEncoding defines the three encodings available to PostScript language programs. *DPSNameEncoding* defines the two encodings for user names in PostScript language programs.

Translation

Translation is the conversion of program encoding or name encoding from one form to another. Any code sent to the context is converted according to the setting of the encoding fields. For a context created with the system-specific routine **DPSCreateTextContext( )**, code is automatically converted to ASCII encoding.

An application sometimes exchanges binary object sequences with another application. Since binary object sequences have user name indexes by default, the sending application must provide name-mapping information to the receiving application which can be lengthy.

Instead, some implementations allow the application to translate name indices back into user names by changing the *nameEncoding* field to *dps_strings*. In many implementations, **DPSChangeEncoding( )** performs this function.

A.6.3   Buffering

For optimal performance, programs and data sent to a context might be buffered by the Client Library. For the most part, you don't need to be concerned with this. Flushing of the buffer happens automatically as required, such as just before waiting for input events.

However, in certain situations, the application can explicitly flush a buffer. **DPSFlushContext( )** allows the application to force any buffered code or data to be sent to the context. Using **DPSFlushContext( )** is usually not necessary. Flushing does not guarantee that code is executed by the context, only that any buffered code is sent to the context.

Unnecessary flushing is inefficient. It is unusual for the application to flush the buffer explicitly. Cases where the buffer might need to be flushed include the following:

- When there is nothing to send to the interpreter for a long time (for example, "going to sleep" or doing a long computation).

- When there is nothing expected from the interpreter for a long time. (Note that getting input automatically flushes the output buffers.)

When the client and the server are separate processes and the buffered code doesn't need to be executed immediately, the application can flush the buffers with **flush** rather than synchronizing with the context.

A.6.4 Synchronizing Application and Context

The PostScript interpreter can run as a separate operating system process (or task) from the application; it can even run on a separate machine. When the processes are separate, you must take into account the communication between the application and the PostScript interpreter. This is important when time-critical actions must be performed based on the current appearance of the display. Also, errors arising from the execution of a wrapped procedure can be reported long after the procedure returns.

The application and the context are synchronized when all code sent to the context has been executed, and it is waiting to execute more code. When the two are not synchronized, the status of code previously sent to the context is unknown to the application. Synchronization can be effected in two ways: as a side effect of calling wraps that return values, or explicitly, by calling the **DPSWaitContext( )** procedure.

A wrapped procedure that has no result values returns as soon as the wrap body is sent to the context. The data buffer is not necessarily flushed in this case. Sometimes, however, the application's next action depends on the completed execution of the wrap body by the PostScript interpreter. The following describes the kind of problem that can occur when the assumption is made that a wrap's code has been executed by the time it returns.

For example, an application calls a wrapped procedure to draw a large, complex picture into an offscreen buffer (such as an X11 pixmap). The wrapped procedure has no return value, so it returns immediately, although the context might not have finished executing the code. The application then calls procedures to copy the screen buffer to a window for display. If the context has not finished drawing the picture in the buffer, only part of the image appears on the screen. This is not what the application programmer intended.

Wrapped procedures that return results flush any code waiting to be sent to the context and then wait until all results have been received. They automatically synchronize the context with the application. The wrapped procedure won't return until the interpreter indicates that all results have been sent. In this case, the application knows that the context is ready to execute more code as soon as the wrapped procedure returns, but the wrapped procedure might return prematurely if an error occurs, depending on how the error handler works.

The preceding discussion describes the side effect of calling a wrap that returns a value, but it is not always convenient or correct to use this method of implementation. Forcing the application to wait for a return result for every wrap is inefficient and might degrade performance.

If an application has a few critical points where synchronization must occur, and a wrap that returns results is not needed, **DPSWaitContext( )** can be used to synchronize the application with the context. It flushes any buffered code, and then waits until the context finishes executing all code that has been sent to it so far. This forces the context to finish before the application continues.

Like wraps that return results, use **DPSWaitContext( )** only when necessary. Performance can be degraded by excessive synchronization.

A.6.5 Forked Contexts

When the **fork** operator is executed in the PostScript interpreter, a new execution context is created. In order to communicate with a forked context, the application must create a *DPSContextRec* for it.

A.7 Programming Tips

This section contains tips for avoiding common mistakes made when using the Client Library interface.

- Don't guess the arguments to a single-operator procedure call; look them up in the listing. See section A.9, "Single-Operator Procedures."

- Variables passed to wrapped procedures and single-operator procedures must be of the correct C type. A common mistake is to pass a pointer to a *short int* (only 16 bits) to a procedure that returns a Boolean. A Boolean is defined as an *int*, which can be 32 bits on some systems.

- Variables passed to **DPSPrintf( )** must be of the right type. Passing type *float* to a format string of %d will yield unpredictable results.

- There are two ways of synchronizing the application with the context: Either call **DPSWaitContext( )**, which causes the application to wait until the interpreter has executed all the code sent to the execution context, or call a wrap that returns a result, which causes synchronization as a side effect. If synchronization is not required, use a wrap that returns results only when results are needed. Unnecessary synchronization by either method degrades performance.

- Don't read from the file returned by the operator **currentfile** from within a wrap. In general, don't read directly from the context's standard input stream %stdin from within a wrap. Since a binary object sequence is a single token, the behavior of the code is different from what it would be in another encoding, such as ASCII. This will lead to unpredictable results. See Appendix B, "pswrap," and the *PostScript Language Reference Manual, Second Edition.*

- If the context is an execution context for a display, do not write PostScript language programs (particularly in wraps) that depend on reading the end-of-file (EOF) indicator. Support for EOF on the communications channel is system specific and should not be relied on. However, PostScript language programs that will be written to a file or spooled to a printer can make use of EOF indicators.

- Before calling **DPSWaitContext( )**, make sure that code that has already been sent to the context is syntactically complete, such as a wrap or a correctly terminated PostScript operator or composite object.

- To avoid unintended recursions, don't call Client Library procedures or wraps from within a callback procedure.

- Program wraps carefully. Copying the entire prolog from a PostScript printer driver into a wrap without change probably won't result in efficient code.

- Avoid doing all your programming in the PostScript language. Because the PostScript language is interpreted, not compiled, the application can generally do arithmetic computation and data manipulation (such as sorting) more efficiently in C. Reserve the PostScript language for what it does best: displaying text and graphics.

A.7.1 Using the Imaging Model

A thorough understanding of the imaging model is essential to writing efficient Display PostScript system applications.

The imaging model helps make your application device independent and resolution independent. Device independence ensures that your application will work and look as you intended on any display or print media.

Resolution independence lets you use the power of the PostScript language to scale, rotate, and transform your graphical display without loss of quality. Use of the imaging model automatically gives you the best possible rendering for any device.

Design your application with the imaging model in mind. Consider issues like converting coordinate systems, representing paths and graphics states with data structures, rendering colors and patterns, setting text, and accessing fonts (to name just a few).

Specific tips are

- Think in terms of color. Avoid programming to the lowest common denominator (low-resolution monochrome). The imaging model always gives the best rendering possible for a device, so use colors even if your application might be run on monochrome or gray-scale devices. Avoid using **setgray** unless you want a black, white, or gray level. Use **setrgbcolor** for all other cases. The imaging model will use a gray level or halftone pattern if the device does not support color, so objects of different colors will be distinguishable from one another.

- Don't use **setlinewidth** with a width of zero to get thin lines. On high-resolution devices the lines are practically invisible. To get lines narrower than one point, use fractions such as 0.3 or 0.25.

A.8 dpsclient.h Header File

The procedures in *dpsclient.h* constitute the core of the Client Library and are system independent. The contents of the header file are described in the following sections.

A.8.1 dpsclient.h Data Structures

The context record *DPSContextRec* is shared by the application and the PostScript interpreter. Except for the *priv* field, this data structure should not be altered directly. The *dpsclient.h* header file provides procedures to alter it.

When calling Client Library procedures, refer to the context record by its handle, *DPSContext*.

DPSContext   /* handle for context record */

See *DPSContextRec*.

DPSContextRec

```
typedef struct_t_DPSContextRec {
    char *priv;
    DPSSpace space;
    DPSProgramEncoding programEncoding;
    DPSNameEncoding nameEncoding;
    DPSProcs procs;
    void (*textProc)( );
    void (*errorProc)( );
    DPSResults resultTable;
    unsigned int resultTableLength;
    struct_t_DPSContextRec *chainParent, *chainChild;
    DPSContextType type;        /* NeXT addition—denotes type of context */
} DPSContextRec, *DPSContext;
```

DPSContextRec defines the data structure pointed to by *DPSContext*.

Note that this record is used by *dpsclient.h* procedures but is actually defined in the *dpsfriends.h* header file.

priv is used by application code. It is initialized to *NULL* and is not touched thereafter by the Client Library implementation.

Although it is possible to read all fields of DPSContextRec directly, do not modify them directly except for priv. Data structures internal to the Client Library depend on the values in these fields and must be notified when they change. Call the procedures provided for this purpose, such as **DPSSetTextProc( ).**

space identifies the space in which the context executes.

programEncoding and *nameEncoding* describe the encoding of the PostScript language that is sent to the interpreter. The values in these fields are established when the context is created. Whether or not the encoding fields can be changed after creation is system specific.

procs points to a *struct* containing procedures that implement the basic context operations, including writing, flushing, interrupting, and so on.

The Client Library calls the *textProc* and *errorProc* procedures to handle interpreter-generated ASCII text and errors.

resultTableLength and *resultTable* define the number, type, and location of results expected by a wrap. They are set up by the wrap procedure before any values are returned.

chainParent and *chainChild* are used for chaining contexts. *chainChild* is a pointer to the context that automatically receives code and data sent to the context represented by this *DPSContextRec*. *chainParent* is a pointer to the context that automatically sends code and data to the context represented by this *DPSContextRec*.

DPSErrorCode   typedef int DPSErrorCode;

DPSErrorCode defines the type of error code used by the Client Library. The following are the standard error codes:

- *dps_err_ps* identifies standard PostScript interpreter errors.

- *dps_err_nameTooLong* flags user names that are too long. 128 characters is the maximum length for PostScript language names.

- *dps_err_resultTagCheck* flags erroneous result tags; these are most likely due to erroneous explicit use of **printobject**.

- *dps_err_resultTypeCheck* flags incompatible result types.

- *dps_err_invalidContext* flags an invalid *DPSContext* argument. An attempt to send PostScript language code to a context that has terminated is probably the cause of this error.

A.8.2   dpsclient.h Procedures

This section contains descriptions of the procedures in the Client Library header file *dpsclient.h*, listed alphabetically.

DPSChainContext

```
int DPSChainContext(parent, child)
    DPSContext parent, child;
```

DPSChainContext( ) links *child* onto the context chain of *parent*. This is the chain of contexts that automatically receive a copy of any code or data sent to *parent*. A context appears on only one such chain.

DPSChainContext( ) returns zero if it successfully chains *child* to *parent*. It fails if *child* is on another context's chain; in that case, it returns -1.

DPSDefaultErrorProc

```
void DPSDefaultErrorProc(ctxt, errorCode, arg1, arg2)
    DPSContext ctxt;
    DPSErrorCode errorCode;
    long unsigned int arg1, arg2;
```

DPSDefaultErrorProc( ) is a sample **DPSErrorProc( )** for handling errors from the PostScript interpreter.

The meaning of *arg1* and *arg2* depend on *errorCode*. See **DPSErrorProc( )**.

DPSDestroyContext

```
void DPSDestroyContext(ctxt)
    DPSContext ctxt;
```

DPSDestroyContext( ) destroys the context represented by *ctxt*. The context is first unchained if it is on a chain.

What happens to buffered input and output when a context is destroyed is system specific.

Destroying a context does not destroy its space; see **DPSDestroySpace( )**.

DPSDestroySpace   void DPSDestroySpace(spc)
    DPSSpace spc;

> **DPSDestroySpace( )** destroys the space represented by *spc*. This is necessary for application termination and cleanup. It also destroys all contexts within *spc*.

DPSErrorProc   typedef void (*DPSErrorProc)(/*
    DPSContext ctxt;
    DPSErrorCode errorCode;
    long unsigned int arg1, arg2;*/);

> **DPSErrorProc( )** handles errors caused by the context. These can be PostScript language errors reported by the interpreter or errors that occur when the Client Library is called with a context. *errorCode* is one of the predefined codes that specify the type of error encountered. *errorCode* determines the interpretation of PostScript language errors *arg1* and *arg2*.
>
> The following list shows how *arg1* and *arg2* are handled for each *errorCode*:

dps_err_ps	*arg1* is the address of the binary object sequence sent by **handleerror** to report the error. The sequence has one object, which is an array of four objects. *arg2* is the number of bytes in the entire binary object sequence.
dps_err_nameTooLong	Error in wrap argument. The PostScript user name and its length are passed as *arg1* and *arg2*. A name of more than 128 characters causes an error.
dps_err_resultTagCheck	Error in formulation of wrap. The pointer to the binary object sequence and its length are passed as *arg1* and *arg2*. There is one object in the sequence.
dps_err_resultTypeCheck	Incompatible result types. A pointer to the binary object is passed as *arg1*; *arg2* is unused.
dps_err_invalidContext	Stale context handle (probably terminated). *arg1* is a context identifier; *arg2* is unused.

DPSFlushContext   void DPSFlushContext(ctxt)
    DPSContext ctxt;

> **DPSFlushContext( )** forces any buffered code or data to be sent to *ctxt*. Some Client Library implementations use buffering to optimize performance.

DPSGetCurrentErrorBackstop

DPSErrorProc DPSGetCurrentErrorBackstop( );

DPSGetCurrentErrorBackstop( ) returns the *errorProc* passed most recently to **DPSSetErrorBackstop( )**, or *NULL* if none was set.

DPSGetCurrentTextBackstop

DPSTextProc DPSGetCurrentTextBackstop( );

DPSGetCurrentErrorBackstop( ) returns the *textProc* passed most recently to **DPSSetTextBackstop( )**, or *NULL* if none was set.

DPSInterruptContext

void DPSInterruptContext(ctxt)
    DPSContext ctxt;

DPSInterruptContext( ) notifies the interpreter to interrupt the execution of the context, resulting in the PostScript language **interrupt** error. The procedure returns immediately after sending the notification.

DPSPrintf

void DPSPrintf(ctxt, fmt, [, arg ...])
    DPSContext ctxt;
    char *fmt;

DPSPrintf( ) sends string *fmt* to *ctxt* with the optional arguments converted, formatted, and logically inserted into the string in a manner identical to the standard C library routine **printf( )**. It is useful for sending formatted data or a short PostScript language program to a context.

DPSResetContext

void DPSResetContext(ctxt)
    DPSContext ctxt;

DPSResetContext( ) resets the context after an error occurs. It ensures that any buffered I/O is discarded and that the context is ready to read and execute more input. **DPSResetContext( )** works in conjunction with **resynchandleerror**.

DPSSetErrorBackstop   void DPSSetErrorBackstop(errorProc)
       DPSErrorProc errorProc;

    DPSSetErrorBackstop( ) establishes *errorProc* as a pointer to the backstop error handler. This error handler handles errors that are not handled by any other error handler. *NULL* will be passed as the *ctxt* argument to the backstop error handler.

DPSSetErrorProc   void DPSSetErrorProc(ctxt, errorProc)
       DPSContext ctxt;
       DPSErrorProc errorProc;

    DPSSetErrorProc( ) changes the context's error handler.

DPSSetTextBackstop   void DPSSetTextBackstop(textProc)
       DPSTextProc textProc;

    DPSSetTextBackstop( ) establishes the procedure pointed to by *textProc* as the handler for text output for which there is no other handler. The text handler acts as a backstop for text output.

DPSSetTextProc   void DPSSetTextProc(ctxt, textProc)
       DPSContext ctxt;
       DPSTextProc textProc;

    DPSSetTextProc( ) changes the context's text handler.

DPSSpaceFromContext   DPSSpace DPSSpaceFromContext(ctxt)
       DPSContext ctxt;

    DPSSpaceFromContext( ) returns the space handle for the specified context. It returns *NULL* if *ctxt* does not represent a valid execution context.

DPSTextProc   typedef void (*DPSTextProc)(/*
       DPSContext ctxt;
       char *buf;
       long unsigned int count; */);

    DPSTextProc( ) handles text emitted from the interpreter, for example, by the == operator. *buf* is a pointer to *count* characters.

DPSUnchainContext   void DPSUnchainContext(ctxt)
　　　　　　　　　　　　DPSContext ctxt;

DPSUnchainContext( ) removes *ctxt* from the chain that it is on, if any. The parent and child pointers of the unchained context are set to *NULL*.

DPSWaitContext   void DPSWaitContext(ctxt)
　　　　　　　　　　　DPSContext ctxt;

DPSWaitContext( ) flushes output buffers belonging to *ctxt* and then waits until the interpreter is ready for more input to *ctxt*. It is not necessary to call **DPSWaitContext( )** after calling a wrapped procedure that returns a value.

Before calling **DPSWaitContext( )**, ensure that the last code sent to the context is syntactically complete, such as a wrap or a correctly terminated PostScript operator or composite object.

DPSWriteData   void DPSWriteData(ctxt, buf, count)
　　　　　　　　　　DPSContext ctxt;
　　　　　　　　　　char *buf;
　　　　　　　　　　unsigned int count;

DPSWriteData( ) sends *count* bytes of data from *buf* to *ctxt*. *ctxt* specifies the destination context. *buf* points to a buffer that contains *count* bytes. The contents of the buffer will not be converted according to the context's encoding parameters.

DPSWritePostScript   void DPSWritePostScript(ctxt, buf, count)
　　　　　　　　　　　　DPSContext ctxt;
　　　　　　　　　　　　char *buf;
　　　　　　　　　　　　unsigned int count;

DPSWritePostScript( ) sends PostScript language to a context in any of the three language encodings. *ctxt* specifies the destination context. *buf* points to a buffer that contains *count* bytes of PostScript language code. The code in the buffer will be converted according to the context's encoding parameters as needed; refer to the system-specific documentation for a list of supported conversions.

A.9 Single-Operator Procedures

For each operator defined in the PostScript language, the Client Library provides a procedure to invoke the most common usage of the operator. These are called the single-operator procedures. If the predefined usage is not the one you need, you can write wraps for variant forms of the operators.

There are two Client Library header files for single-operator procedures: *dpsops.h* and *psops.h*. The name of the Client Library single-operator procedure is the name of the PostScript operator preceded by either DPS or PS:

DPS prefix

Used when the context is explicitly specified; for example, **DPSgsave( )**. The first argument must be of type *DPSContext*. These single-operator procedures are defined in *dpsops.h*.

PS prefix

Used when the context is assumed to be the current context; for example, **PSgsave( )**. These single-operator procedures are defined in *psops.h*. The procedure **DPSSetContext( )**, defined in *dpsclient.h*, sets the current context.

For example, to execute the PostScript operator **translate**, the application can call

    DPStranslate(ctxt, 1.23, 43.56)

where *ctxt* is a variable of type *DPSContext*, the handle that represents a PostScript execution context.

Note   *Most PostScript operator names are lowercase, but some contain uppercase letters; for example **FontDirectory**. In either case, the name of the corresponding single-operator procedure is formed by using PS or DPS as a preface.*

The **DPStranslate( )** procedure sends the binary encoding of

    1.23 43.56 translate

to execute in *ctxt*.

A.9.1 Setting the Current Context

The single-operator procedures in *psops.h* assume the current context. The **DPSSetContext( )** procedure, defined in *dpsclient.h*, sets the current context. When the application deals with only one context it is convenient to use the procedures in *psops.h* rather than those in *dpsops.h*. In this case, the application would set the current context during its initialization phase:

    DPSSetContext(ctxt);

In subsequent calls on the procedures in *psops.h*, *ctxt* is used implicitly. For example:

    PStranslate(1.23, 43.56);

has the same effect as

    DPStranslate(ctxt, 1.23, 43.56);

The explicit method is preferred for situations that require intermingling of calls to multiple contexts.

Note   *It is important to pass the correct C types to the single-operator procedures. In general, if a PostScript operator takes operands of arbitrary numeric type, the corresponding single-operator procedure takes parameters of type float. Coordinates are always type float. Passing an integer literal to a procedure that expects a floating-point literal is a common error:*

incorrect: PSlineto(72, 72);

correct: PSlineto(72.0, 72.0);

Procedures that appear to have no input arguments might actually take their operands from the operand stack, for example, **PSdef( )** and **DPSdef( )**.

A.9.2 Types in Single-Operator Procedures

When using single-operator procedures, inspect the calling protocol (that is, order and types of formal parameters) for every procedure to be called.

Note   *Throughout this section, references to single-operator procedures with a DPS prefix are applicable to the equivalent procedures with a PS prefix.*

A.9.3 Guidelines for Associating Data Types with Single-Operator Procedures

There is no completely consistent system for associating data types with particular single-operator procedures. In general, look up the definition in the header file. However, there are a few rules that can be applied. All these rules have exceptions.

- Coordinates are specified as type *float*. For example, all of the standard path construction operators (**moveto**, **lineto**, **curveto**, and so on) take type *float*.

- Booleans are specified as type *int*. The comment /* *int *b* */ or /* *int *it* */ in the header file means that the procedure returns a Boolean.

- If the operator takes either integer or floating-point numbers, the corresponding procedure takes type *float*. If the operator specifies a number type (such as *rand* and *vmreclaim*), the procedure takes arguments of that type (typically type *int*).

- Operators that return values must always be specified with a pointer to the appropriate data type. For example, **currentgray** returns the current gray value of the graphics state. You must pass **DPScurrentgray( )** a pointer to a variable of type *float*.

- If an operator takes a data type that does not have a directly analogous C type, such as dictionaries, graphics states, and executable arrays, the single-operator procedure takes no arguments. It is assumed that you will arrange for the appropriate data to be on the operand stack before calling the procedure; see **DPSsendchararray( )** and **DPSsendfloat( )**, among others.

- If a single-operator procedure takes or returns a matrix, the matrix is specified as *float m[ ]*, which is an array of six floating-point numbers.

- In general, the integer parameter *size* is used to specify the length of a variable-length array; see, for example, **DPSxshow( )**. For single-operator procedures that take two variable-length arrays as parameters, the length of the first array is specified by the integer n; the length of the second array is specified by the integer l; see, for example, **DPSustroke( )**.

The following operators are worth noting for unusual order and types of arguments, or for other irregularities. After reading these descriptions, inspect the declarations in the listing or in the header file.

- **DPSdefineuserobject( )** takes no arguments. One would expect it to take at least the index argument, but because of the requirement to have the arbitrary object on the top of the stack, it is better to send the index down separately, perhaps with **DPSsendint( )**.

- **DPSgetchararray( )**, **DPSgetfloatarray( )**, and other get array operators specify the length of the array first, followed by the array. (Mnemonic: get the array last.)

- **DPSsendchararray( )**, **DPSsendfloatarray( )**, and other send array operators specify the array first, followed by the length of the array. (Mnemonic: send the array first.)

- **DPSinfill( )**, **DPSinstroke( )**, and **DPSinufill( )** support only the x, y coordinate version of the operator. The optional second userpath argument is not supported.

- **DPSinueofill( )**, **DPSinufill( )**, **DPSinustroke( )**, **DPSuappend( )**, **DPSueofill( )**, **DPSufill( )**, **DPSustroke( )**, and **DPSustrokepath( )** take a userpath in the form of an encoded number string and operator string. The lengths of the strings follow the strings themselves as argument.

- **DPSsetdash( )** takes an array of numbers of type *float* for the dash pattern.

- **DPSselectfont( )** takes type *float* for the font scale parameter.

- **DPSsetgray( )** takes type *float*. (DPSsetgray(1) is wrong.)

- **DPSxshow( )**, **DPSxyshow( )**, and **DPSyshow( )** take an array of numbers of type *float* for specifying the coordinates of each character.

- **DPSequals( )** is the procedure equivalent to the = operator.

- **DPSequalsequals( )** is the procedure equivalent to the == operator.

- **DPSversion( )** returns the version number in a character array *buf[ ]* whose length is specified by *bufsize*.

Special Cases

A few of the single-operator procedures have been optimized to take user objects for arguments, since they are most commonly used in this way. In the list in section A.9.4, these user object arguments are specified as type *int*, which is the correct type of a user object.

- **DPScurrentgstate( )** takes a user object that represents the graphics state object into which the current gstate should be stored. The gstate object is left on the stack.

- **DPSsetfont( )** takes a user object that represents the font dictionary.

- **DPSsetgstate( )** takes a user object that represents the graphics state object that the current gstate should be set to.

A.9.4 psops.h Procedure Declarations

The procedures in *dpsops.h* and *psops.h* are identical except for the first argument. *dpsops.h* procedures require the *ctxt* argument; *psops.h* procedures do not. The procedure name is the lowercase PostScript language operator name preceded by *DPS* or *PS* as appropriate. Only the *psops.h* procedures are listed here.

Note   **DPSSetContext( )** *must have been called before calling any procedure in* psops.h.

```
void PSFontDirectory(void)
void PSISOLatin1Encoding(void)
void PSSharedFontDirectory(void)
void PSStandardEncoding(void)
void PSabs(void)
void PSadd(void)
void PSaload(void)
void PSanchorsearch(int *truth)
void PSand(void)
void PSarc(float x, float y, float r, float angle1, float angle2)
void PSarcn(float x, float y, float r, float angle1, float angle2)
void PSarct(float x1, float y1, float x2, float y2, float r)
void PSarcto(float x1, float y1, float x2, float y2, float r, float *xt1, float *yt1, float
    *xt2, float *yt2)
void PSarray(int len)
void PSashow(float x, float y, char *s)
void PSastore(void)
void PSatan(void)
void PSawidthshow(float cx, float cy, int c, float ax, float ay, char *s)
```

void PSbanddevice(void)
void PSbegin(void)
void PSbind(void)
void PSbitshift(int shift)
void PSbytesavailable(int *n)
void PScachestatus(int *bsize, int *bmax, int *msize)
void PSceiling(void)
void PScharpath(char *s, int b)
void PSclear(void)
void PScleartomark(void)
void PSclip(void)
void PSclippath(void)
void PSclosefile(void)
void PSclosepath(void)
void PScolorimage(void)
void PSconcat(float m[ ])
void PSconcatmatrix(void)
void PScondition(void)
void PScopy(int n)
void PScopypage(void)†
void PScos(void)
void PScount(int *n)
void PScountdictstack(int *n)
void PScountexecstack(int *n)
void PScounttomark(int *n)
void PScurrentblackgeneration(void)
void PScurrentcacheparams(void)
void PScurrentcmykcolor(float *c, float *m, float *y, float *k)
void PScurrentcolorscreen(void)
void PScurrentcolortransfer(void)
void PScurrentcontext(int *cid)
void PScurrentdash(void)
void PScurrentdict(void)
void PScurrentfile(void)
void PScurrentflat(float *flatness)
void PScurrentfont(void)
void PScurrentgray(float *gray)
void PScurrentgstate(int gst)
void PScurrenthalftone(void)
void PScurrenthalftonephase(float *x, float *y)
void PScurrenthsbcolor(float *h, float *s, float *b)
void PScurrentlinecap(int *linecap)
void PScurrentlinejoin(int *linejoin)
void PScurrentlinewidth(float *width)
void PScurrentmatrix(void)
void PScurrentmiterlimit(float *limit)
void PScurrentobjectformat(int *code)
void PScurrentpacking(int *b)
void PScurrentpoint(float *x, float *y)

```
void PScurrentrgbcolor(float *r, float *g, float *b)
void PScurrentscreen(void)
void PScurrentshared(int *b)
void PScurrentstrokeadjust(int *b)
void PScurrenttransfer(void)
void PScurrentundercolorremoval(void)
void PScurveto(float x1, float y1, float x2, float y2, float x3, float y3)
void PScvi(void)
void PScvlit(void)
void PScvn(void)
void PScvr(void)
void PScvrs(void)
void PScvs(void)
void PScvx(void)
void PSdef(void)
void PSdefaultmatrix(void)
void PSdefinefont(void)
void PSdefineusername(int i, char *username)
void PSdefineuserobject(void)
void PSdeletefile(char *filename)
void PSdetach(void)
void PSdeviceinfo(void)
void PSdict(int len)
void PSdictstack(void)
void PSdiv(void)
void PSdtransform(float x1, float y1, float *x2, float *y2)
void PSdup(void)
void PSecho(int b)
void PSend(void)
void PSeoclip(void)
void PSeofill(void)
void PSeoviewclip(void)
void PSeq(void)
void PSequals(void)
void PSequalsequals(void)
void PSerasepage(void)†
void PSerrordict(void)
void PSexch(void)
void PSexec(void)
void PSexecstack(void)
void PSexecuserobject(int index)
void PSexecuteonly(void)
void PSexit(void)
void PSexp(void)
void PSfalse(void)
void PSfile(char *name, char *access)
void PSfilenameforall(void)
void PSfileposition(int *pos)
void PSfill(void)
```

void PSfindfont(char *name)
void PSflattenpath(void)
void PSfloor(void)
void PSflush(void)
void PSflushfile(void)
void PSfor(void)
void PSforall(void)
void PSfork(void)
void PSframedevice(void)
void PSge(void)
void PSget(void)
void PSgetboolean(int *it)
void PSgetchararray(int size, char s[ ])
void PSgetfloat(float *it)
void PSgetfloatarray(int size, float a[ ])
void PSgetint(int *it)
void PSgetintarray(int size, int a[ ])
void PSgetinterval(void)
void PSgetstring(char *s)
void PSgrestore(void)
void PSgrestoreall(void)
void PSgsave(void)
void PSgstate(void)
void PSgt(void)
void PSidentmatrix(void)
void PSidiv(void)
void PSidtransform(float x1, float y1, float *x2, float *y2)
void PSif(void)
void PSifelse(void)
void PSimage(void)†
void PSimagemask(void)
void PSindex(int i)
void PSineofill(float x, float y, int *b)
void PSinfill(float x, float y, int *b)
void PSinitclip(void)
void PSinitgraphics(void)
void PSinitmatrix(void)
void PSinitviewclip(void)
void PSinstroke(float x, float y, int *b)
void PSinueofill(float x, float y, char nums[ ], int n, char ops[ ], int l, int *b)
void PSinufill(float x, float y, char nums[ ], int n, char ops[ ], int l, int *b)
void PSinustroke(float x, float y, char nums[ ], int n, char ops[ ], int l, int *b)
void PSinvertmatrix(void)
void PSitransform(float x1, float y1, float *x2, float *y2)
void PSjoin(void)
void PSknown(int *b)
void PSkshow(char *s)
void PSle(void)
void PSlength(int *len)

```
void PSlineto(float x, float y)
void PSln(void)
void PSload(void)
void PSlock(void)
void PSlog(void)
void PSloop(void)
void PSlt(void)
void PSmakefont(void)
void PSmark(void)
void PSmatrix(void)
void PSmaxlength(int *len)
void PSmod(void)
void PSmonitor(void)
void PSmoveto(float x, float y)
void PSmul(void)
void PSne(void)
void PSneg(void)
void PSnewpath(void)
void PSnoaccess(void)
void PSnot(void)
void PSnotify(void)
void PSnull(void)
void PSnulldevice(void)
void PSor(void)
void PSpackedarray(void)
void PSpathbbox(float *llx, float *lly, float *urx, float *ury)
void PSpathforall(void)
void PSpop(void)
void PSprint(void)
void PSprintobject(int tag)
void PSprompt(void)
void PSpstack(void)
void PSput(void)
void PSputinterval(void)
void PSquit(void)
void PSrand(void)
void PSrcheck(int *b)
void PSrcurveto(float x1, float y1, float x2, float y2, float x3, float y3)
void PSread(int *b)
void PSreadhexstring(int *b)
void PSreadline(int *b)
void PSreadonly(void)
void PSreadstring(int *b)
void PSrealtime(int *i)
void PSrectclip(float x, float y, float w, float h)
void PSrectfill(float x, float y, float w, float h)
void PSrectstroke(float x, float y, float w, float h)
void PSrectviewclip(float x, float y, float w, float h)
void PSrenamefile(char *old, char *new)
```

void PSrenderbands(void)
void PSrepeat(void)
void PSresetfile(void)
void PSrestore(void)
void PSreversepath(void)
void PSrlineto(float x, float y)
void PSrmoveto(float x, float y)
void PSroll(int n, int j)
void PSrotate(float angle)
void PSround(void)
void PSrrand(void)
void PSrun(char *filename)
void PSsave(void)
void PSscale(float x, float y)
void PSscalefont(float size)
void PSscheck(int *b)
void PSsearch(int *b)
void PSselectfont(char *name, float scale)
void PSsendboolean(int it)
void PSsendchararray(char s[ ], int size)
void PSsendfloat(float it)
void PSsendfloatarray(float a[ ], int size)
void PSsendint(int it)
void PSsendintarray(int a[ ], int size)
void PSsendstring(char *s)
void PSsetbbox(float llx, float lly, float urx, float ury)
void PSsetblackgeneration(void)
void PSsetcachedevice(float wx, float wy, float llx, float lly, float urx, float ury)
void PSsetcachelimit(float n)
void PSsetcacheparams(void)
void PSsetcharwidth(float wx, float wy)
void PSsetcmykcolor(float c, float m, float y, float k)
void PSsetcolorscreen(void)
void PSsetcolortransfer(void)
void PSsetdash(float pat[ ], int size, float offset)
void PSsetfileposition(int pos)
void PSsetflat(float flatness)
void PSsetfont(int f)
void PSsetgray(float gray)
void PSsetgstate(int gst)
void PSsethalftone(void)
void PSsethalftonephase(float x, float y)
void PSsethsbcolor(float h, float s, float b)
void PSsetlinecap(int linecap)
void PSsetlinejoin(int linejoin)
void PSsetlinewidth(float width)
void PSsetmatrix(void)
void PSsetmiterlimit(float limit)
void PSsetobjectformat(int code)

```
void PSsetpacking(int b)
void PSsetrgbcolor(float r, float g, float b)
void PSsetscreen(void)
void PSsetshared(int b)
void PSsetstrokeadjust(int b)
void PSsettransfer(void)
void PSsetucacheparams(void)
void PSsetundercolorremoval(void)
void PSsetvmthreshold(int i)
void PSshareddict(void)
void PSshow(char *s)
void PSshowpage(void)†
void PSsin(void)
void PSsqrt(void)
void PSsrand(void)
void PSstack(void)
void PSstart(void)
void PSstatus(int *b)
void PSstatusdict(void)
void PSstop(void)
void PSstopped(void)
void PSstore(void)
void PSstring(int len)
void PSstringwidth(char *s, float *xp, float *yp)
void PSstroke(void)
void PSstrokepath(void)
void PSsub(void)
void PSsystemdict(void)
void PStoken(int *b)
void PStransform(float x1, float y1, float *x2, float *y2)
void PStranslate(float x, float y)
void PStrue(void)
void PStruncate(void)
void PStype(void)
void PSuappend(char nums[ ], int n, char ops[ ], int l)
void PSucache(void)
void PSucachestatus(void)
void PSueofill(char nums[ ], int n, char ops[ ], int l)
void PSufill(char nums[ ], int n, char ops[ ], int l)
void PSundef(char *name)
void PSundefinefont(char *name)
void PSundefineuserobject(int index)
void PSupath(int b)
void PSuserdict(void)
void PSuserobject(void)
void PSusertime(int *milliseconds)
void PSustroke(char nums[ ], int n, char ops[ ], int l)
void PSustrokepath(char nums[ ], int n, char ops[ ], int l)
void PSversion(int bufsize, char buf[ ])
```

```
void PSviewclip(void)
void PSviewclippath(void)
void PSvmreclaim(int code)
void PSvmstatus(int *level, int *used, int *maximum)
void PSwait(void)
void PSwcheck(int *b)
void PSwhere(int *b)
void PSwidthshow(float x, float y, int c, char *s)
void PSwrite(void)
void PSwritehexstring(void)
void PSwriteobject(int tag)
void PSwritestring(void)
void PSwtranslation(float *x, float *y);
void PSxcheck(int *b)
void PSxor(void)
void PSxshow(char *s, float numarray[ ], int size)
void PSxyshow(char *s, float numarray[ ], int size)
void PSyield(void)
void PSyshow(char *s, float numarray[ ], int size)
```

†*These functions behave differently in NeXTstep than they do in the standard NeXT implementation.*

A.10   Run Time Support for Wrapped Procedures

This section describes the procedures in the *dpsfriends.h* header file that are called by wrapped procedures: the C-callable procedures that are output by the pswrap translator. This information is not normally required by the application programmer.

A description of *dpsfriends.h* is provided for those who need finer control over the following areas:

- Transmission of code for execution

- Handling of result values

- Mapping of user names to user name indexes

A.10.1 Sending Code for Execution

One of the primary purposes of the Client Library is to provide runtime support for the code generated by pswrap. Each wrapped procedure builds a binary object sequence that represents the PostScript language code to be executed. Since a binary object sequence is structured, the procedures for sending a binary object sequence are designed to take advantage of this structure.

The following procedures efficiently process binary object sequences generated by wrapped procedures:

DPSBinObjSeqWrite( )   sends the beginning of a new binary object sequence. This part includes, at minimum, the header and the top-level sequence of objects. It can also include subsidiary array elements and/or string characters if those arrays and strings are static (lengths are known at compile time and there are no intervening arrays or strings of varying length). **DPSBinObjSeqWrite( )** can convert the binary object sequence to another encoding, depending on the *DPSContextRec* encoding variables. For a particular wrapped procedure, **DPSBinObjSeqWrite( )** is called once.

DPSWriteTypedObjectArray( )   sends arrays (excluding strings) that were specified as input arguments to a wrapped procedure. It writes PostScript language code specified by the context's format and encoding variables, performing appropriate conversions as needed. For a particular wrapped procedure, **DPSWriteTypedObjectArray( )** is called zero or more times, once for each input array specified.

DPSWriteStringChars( )   sends the text of strings or names. It appends characters to the current binary object sequence. For a particular wrapped procedure, **DPSWriteStringChars( )** is called zero or more times to send the text of names and strings.

The length of arrays and strings sent by **DPSWriteTypedObjectArray( )** and **DPSWriteStringChars( )** must be consistent with the length information specified in the binary object sequence header sent by **DPSBinObjSeqWrite( )**. In particular, don't rely on *sizeof( )* to return the correct size value of the binary object sequence.

A.10.2 Receiving Results

Each wrapped procedure with output arguments constructs an array containing elements of type *DPSResultsRec*. This array is called the result table. The index position of each element corresponds to the ordinal position of each output argument as defined in the wrapped procedure: The first table entry (index 0) corresponds to the first output argument, the second table entry (index 1) corresponds to the second argument, and so on.

Each entry defines one of the output arguments of a wrapped procedure by specifying a data type, a count, and a pointer to the storage for the value. **DPSSetResultTable( )** registers the result table with the context.

The interpreter sends return values to the application as binary object sequences. Wrapped procedures that have output arguments use the **printobject** operator to tag and send each return value. The tag corresponds to the index of the output argument in the result table. After the wrapped procedure finishes sending the PostScript language program, it calls **DPSAwaitReturnValues( )** to wait for all of the results to come back.

As the Client Library receives results from the interpreter, it places each result into the output argument specified by the result table. The tag of each result object in the sequence is used as an index into the result table. When the Client Library receives a tag that is greater than the last defined tag number, **DPSAwaitReturnValues( )** returns. This final tag is called the termination tag.

Certain conventions must be followed to handle return values for wrapped procedures properly:

- The tag associated with the return value is the ordinal of the output parameter, as listed in the definition of the wrapped procedure, starting from 0 and counting from left to right (see the following example).

- If the *count* field of the *DPSResultsRec* is -1, the expected result is a single element, or scalar. Return values with the same tag overwrite previous values. Otherwise, the *count* indicates the number of array elements that remain to be received. In this case, a series of return values with the same tag are stored in successive elements of the array. If the value of *count* is zero, further array elements of the same tag value are ignored.

- **DPSAwaitReturnValues( )** returns when it notices that the *resultTable* pointer in the *DPSContextRec* data object is *NULL*. The code that handles return values should note the reception of the termination tag by setting *resultTable* to *NULL* to indicate that there are no more return values to receive for this wrapped procedure.

The following is an example of a wrap with return values:

```
defineps Example(| int *x, *y, *z)
    10 20 30 x y z
endps
```

The code generated for this wrapped procedure is

```
10 20 30
0 printobject
    % pop integer 30 off the operand stack,
    % use tag = 0 (result table index = 0, first parameter 'x')
    % write binary object sequence
1 printobject
    % pop integer 20 off the operand stack,
    % use tag = 1 (result table index = 1, second parameter 'y')
    % write binary object sequence
2 printobject
    % pop integer 10 off the operand stack,
    % use tag = 2 (result table index = 2, third parameter 'z')
    % write binary object sequence
0 3 printobject
    % push dummy value 0 on operand stack
    % pop integer 0 off operand stack,
    % use tag = 3 (termination tag)
    % write binary object sequence
flush
    % make sure all data is sent back to the application
```

A.10.3 Managing User Names

Name indexes are the most efficient way to specify names in a binary object sequence. The Client Library manages the mapping of user names to indexes. Wrapped procedures map user names automatically. The first time a wrapped procedure is called, it calls **DPSMapNames( )** to map all user names specified in the wrapped procedure into indexes. The application can also call **DPSMapNames( )** directly to obtain name mappings.

A name map is stored in a space. All contexts associated with that space have the same name map. The name mapping for the context is automatically kept up-to-date by the Client Library in the following way:

- Every wrapped procedure calls **DPSBinObjSeqWrite( )**, which, in addition to sending the binary object sequence, checks to see if the user name map is up-to-date.

- **DPSBinObjSeqWrite( )** calls **DPSUpdateNameMap( )** if the name map of the space does not agree with the Client Library's name map. **DPSUpdateNameMap( )** can send a series of **defineusername** operators to the PostScript interpreter.

DPSNameFromIndex( ) returns the text for the user name with the given index. The string returned is owned by the Client Library; treat it as a read-only string.

A.10.4   Binary Object Sequences

Syntactically, a binary object sequence is a single token. The structure is described in section 3.12.1 of the *PostScript Language Reference Manual, Second Edition*. The definitions in this section correspond to the components of a binary object sequence.

```
#define DPS_HEADER_SIZE        4

#define DPS_HI_IEEE            128
#define DPS_LO_IEEE            129
#define DPS_HI_NATIVE          130
#define DPS_LO_NATIVE          131

#ifndef DPS_DEF_TOKENTYPE
#define DPS_DEF_TOKENTYPE      DPS_HI_IEEE
#endif DPS_DEF_TOKENTYPE

typedef struct {
    unsigned char tokenType;
    unsigned char nTopElements;
    unsigned short length;
    DPSBinObjRec objects[1];
} DPSBinObjSeqRec, *DPSBinObjSeq;
```

A binary object sequence begins with a 4-byte header. The first byte indicates the token type. A binary object is defined by one of the four token type codes listed. *DPS_DEF_TOKENTYPE* defines the default token type for binary object sequences generated by a particular implementation of the Client Library. It must be consistent with the machine architecture upon which the Client Library is implemented.

The *nTopElements* byte indicates the number of top-level objects in the sequence. A binary object sequence can have from 1 to 255 top-level objects. If more top-level objects are required, use an extended binary object sequence.

The next two bytes form a nonzero 16-bit integer that is the total byte length of the binary object sequence.

The header is followed by a sequence of objects:

```
#define DPS_NULL            0
#define DPS_INT             1
#define DPS_REAL            2
#define DPS_NAME            3
#define DPS_BOOL            4
#define DPS_STRING          5
#define DPS_IMMEDIATE       6
#define DPS_ARRAY           9
#define DPS_MARK            10
```

The first byte of an object describes its attributes and type. The types listed here correspond to the PostScript language objects that pswrap generates.

```
#define DPS_LITERAL         0
#define DPS_EXEC            0x080
```

The high-order bit indicates whether the object has the literal (0) or executable (1) attribute. The next byte is the tag byte, which must be zero for objects sent to the interpreter. Result values sent back from the interpreter use the tag field.

The next two bytes form a 16-bit integer that is the length of the object. The unit value of the length field depends on the type of the object. For arrays, the length indicates the number of elements in the array. For strings, the length indicates the number of characters.

The last four bytes of the object form the value field. The interpretation of this field depends on the type of the object.

```
typedef struct {
    unsigned char attributedType;
    unsigned char tag;
    short length;
    long int val;
} DPSBinObjGeneric;          /* boolean, int, string, name and array */

typedef struct {
    unsigned char attributedType;
    unsigned char tag;
    short length;
    float realVal;
} DPSBinObjReal;             /* float */
```

DPSBinObjGeneric and *DPSBinObjReal* are defined for the use of wraps.
They make it easier to initialize the static portions of the binary object
sequence.

```
typedef struct {
    unsigned char attributedType;
    unsigned char tag;
    short length;
    union{
        long int integerVal;
        float realVal;
        long int nameVal;        /* offset or index */
        long int booleanVal;
        long int stringVal;      /* offset */
        long int arrayVal;       /* offset */
    } val;
} DPSBinObjRec;
```

DPSBinObjRec is a general-purpose variant record for interpreting an
object in a binary object sequence.

A.10.5 Extended Binary Object Sequences

An *extended binary object sequence* is required if there are more than 255 top-level objects in the sequence. The extended binary object sequence is represented by *DPSExtendedBinObjSeqRec*, as follows:

Byte 0	Same as for a normal binary object sequence; it represents the token type.
Byte 1	Set to zero; indicates that this is an extended binary object sequence. (In a normal binary object sequence, this byte represents the number of top-level objects.)
Bytes 2-3	A 16-bit value representing the number of top-level elements.
Bytes 4-7	A 32-bit value representing the overall length of the extended binary object sequence.

The bytes are ordered in numeric fields according to the number representation specified by the token type. The layout of the remainder of the extended binary object sequence is identical to that of a normal binary object sequence.

A.10.6 dpsfriends.h Data Structures

This section describes the data structures used by pswrap as part of its support for wrapped procedures.

Note   *The DPSContextRec data structure and its handle, DPSContext, are part of the dpsfriends.h header file. They are documented in section A.8.1 because they are also used by dpsclient.h procedures.*

DPSBinObjGeneric

```
typedef struct {
    unsigned char attributedType;
    unsigned char tag;
    unsigned short length;
    long int val;
} DPSBinObjGeneric;        /* boolean, int, string, name and array */
```

DPSBinObjGeneric is defined for the use of wraps. It is used to initialize the static portions of the binary object sequence. See *DPSBinObjReal* for type *real*.

DPSBinObjReal

```
typedef struct {
    unsigned char attributedType;
    unsigned char tag;
    unsigned short length;
    float realVal;
} DPSBinObjReal;          /* float */
```

DPSBinObjReal is similar to *DPSBinObjGeneric* but represents a real number.

DPSBinObjRec

```
typedef struct {
    unsigned char attributedType;
    unsigned char tag;
    unsigned short length;
    union {
        long int integerVal;
        float realVal;
        long int nameVal;          /* offset or index */
        long int booleanVal;
        long int stringVal;      /* offset */
        long int arrayVal;     /* offset */
    } val;
} DPSBinObjRec;
```

DPSBinObjRec is a general-purpose variant record for interpreting an object in a binary object sequence.

DPSBinObjSeqRec

```
typedef struct {
    unsigned char token Type;
    unsigned char nTopElements;
    unsigned short length;
    DPSBinObjRec objects[1];
} DPSBinObjSeqRec, *DPSBinObjSeq;
```

DPSBinObjSeqRec is provided as a convenience for accessing a binary object sequence copied from an I/O buffer.

DPSDefinedType

```
typedef enum {
    dps_tBoolean,
    dps_tChar, dps_tUChar,
    dps_tFloat, dps_tDouble,
    dps_tShort, dps_tUShort,
    dps_tInt, dps_tUInt,
    dps_tLong, dps_tULong} DPSDefinedType;
```

DPSDefinedType enumerates the C data types used to describe wrap arguments.

DPSExtendedBinObjSeqRec

```
typedef struct {
    unsigned char tokenType;
    unsigned char escape; /* zero if this is an extended sequence */
    unsigned short nTopElements;
    unsigned long length;
    DPSBinObjRec objects[1];
} DPSExtendedBinObjSeqRec, *DPSExtendedBinObjSeq;
```

DPSExtendedBinObjSeqRec has a purpose similar to *DPSBinObjSeqRec* but it is used for extended binary object sequences.

DPSNameEncoding

```
typedef enum {
    dps_indexed, dps_strings
} DPSNameEncoding;
```

DPSNameEncoding defines the two possible encodings for user names in the *dps_binObjSeq* and *dps_encodedTokens* forms of PostScript language programs.

DPSProcs

/* pointer to procedures record */

See *DPSProcsRec*.

DPSProcsRec
```
typedef struct {
    void (*BinObjSeqWrite)( /* DPSContext ctxt, char *buf, unsigned int count */ );
    void (*WriteTypedObjectArray)( /*
        DPSContext ctxt,
        DPSDefinedType type;
        char *array,
        unsigned int length */ );
    void (*WriteStringChars)( /* DPSContext ctxt; char *buf; unsigned int count; */ );
    void (*WriteData)( /* DPSContext ctxt, char *buf, unsigned int count */ );
    void (*WritePostScript)( /* DPSContext ctxt, char *buf, unsigned int count */ );
    void (*FlushContext)( /* DPSContext ctxt */ );
    void (*ResetContext)( /* DPSContext ctxt */ );
    void (*UpdateNameMap)( /* DPSContext ctxt */ );
    void (*AwaitReturnValues)( /* DPSContext ctxt */ );
    void (*Interrupt)( /* DPSContext ctxt */ );
    void (*DestroyContext)( /* DPSContext ctxt */ );
    void (*WaitContext)( /* DPSContext ctxt */ );
    void (*Printf)( /* DPSContext ctxt, const char *fmt, va_list argList */ );
        /* NeXT addition */
} DPSProcsRec, *DPSProcs;
```

DPSProcsRec defines the data structure pointed to by *DPSProcs*.

This record contains pointers to procedures that implement all the operations that can be performed on a context. These procedures are analogous to the instance methods of an object in an object-oriented language.

Note   *You do not need to be concerned with the contents of this data structure. Do not change the DPSProcs pointer or the contents of DPSProcsRec.*

DPSProgramEncoding
```
typedef enum {
    dps_ascii, dps_binObjSeq, dps_encodedTokens
} DPSProgramEncoding;
```

DPSProgramEncoding defines the three possible encodings of PostScript language programs: ASCII encoding, binary object sequence encoding, and binary token encoding.

DPSResultsRec   typedef struct {
    DPSDefinedType type;
    int count;
    char *value;
    } DPSResultsRec, *DPSResults;

Each wrapped procedure constructs an array called the *result table*, which consists of elements of type *DPSResultsRec*. The index position of each element corresponds to the ordinal position of each output parameter as defined in the wrapped procedure; for example, index 0 (the first table entry) corresponds to the first output parameter, index 1 corresponds to the second output parameter, and so on.

type specifies the format type of the return value. *count* specifies the number of values expected; this supports array formats. *value* points to the location of the first value; the storage beginning must have room for *count* values of type *type*. If *count* is -1, *value* points to a scalar (single) result argument. If *count* is zero, any subsequent return values are ignored.

DPSSpace   /* handle for space record */

See *DPSSpaceRec.*

DPSSpaceProcsRec   typedef struct {
    void (*DestroySpace)(/* DPSSpace space */);
    } DPSSpaceProcsRec, *DPSSpaceProcs;

See **DPSDestroySpace( )** in *dpsclient.h.*

DPSSpaceRec   typedef struct {
    int lastNameIndex;   /* NeXT addition */
    DPSSpaceProcs procs;
    } DPSSpaceRec, *DPSSpace;

DPSSpaceRec provides a representation of a space. See also **DPSDestroySpace( )**.

A.10.7   dpsfriends.h Procedures

The following is an alphabetical listing of the procedures in the Client Library header file *dpsfriends.h*. These procedures are for experts only; most application developers don't need them. The pswrap translator inserts calls to these procedures when it creates the C-callable wrapped procedures you specify.

DPSAwaitReturnValues

void DPSAwaitReturnValues(ctxt)
    DPSContext ctxt;

DPSAwaitReturnValues( ) waits for all results described by the result table; see *DPSResultRec*. It uses the tag of each object in the sequence to find the corresponding entry in the result table. When **DPSAwaitReturnValues( )** receives a tag that is greater than the last defined tag number, there are no more return values to be received and the procedure returns. This final tag is called the termination tag. **DPSSetResultTable( )** must be caged to set the result table before any calls to **DPSBinObjSeqWrite( )**.

DPSAwaitReturnValues( ) can call the context's error procedure with *dps_err_resultTagCheck* or *dps_err_resultTypeCheck*. It returns prematurely if it encounters a *dps_err_ps* error.

DPSBinObjSeqWrite

void DPSBinObjSeqWrite(ctxt, buf, count)
    DPSContext ctxt;
    char *buf;
    unsigned int count;

DPSBinObjSeqWrite( ) sends the beginning of a binary object sequence generated by a wrap. *buf* points to a buffer containing *count* bytes of a binary object sequence. *buf* must point to the beginning of a sequence, which includes at least the header and the entire top-level sequence of objects.

DPSBinObjSeqWrite( ) can also include subsidiary array elements and/or strings. It writes PostScript language as specified by the format and encoding variables of *ctxt*, doing appropriate conversions as needed. If the buffer does not contain the entire binary object sequence, one or more calls to **DPSWriteTypedObjectArray( )** and/or **DPSWriteStringChars( )** must follow immediately; *buf* and its contents must remain valid until the entire binary object sequence has been written. **DPSBinObjSeqWrite( )** ensures that the user name map is up-to-date.

DPSGetCurrentContext   DPSContext DPSGetCurrentContext( );

DPSGetCurrentContext( ) returns the current context.

DPSMapNames   void DPSMapNames(ctxt, nNames, names, indices)
        DPSContext ctxt;
        unsigned int nNames;
        char **names;
        long int **indices;

DPSMapNames( ) maps all specified names into user name indices, sending new **defineusername** definitions as needed. *names* is an array of strings whose elements are the user names. *nNames* is the number of elements in the array. *indices* is an array of pointers to *(long int*)* integers, which are the storage locations for the indexes.

DPSMapNames( ) is normally called automatically from within wraps. The application can also call this procedure directly to obtain name mappings. **DPSMapNames( )** calls the context's error procedure with *dps_err_nameTooLong*.

Note that the caller must ensure that the string pointers remain valid after the procedure returns. The Client Library becomes the owner of all strings passed to it with **DPSMapNames( )**.

The same name can be used several times in a wrap. To reduce string storage, duplicates can be eliminated by using an optimization recognized by **DPSMapNames( )**. If the pointer to the string in the array *names* is null, that is *(char *)0*, **DPSMapNames( )** uses the nearest non null name that precedes the *(char *)0* entry in the array. The first element of *names* must be non null. This optimization works best if you sort the names so that duplicate occurrences are adjacent.

For example, **DPSMapNames( )** treats the following arrays as equivalent, but the one on the right saves storage.

```
{                          {
"boxes",                   "boxes",
"drawMe",                  "drawMe",
"drawMe",                  (char *)0,
"init",                    "init",
"makeAPath",               "makeAPath",
"returnAClip",             "returnAClip",
"returnAClip",             (char *)0,
"returnAClip"              (char *)0
}                          }
```

DPSNameFromIndex   char *DPSNameFromIndex(index)
                            long int index;

DPSNameFromIndex( ) returns the text for the user name with the given index. The string returned must be treated as read-only. *NULL* is returned if *index* is invalid.

DPSSetContext   void DPSSetContext(ctxt)
                            DPSContext ctxt;

DPSSetContext( ) sets the current context. Call **DPSSetContext( )** before calling any procedures defined in *psops.h*.

DPSSetResultTable   void DPSSetResultTable(ctxt, tbl, len)
                            DPSContext ctxt;
                            DPSResults tbl;
                            unsigned int len;

DPSSetResultTable( ) sets the result table and its length in *ctxt*. This operation must be performed before a wrap body that can return a value is sent to the interpreter.

DPSUpdateNameMap   void DPSUpdateNameMap(ctxt)
                            DPSContext ctxt;

DPSUpdateNameMap( ) sends a series of **defineusername** commands to the interpreter. This procedure is called if the name map of the context's space is not synchronized with the Client Library name map.

DPSWriteStringChars   void DPSWriteStringChars(ctxt, buf, count);
                            DPSContext ctxt;
                            char *buf;
                            unsigned int count;

DPSWriteStringChars( ) appends strings to the current binary object sequence. *buf* contains *count* characters that form the body of one or more strings in a binary object sequence. *buf* and its contents must remain valid until the entire binary object sequence has been sent.

DPSWriteTypedObjectArray   void DPSWriteTypedObjectArray(ctxt, type, array, length)
                DPSContext ctxt;
                DPSDefinedType type;
                char *array;
                unsigned int length;

DPSWriteTypedObjectArray( ) writes PostScript language code as specified by the format and encoding variables of *ctxt*, doing appropriate conversions as needed. *array* points to an array of *length* elements of type *type*. *array* contains the element values for the body of a subsidiary array that was passed as an input argument to pswrap. *array* and its contents must remain valid until the entire binary object sequence has been sent.

A.11   Example Error Handler

An error handler must deal with all errors defined in *dpsclient.h* as well as any additional errors defined in system-specific header files.

A.11.1   Error Handler Implementation

An example implementation of an error handler, **DPSDefaultErrorProc( )**, follows. The code is followed by explanatory text.

```
#include "dpsclient.h"

void DPS
DefaultErrorProc(ctxt, errorCode, arg1, arg2)
  DPSContext ctxt;
  DPSErrorCode errorCode;
  long unsigned int arg1, arg2;

  DPSTextProc textProc = DPSGetCurrentTextBackstop( );

  char *prefix = *%%[ Error: ";
  char *suffix = "]%%\n";

  char *infix = "; OffendingCommand: ";
  char *nameinfix = "User name too long; Name: ";
  char *contextinfix = "Invalid context: ";
  char *taginfix = "Unexpected wrap result tag: ";
  char *typeinfix = "Unexpected wrap result type; tag: ";

  switch (errorCode) {
    case dps_err_ps: {
      char *buf = (char *)arg1;
      DPSBinObj ary = (DPSBinObj) (buf+DPS_HEADER_SIZE);
```

```
            DPSBinObj elements;
            char *error, *errorName;
            integer errorCount, errorNameCount;
            boolean resyncFlg;

            Assert((ary->attributedType & 0x7f) == DPS_ARRAY);
            Assert(ary->length == 4);

            elements = (DPSBinObj)(((char *) ary) + ary->val.arrayVal);
            errorName = (char *)(((char *) ary) + elements[1].val.nameVal);
            errorNameCount = elements[1].length;

            error = (char *)(((char *) ary) + elements[2].val.nameVal);
            errorCount = elements[2].length;

            resyncFlg = elements[3].val.booleanVal;

            if (textProc != NIL) {
              (*textProc)(ctxt, prefix, strlen(prefix));
              (*textProc)(ctxt, errorName, errorNameCount);
              (*textProc)(ctxt, infix, strlen(infix));
              (*textProc)(ctxt, error, errorCount);
              (*textProc)(ctxt, suffix, strlen(suffix));
            }
          if (resyncFlg && (ctxt != dummyCtx)) {
            RAISE(dps_err_ps, ctxt);
            CantHappen( );
            }
          break;
          }
        case dps_err_nameTooLong:
          if (textProc != NIL) {
            char *buf = (char *)arg1;
            (*textProc)(ctxt, prefix, strlen(prefix));
            (*textProc)(ctxt, nameinfix, strlen(nameinfix));
            (*textProc)(ctxt, buf, arg2);
            (*textProc)(ctxt, suffix, strlen(suffix));
            }
          break;
        case dps_err_invalidContext:
          if (textProc != NIL) {
            char m[100];
            (void) sprintf(m, "%s%s%d%s", prefix, contextinfix, arg1, suffix);
            (*textProc)(ctxt, m, strlen(m));
            }
          break;
        case dps_err_resultTagCheck:
        case dps_err_resultTypeCheck:
          if (textProc != NIL) {
```

```
      char m[100];
      unsigned char tag = *((unsigned char *) arg1 +1);
      (void) sprintf(m, "%s%s%d%s", prefix, typeinfix, tag, suffix);
      (*textProc)(ctxt, m, strlen(m));
      }
   break;
 case dps_err_invalidAccess:
   if (textProc != NIL)
     {
     char m[100];
     (void) sprintf (m, "%sInvalid context access.%s", prefix, suffix);
     (*textProc) (ctxt, m, strlen (m));
     }
   break;
 case dps_err_encodingCheck:
   if (textProc != NIL)
     {
     char m[100];
     (void) sprintf (m, "%sInvalid name/program encoding: %d/%d.%s",
                 prefix, (int) arg1, (int) arg2, suffix);
     (*textProc) (ctxt, m, strlen (m));
     }
   break;
 case dps_err_closedDisplay:
   if (textProc != NIL)
     {
     char m[100];
     (void) sprintf (m, "%sBroken display connection %d.%s",
                 prefix, (int) arg1, suffix);
     (*textProc) (ctxt, m, strlen (m));
     }
   break;
 case dps_err_deadContext:
   if (textProc != NIL)
     {
     char m[100];
     (void) sprintf (m, "%sDead context 0x0%x.%s", prefix,
                 (int) arg1, suffix);
     (*textProc) (ctxt, m, strlen (m));
     }
   break;
 default:;
  }
} /* DPSDefaultErrorProc */
```

A.11.2 Description of the Error Handler

DPSDefaultErrorProc( ) handles errors that arise when a wrap or Client Library procedure is called for the context. The error code indicates which error occurred. Interpretation of the *arg1* and *arg2* values is based on the error code.

The error handler initializes itself by getting the current backstop text handler and assigning string constants that will be used to formulate and report a text message. The section of the program that deals with the various error codes begins with the switch statement. Each error code can be handled differently.

If a *textProc* was specified, the error handler calls the text handler to formulate an error message, passing it the name of the error, the object that caused the error, and the string constants used to format a standard error message. For example, a **typecheck** error reported by the **cvn** operator is reported as a *dps_err_ps* error code and printed as follows:

%%[Error: typecheck; OffendingCommand: cvn]%%

The following error codes are common to all Client Library implementations:

dps_err_ps	represents all PostScript language errors reported by the interpreter, that is, the errors listed under each operator in the *PostScript Language Reference Manual, Second Edition*.
dps_err_nameTooLong	arises if a binary object sequence or encoded token has a name whose length exceeds 128 characters. *arg1* is the PostScript user name; *arg2* is its length.
dps_err_invalidcontext	arises if a Client Library routine was called with an invalid context. This can happen if the client is unaware that the execution context in the interpreter has terminated. *arg1* is a context identifier; *arg2* is unused.
dps_err_resultTagCheck	occurs when an invalid tag is received for a result value. There is one object in the sequence. *arg1* is a pointer to the binary object sequence; *arg2* is the length of the binary object sequence.
dps_err_resultTypeCheck	occurs when the value returned is of a type incompatible with the output parameter (for example, a string returned to an integer output parameter). *arg1* is a pointer to the binary object (the result with the wrong type); *arg2* is unused.

A.11.3 Handling PostScript Language Errors

The following discussion applies only to the *dps_err_ps* error code. This error code represents all possible PostScript operator errors. Because the interpreter provides a binary object sequence containing detailed information about the error, more options are available to the error handler than for other client errors.

arg1 points to a binary object sequence that describes the error. The binary object sequence is a four-element array consisting of the name *Error*, the name that identifies the specific error, the object that was executed when the error occurred, and a Boolean indicating whether the context expects to be resynchronized.

The type and length of the array are checked with assertions. The body of the array is pointed to by the *elements* variable. Each element of the array is derived and placed in a variable.

DPSDefaultErrorProc( ) raises an exception only if the context executed **resyncstart** to install **resynchandleerror**. The *resyncFlag* variable contains the value of the fourth element of the binary object sequence array, the Boolean that indicates whether resynchronization is needed. *resyncFlag* will be *false* if **handleerror** handled the error. It will be *true* if **resynchandleerror** handled the error.

If *resyncFlag* is *true* and the context handling the error is a context created by the application, the error handler raises the exception by calling *RAISE*. This call never returns.

A.12 Exception Handling

This section describes a general-purpose exception-handling facility. It provides help for a narrowly defined problem area handling PostScript language errors. Most application programmers need not be concerned with exception handling. These facilities can be used in conjunction with PostScript language code and a sophisticated error handler such as **DPSDefaultErrorProc( )** to provide a certain amount of error recovery capability. Consult the system-specific documentation for alternative means of error recovery.

An *exception* is an unexpected condition such as a PostScript language error that prevents a procedure from running to normal completion. The procedure could simply return, but data structures might be left in an inconsistent state and returned values might be incorrect.

Instead of returning, the procedure can raise the exception, passing a code that indicates what has happened. The exception is intercepted by some caller of the procedure that raised the exception (any number of procedure calls deep); execution then resumes at the point of interception. As a result, the procedure that raised the exception is terminated, as are any intervening procedures between it and the procedure that intercepted the exception, an action called "unwinding the call stack."

The Client Library provides a general-purpose exception-handling mechanism in *dpsexcept.h*. This header file provides facilities for placing exception handlers in application subroutines to respond cleanly to exceptional conditions.

Note   *Application programs might need to contain the following statement:*

```
#include "dpsexcept.h"
```

As an exception propagates up the call stack, each procedure encountered can deal with the exception in one of three ways:

- It ignores the exception, in which case the exception continues on to the caller of the procedure.

- It intercepts the exception and handles it, in which case all procedure calls below the handler are unwound and discarded.

- It intercepts, handles, and then raises the exception, allowing handlers higher in the stack to notice and react to the exception.

The body of a procedure that intercepts exceptions is written as follows:

```
DURING
    statement1;
    statement2;
    ...
HANDLER
    statement3
    statement4;
    ...
END_HANDLER
```

The statements between *HANDLER* and *END_HANDLER* make up the exception handler for exceptions occurring between *DURING* and *HANDLER*. The procedure body works as follows:

- Normally, the statements between *DURING* and *HANDLER* are executed.

- If no exception occurs, the statements between *HANDLER* and *END_HANDLER* are bypassed; execution resumes at the statement after *END_HANDLER*.

- If an exception is raised while executing the statements between *DURING* and *HANDLER* (including any procedure called from those statements), execution of those statements is aborted and control passes to the statements between *HANDLER* and *END_HANDLER*.

In terms of C syntax, treat these macros as if they were C code brackets, as shown in Table A.1.

Table A.1 *C equivalents for exception macros*

Macro	C Equivalent
DURING	{{
HANDLER	}{
END_HANDLER	}}

In general, exception-handling macros either should entirely enclose a code block (the preferred method, Example A.2) or should be entirely within the block (Example A.3).

Example A.2 *Exception handling macros–enclose a code block*

```
DURING
   while ( /* Example 1 */) {
      ...
   }
HANDLER
   ...
END_HANDLER
```

Example A.3 *Exception handling macros–within a code block*

```
while (/* Example 2 */) {
   DURING
   ...
   HANDLER
   ...
   END_HANDLER
}
```

When a procedure detects an exceptional condition, it can raise an exception by calling *RAISE*. *RAISE* takes two arguments. The first is an error code (for example, one of the values of **DPSErrorCode( )**). The second is a pointer, *char **, which can point to any kind of data structure, such as a string of ASCII text or a binary object sequence.

The exception handler has two local variables: *Exception.Code* and *Exception.Message*. When the handler is entered, the first argument that was passed to *RAISE* gets assigned to *Exception.Code* and the second argument gets assigned to *Exception.Message*. These variables have valid contents only between *HANDLER* and *END_HANDLER*.

If the exception handler executes *END_HANDLER* or returns, propagation of the exception ceases. However, if the exception handler calls *RERAISE*, the exception, along with *Exception.Code* and *Exception.Message*, is propagated to the next outer dynamically enclosing occurrence of *DURING...HANDLER*.

A procedure can choose not to handle an exception, in which case one of its callers must handle it. There are two common reasons for wanting to handle exceptions:

- To deallocate dynamically allocated storage and clean up any other local state, then allow the exception to propagate further. In this case, the handler should perform its cleanup, then call *RERAISE*.

- To recover from certain exceptions that might occur, then continue normal execution. In this case, the handler should compare *Exception.Code* with the set of exceptions it can handle. If it can handle the exception, it should perform the recovery and execute the statement that follows *END_HANDLER*; if not, it should call *RERAISE* to propagate the exception to a higher-level handler.

Warning *It is illegal to execute a statement between DURING and HANDLER that would transfer control outside of those statements. In particular, return is illegal: an unspecified error will occur. This restriction does not apply to the statements between HANDLER and END_HANDLER. To return from the exception handler, call* **E_RETURN_VOID( )***; to perform return(x), call* **E_RETURN(x)***.*

A.12.1 Recovering from PostScript Language Errors

The example **DPSDefaultErrorProc( )** procedure can be used with the PostScript operator **resyncstart** to recover from PostScript language errors. If you use this strategy, an exception can be raised by any of the Client Library procedures that write code or data to the context: any wrap, any single-operator procedure, **DPSWritePostScript( )**, and so on. The strategy is as follows:

1. Send **resyncstart** to the context immediately after it is created. **resyncstart** is a simple, read-evaluate-print loop enclosed in a *stopped* clause which, on error, executes **resynchandleerror**.

   resynchandleerror reports PostScript errors back to the client in the form of a binary object sequence of a single object: an array of four elements as described in section 3.12.2 of the *PostScript Language Reference Manual, Second Edition*. The fourth element of the binary object sequence, a Boolean, is set to *true* to indicate that **resynchandleerror** is executing. The *stopped* clause itself executes within an outer loop.

2. When a PostScript language error is detected, **resynchandleerror** writes the binary object sequence describing the error, flushes the output stream %stdout, then reads and discards any data on the input stream %stdin until *EOF* (an end-of-file marker) is received. This effectively clears out any pending code and data, and makes the context do nothing until the client handles the error.

3. The binary object sequence sent by **resynchandleerror** is received by the client and passed to the context's error handler. The error handler formulates a text message from the binary object sequence and displays it, for example, by calling the backstop text handler.

   It then inspects the binary object sequence and notices that the fourth element of the array, a Boolean, is *true*. This means **resynchandleerror** is executing and waiting for the client to recover from the error. The error handler can then raise an exception by calling *RAISE* with *dps_err_ps* and the *DPSContext* pointer in order to allow an exception handler to perform error recovery.

4. The *dps_err_ps* exception is caught by one of the handlers in the application program. This causes the C stack to be unwound, and the handler body to be executed. To handle the exception, the application can reset the context that reported the error, discarding any waiting code.

5. The handler body calls **DPSResetContext( )**, which resets the context after an error occurs. This procedure guarantees that any buffered I/O is discarded and that the context is ready to read and execute more input. Specifically, **DPSResetContext( )** causes *EOF* to be put on the context's input stream.

6. We have come full circle now. *EOF* is received by **resynchandleerror**, which causes it to terminate. The outer loop of **resyncstart** then reopens the context's input stream %stdin, which clears the end-of-file indication and resumes execution at the top of the loop. The context is now ready to read new code.

Although this strategy works well for some applications, it leaves the context and the contents of its private VM in an unknown state. For example, the dictionary and operand stacks might be cluttered, free-running forked contexts might have been created, or the contents of **userdict** might have been changed. Clearing the state of such a context can be very complicated.

You might not get PostScript language error exceptions when you expect them. Because of delays related to buffering and scheduling, a PostScript language error can be reported long after the C procedure responsible for the error has returned. This makes it difficult to write an exception handler for a given section of code. If this code can cause a PostScript language error and therefore cause **DPSDefaultErrorProc( )** to raise an exception, you can ensure that you get the exception in a timely manner by using synchronization.

Warning   *In multicontext applications that require error recovery, the code to recover from PostScript errors can get complicated. An exception reporting a PostScript error caused by one context can be raised by any call on the Client Library, even one on behalf of some other context, including calls made from wraps. Although **DPSDefaultErrorProc( )** passes the context that caused the error as an argument to RAISE, it is difficult in general to deal with an exception from one context that arises while the application is working with another.*

When the **handleerror** procedure is called to report an error, no recovery is possible except to display an error message and destroy the context.

A.12.2   Example Exception Handler

A typical application might have the following main loop. Assume that a context has already been created with **DPSDefaultErrorProc( )** as its error procedure, and that **resyncstart** has been executed by the context.

Example A.4 *Exception handler*

```
#include <dpsexcept.h>

        while (/* the user hasn't quit */) {
            /* get an input event */
            event = GetEventFromQueue( );
            /* react to event */
            DURING
              switch (event) {
                case EVENT_A:
                    UserWrapA(context, ...);
                    break;
                case EVENT_B:
                    UserWrapB(context, ...);
                    break;
                case EVENT_C:
                    ProcThatCallsSeveralWraps(context);
                    break;
                /* ... */
                default:;
              }
            HANDLER
              /* the context's error proc has already posted an
                 error for this exception, so just reset.
                 Make sure the context we're using is the
                 one that caused the error! */
              if (Exception.Code == dps_err_ps)
                  DPSResetContext((DPSContext)Exception.Message);
            END_HANDLER
        }
```

Most of the calls in the *switch* statement are either direct calls to wrapped procedures or indirect calls (that is, calls to procedures that make direct calls to wrapped procedures or to the Client Library). All of the procedure calls between *DURING* and *HANDLER* can potentially raise an exception. The code between *HANDLER* and *END_HANDLER* is executed only if an exception is raised by the code between *DURING* and *HANDLER*. Otherwise, the handler code is skipped.

Suppose **ProcThatCallsSeveralWraps( )** is defined as follows:

```
void ProcThatCallsSeveralWraps(context)
DPSContext context;
{
    char *s = ProcThatAllocsAString (...);
    int n;
```

```
            DURING
                UserWrapC1 (context, ...);
                UserWrapC2(context, &n); /* user wrap returns a value */
                DPSPrintf(context, "/%s %d def\n", s, n); /* client lib proc */
            HANDLER
                if ((DPSContext)Exception.Message == context)
                    {
                    /* clean up the allocated string */
                    free(s);
                    s = NULL;
                    }
                /* let the caller handle resetting the context */
                RERAISE;
            END_HANDLER

            /* clean up, if we haven't already */
            if (s != NULL) free(s);
        }
```

This procedure unconditionally allocates storage, then calls procedures that might raise an exception. If no handlers are here and the exception is propagated to the main loop, the storage allocated for the string would never be reclaimed. The solution is to define a handler that frees the storage and then calls *RERAISE* to allow another handler to do the final processing of the exception.

pswrap

This appendix is a reference guide to the pswrap translator. The pswrap translator provides a way for an application developer or toolkit implementor to compose a package of C-callable procedures that send PostScript language code to the PostScript interpreter. These C-callable procedures are known as *wrapped procedures* or *wraps*. (A wrap is a procedure that consists of a C declaration with a PostScript language body. A wrap body is the PostScript language program fragment within a wrap.)

Note   *This is the August 30, 1990 edition of "pswrap."*

The following steps show how pswrap fits into the Display PostScript system:

1. Write the PostScript language programs required by your application using the pswrap syntax to define a C-callable procedure and specify input and output arguments.

2. Run pswrap to translate PostScript language programs into wrapped procedures.

3. Compile and link these wraps with the application program.

4. When a wrap is called by the application, it sends encoded PostScript language to the PostScript interpreter and receives the values returned by the interpreter.

A pswrap source file associates PostScript language code with declarations of C procedures; pswrap writes C source code for the declared procedures, in effect wrapping C code around the PostScript language code. Wrapped procedures can take both input and output arguments.

- Input arguments are values a wrap sends to the PostScript interpreter as PostScript objects.

- Output arguments are pointers to variables where the wrap stores values returned by the PostScript interpreter.

Wraps are the most efficient way for an application to communicate with the PostScript interpreter.

B.1 Using pswrap

The form of the pswrap command line (UNIX- and C-specific) is:

pswrap [-apr] [-o outputCfile] [-h outputHfile] [-s maxstring] [inputFile]

where square brackets [ ] indicate optional items.

B.1.1 Command-Line Options

The pswrap command-line options are as follows:

inputFile   A file that contains one or more wrap definitions. pswrap transforms the definitions in *inputFile* into C procedure definitions. If no input file is specified, the standard input (which can be redirected from a file or pipe) is used. The input file can include text other than procedure definitions. pswrap converts procedure definitions to C procedures and passes the other text through unchanged. Therefore, it is possible to intersperse C-language source code with wrap definitions in the input file.

Note   *Although C code is allowed in a pswrap input file, it is not allowed within a wrap body. In particular, C #define macros cannot be used inside a wrap.*

-a Generates ANSI C procedure prototypes for procedure declarations in *outputCfile* and, optionally, *outputHfile*. The **-a** option allows compilers that recognize the ANSI C standard to do more complete typechecking of parameters. To save space, the **-a** option also causes pswrap to generate *const* declarations.

Note *ANSI C procedure prototype syntax is not recognized by most non-ANSI C compilers, including many compilers based on the Portable C Compiler. Use the -a option only in conjunction with a compiler that conforms to the ANSI C Standard.*

-h *outputHFile* Generates a header file that contains *extern* declarations for non-static wraps. This file can be used in *#include* statements in modules that use wraps. If the **-a** option is specified, the declarations in the header file are ANSI C procedure prototypes. If the **-h** option is omitted, a header file is not produced.

-o *outputCFile* Specifies the file to which the generated wraps and passed-through text are written. If omitted, the standard output is used. If the **-a** option is also specified, the procedure declarations generated by pswrap are in ANSI C procedure prototype syntax.

-p Specifies that strings passed by wraps are padded so that the next field begins on a long-word (4-byte) boundary.

-r Generates reentrant code for wraps shared by more than one process (as in shared libraries). Since the **-r** option causes pswrap to generate extra code, use it only when necessary.

-s *maxstring* Sets the maximum allowable length of a PostScript string object or PostScript hex string object in the wrap body input. A syntax error is reported if a string is not terminated with) or > within *maxstring* characters. *maxstring* cannot be set lower than 80; the default is 200.

B.1.2   #line Directives

Since the C source code generated for wrapped procedures usually contains more lines than the input wrap body does, pswrap inserts *#line* directives into the output wrap. These directives record input line numbers in the output wrap source file so that a source-code debugger can display them. Since a debugger displays C source code, not the PostScript language code in the wrap body, pswrap inserts *#line* directives for both the *inputFile* and the *outputCfile*.

Note   *Using the standard input and standard output streams is discouraged. Unless both the input and output files are named on the command line, the #line directives will be incomplete; in the latter case, they will lack the name of the C source file pswrap produces.*

pswrap writes diagnostic output to the standard error if there are errors in the command line or in the input. If pswrap encounters errors during processing, it reports the error and exits with a nonzero termination status.

B.2   Writing a Wrap

Example B.1 is a sample wrap definition. It declares the **PSWGrayCircle( )** procedure, which creates a solid gray circle with a radius of 5.0 centered at (10.0, 10.0).

Example B.1 *Sample wrap definition:* ***PSWGrayCircle( )*** *procedure*

Wrap definition

```
defineps PSWGrayCircle( )
  newpath
  10.0 10.0 5.0 0.0 360.0 arc
  closepath
  0.5 setgray
  fill
endps
```

Procedure call

```
PSWGrayCircle( );
```

PostScript language code equivalent

```
newpath
10.0 10.0 5.0 0.0 360.0 arc
closepath
0.5 setgray
fill
```

B.2.1   The Wrap Definition

Following are the rules for defining a wrapped procedure. Each wrap definition consists of four parts:

- *defineps* begins the definition. It must appear at the beginning of a line without any preceding spaces or tabs.

- *Declaration of the C-callable procedure* is the name of the procedure followed by a list in parentheses of the arguments it takes. The arguments are optional. Parentheses are required even for a procedure without arguments. (Wraps do not return values; they are declared void.)

- *Wrap body* is a PostScript language program fragment, which is sent to the PostScript interpreter. It includes a series of PostScript operators and operands separated by spaces, tabs, and newline characters.

- *endps* ends the definition. Like *defineps*, *endps* must appear at the beginning of a line.

By default, wrap definitions introduce external (that is, global) names that can be used outside the file in which the definition appears. To introduce private (local) procedures, declare the wrapped procedure as static. For example, the **PSWGrayCircle( )** wrap in Example B.1 can be made static by substituting the following statement for the first line:

```
defineps static PSWGrayCircle( )
```

Note   *It is helpful for the application to give wraps names that identify them as such; for example,* **PSWDrawBox( )***,* **PSWShowTitle( )***,* **PSWDrawSlider( )***, and so on.*

B.2.2 Comments

C comments can appear anywhere outside a wrap definition. PostScript language comments can appear anywhere after the procedure is declared and before the definition ends. pswrap strips PostScript language comments from the wrap body. Comments cannot appear within PostScript string objects.

Example B.2 *C comment*

```
/*This is a C comment*/
defineps PSWNoComment( )
   (/*This is not a comment*/)show
   (%Nor is this.)length
   %This is a PS comment
endps
```

Wraps cannot be used to send PostScript language comments that contain structural information (%% and %!). Use another Client Library facility, such as **DPSWriteData( )**, to send comments.

B.2.3 The Wrap Body

pswrap accepts any valid PostScript language code as specified in the *PostScript Language Reference Manual, Second Edition* and *PostScript Language Color Extensions*. If the PostScript language code in a wrap body includes any of the following symbols, the opening and closing marks must balance:

{ }   Braces (to delimit a procedure)

[ ]   Square brackets (to define an array)

( )   Parentheses (to enclose a string)

< >   Angle brackets (to mark a hexadecimal string)

Parentheses within a string body must balance or be quoted with \ according to standard PostScript language syntax.

Note   *pswrap does not check a wrap definition for valid or sensible PostScript language code.*

pswrap attempts to wrap whatever it encounters. Everything between the closing parenthesis of the procedure declaration and the end of the wrap definition is assumed to be an element of the PostScript language unless it is part of a comment or matches one of the wrap arguments.

Note *pswrap does not support the double slash (//) PostScript language syntax for immediately evaluated names. See the "PostScript Language Reference Manual, Second Edition" for more information about immediately evaluated names.*

B.2.4 Arguments

Argument names in the procedure header are declared using C types. For instance, the following example declares two variables, *x* and *y*, of type *long int*.

```
defineps PSWMyFunc(long int x,y)
```

In addition, the following holds true for arguments:

- There can be an unlimited number of input and output arguments.

- Input arguments must be listed before output arguments in the wrap header.

- Precede the output arguments, if any, with a vertical bar |.

- Separate arguments of the same type with a comma.

- Separate arguments of different types with a semicolon.

- A semicolon is optional before a vertical bar or a right parenthesis; these two examples are equivalent:

```
defineps PSWNewFunc(float x,y; int a | int *i)
defineps PSWNewFunc(float x,y; int a; | int *i;)
```

B.2.5 Input Arguments

Input arguments describe values that the wrap converts to encoded PostScript objects at run time. When an element within the wrap body matches an input argument, the value that was passed to the wrap replaces the element in the wrap body. Input arguments represent placeholders for values in the wrap body. They are not PostScript language variables (names). Think of them as macro definitions that are substituted at run time.

For example, the **PSWGrayCircle( )** procedure can be made more useful by providing input arguments for the radius and center coordinates, as in Example B.3.

Example B.3 *PSWGrayCircle( ) with input arguments for radius and center coordinates*

Wrap definition

```
defineps PSWGrayCircle(float x,y, radius)
  newpath
  x y radius 0.0 360.0 arc
  closepath
  0.5 setgray
  fill
endps
```

Procedure call

```
PSWGrayCircle(25.4,17.7, 40.0);
```

PostScript language code equivalent

```
newpath
25.4 17.7 40.0 0.0 360.0 arc
closepath
0.5 setgray
fill
```

The value of input argument x replaces each occurrence of x in the wrap body. This version of **PSWGrayCircle( )** draws a circle of a specified size at a specified location.

B.2.6   Output Arguments

Output arguments describe values that PostScript operators return. For example, the PostScript operator **currentgray** returns the gray-level setting in the current graphics state. PostScript operators place their return values on the top of the operand stack. To return a value to the application, place the name of the output argument in the wrap body at a time when the desired value is on the top of the operand stack. In Example B.4, the wrap gets the value returned by **currentgray**.

Example B.4 *Wrap value returned by* **currentgray**

Wrap definition

```
defineps PSWGetGray( | float *level)
    currentgray level
endps
```

Procedure call

```
float aLevel;
PSWGetGray(&aLevel);
```

PostScript language code equivalent

```
currentgray
% Pop current gray level off operand stack
% and store in aLevel.
```

Note   *See section A.10, "Run Time Support for Wrapped Procedures," in Appendix A for a discussion about how pswrap uses* **printobject** *to return results.*

When an element within a wrap body matches an output argument in this way, pswrap replaces the output argument with code that returns the top object on the operand stack. For every output argument, the wrap performs the following operations:

1. Pops an object off the operand stack.

2. Sends it to the application.

3. Converts it to the correct C data type.

4. Stores it at the place designated by the output argument.

Each output argument must be declared as a pointer to the location where the procedure stores the returned value. To get a *long int* back from a pswrap-generated procedure, declare the output argument as *long int*, as in Example B.5.

Example B.5 *Output argument as long int*

Wrap definition

```
defineps PSWCountExecStack( | long int *n)
     countexecstack n
endps
```

Procedure call

```
long int aNumber;
PSWCountExecStack(&aNumber);
```

PostScript language code equivalent

```
countexecstack
% Pop count of objects on exec stack
%    and return in aNumber.
```

To receive information back from the PostScript interpreter, use only the syntax for output arguments described here. Do not use operators that write to the standard output (such as =, ==, **print**, or **pstack**). These operators send ASCII strings to the application that pswrap-generated procedures cannot handle.

Warning   *For an operator that returns results, the operator description shows the order in which results are placed on the operand stack, reading from left to right. When you specify a result value in a wrap body, the result is taken from the top of the operand stack. Therefore, the order in which wrap results are stated must be the reverse of their order in the operator description.*

For instance, the PostScript operator description for **currentpoint** *returns two values, x and y:*

*– **currentpoint** x y*

The corresponding wrap definition must be written

```
defineps PSWcurrentpoint (| float *x, *y)
    currentpoint y x      % Note: y before x.
endps
```

B.3   Declaring Input Arguments

This section defines the data types allowed as input arguments in a wrap. In the following list, square brackets indicate optional elements.

- *DPSContext*. If the wrap specifies a context, it must appear as the first input argument. (*DPSContext* is a handle to the context record.)

- One of the following pswrap data types (equivalent to C data types except for *boolean* and *userobject*, which are exclusive to pswrap):

boolean	userobject
int	unsigned [int]
short [int]	unsigned short [int]
long [int]	unsigned long [int]
float	double

- An array of a pswrap data type.

- A character string (*char** or *unsigned char**).

- A character array (*char [ ]* or *unsigned char [ ]*). (The square brackets are part of C syntax.)

A string (*char**) passed as input can't be more than 65,535 characters. An array can't contain more than 65,535 elements.

B.3.1   Sending Boolean Values

If an input argument is declared as *boolean*, the wrap expects to be passed a variable of type *int*. If the variable has a value of zero, it is translated to a PostScript Boolean object with the value *false*. Otherwise, it is translated to a PostScript Boolean object with the value *true*.

B.3.2   Sending User Object Values

Input parameters declared as type *userobject* should be passed as type *long int*. The value of a *userobject* argument is an index into the **UserObjects** array.

When pswrap encounters an argument of type *userobject*, it generates PostScript language code to obtain the object associated with the index, as in Example B.6.

Example B.6 *PSWAccessUserObject( ) wrap definition*

Wrap definition

```
defineps PSWAccessUserObject(userobject x)
   x
endps
```

Procedure call

```
long int aUserObject;

   ...
/* assume aUserObject = 6 */
PSWAccessUserObject(aUserObject);
```

PostScript language code equivalent

```
6 execuserobject
```

If the object is executable, it executes; if it's not, it is pushed on the operand stack.

If you want to pass the index of a user object without having it translated by pswrap as described in Example B.6, declare the argument to be of type *long int* rather than type *userobject*. Example B.7 is a wrap that defines a user object.

Example B.7 *Wrap that defines a user object*

Wrap definition

```
defineps PSWDefUserObject(long int d)
   d 10 dict defineuserobject
endps
```

Procedure call

```
long int anIndex;

   ...
/* assume anIndex = 12 */
PSWDefUserObject(anIndex);
```

PostScript language code equivalent

```
12 10 dict defineuserobject
```

B.3.3   Sending Numbers

An input argument declared as one of the *int* types is converted to a 32-bit PostScript integer object before it is sent to the interpreter. A *float* or *double* input argument is converted to a 32-bit PostScript real object. These conversions follow the C conversion rules.

See *The C Programming Language*, R.W. Kernighan and D.M. Ritchie (Englewood Cliffs, N.J., Prentice-Hall, 1978) or *C: A Reference Manual*, Harbison and G. L. Steele, Jr. (Englewood Cliffs, N.J., Prentice-Hall, 1984).

Note   *Since the PostScript language doesn't support unsigned integers, unsigned integer input arguments are converted to signed integers in the body of the wrap.*

B.3.4   Sending Characters

An input argument composed of characters is treated as a PostScript name object or string object. The argument can be declared as a character string or a character array.

pswrap expects arguments that are passed to it as character strings (*char** or *unsigned char**) to be null terminated (\0). Character arrays are not null terminated. The number of elements in the array must be specified as an integer constant or an input argument of type *int*. In either case, the integer value must be positive.

Text Arguments

A text argument is an input argument declared as a character string or character array and converted to a single PostScript name object or string object.

The PostScript language interpreter does not process the characters of text arguments. It assumes that any escape sequences (\n, \t, and so on) have been processed before the wrap is called.

To make pswrap treat a text argument as a PostScript literal name object, precede it with a slash, as in the **PSWReadyFont( )** wrap definition in Example B.8. (Only names and text arguments are preceded by a slash.)

Example B.8 *PSWReadyFont( ) wrap definition*

Wrap definition

```
defineps PSWReadyFont(char *fontname; int size)
    /fontname size selectfont
endps
```

Procedure call

```
PSWReadyFont("Sonata", 6);
```

PostScript language code equivalent

```
/Sonata 6 selectfont
```

To make pswrap treat a text argument as a PostScript string object, enclose it within parentheses. The **PSWPutString( )** wrap definition in Example B.9, shows a text argument, *str.*

Example B.9 *PSWPutString( ) wrap definition*

Wrap definition

```
defineps PSWPutString(char *str; float x, y)
    x y moveto
    (str) show
endps
```

Procedure call

```
PSWPutString("Hello World", 72.0, 72.0);
```

PostScript language code equivalent

```
72.072.0 moveto
(Hello World) show
```

Note   *Text arguments are recognized within parentheses only if they appear alone, without any surrounding white space or additional elements. In the following wrap definition, only the first string is replaced with the value of the text argument. The second and third strings are sent unchanged to the interpreter.*

```
defineps PSWThreeStrings(char *str)
    (str) (  str  ) (a str)
endps
```

If a text argument is not marked by either a slash or parentheses, pswrap treats it as an executable PostScript name object. In Example B.10, *mydict* is treated as executable.

Example B.10 *mydict as executable*

Wrap definition

```
defineps PSWDoProcedure(char *mydict)
  mydict /procedure get exec
endps
```

Procedure call

```
PSWDoProcedure("lexicon");
```

PostScript language code equivalent

```
lexicon /procedure get exec
```

B.3.5   Sending Arrays of Numbers or Booleans

Each element in the wrap body that names an input array argument represents a PostScript literal array object that has the same element values. In Example B.11, the current transformation matrix is set using an array of six floating-point values.

Example B.11 *PSWSetMyMatrix( ) wrap definition*

Wrap definition

```
defineps PSWSetMyMatrix (float mtx[6])
  mtx setmatrix
endps
```

Procedure call

```
static float anArray[ ] = {1.0, 0.0, 0.0, -1.0, 0.0, 0.0};
PSWSetMyMatrix(anArray);
```

PostScript language code equivalent

```
[1.0 0.0 0.0 -1.0 0.0 0.0] setmatrix
```

The **PSWDefineA( )** wrap in Example B.12 sends an array of variable length to the PostScript interpreter.

Example B.12 *Sending an array of variable length to the PostScript interpreter*

Wrap definition

```
defineps PSWDefineA (int data[x]; int x)
  /A data def
endps
```

Procedure call

```
static int d1[ ] ={1, 2, 3};
static int d2[ ] = {4, 5};

   ...
PSWDefineA(d1, 3);
PSWDefineA(d2, 2);
```

PostScript language code equivalent

```
/A [1 2 3] def
/A [4 5] def
```

B.3.6   Sending a Series of Numeric or Boolean Values

Occasionally, it is useful to group several numeric or Boolean values
into a C array, and pass the array to a wrap that will send the individual
elements of the array to the PostScript interpreter, as in Example B.13.

Example B.13 *PSWGrayCircle( ) wrap definition*

Wrap definition

```
defineps PSWGrayCircle(float nums[3], gray)
   newpath
   \nums[0] \nums[1] \nums[2] 0.0 360.0 arc
   closepath
   gray setgray
   fill
endps
```

Procedure call

```
static float xyRadius = {40.0, 200.0, 55.0};
PSWGrayCircle(xyRadius, .75);
```

PostScript language code equivalent

```
newpath
40.0 200.0 55.0 0.0 360.0 arc
closepath
.75 setgray
fill
```

In Example B.13, \nums[i] identifies an element of an input array in
the wrap body, where *nums* is the name of an input boolean array or
numeric array argument, and i is a nonnegative integer literal. No white
space is allowed between the backslash (\) and the right bracket (]).

Specifying the Size of an Input Array

As the previous examples illustrate, you can specify the size of an input array in two ways:

- Give an integer constant size when you define the procedure, as in the **PSWGrayCircle( )** wrap definition

- Give an input argument that evaluates to an integer at run time, as in the **PSWDefineA( )** wrap definition

In either case, the size of the array must be a positive integer with a value not greater than 65,535.

Sending Encoded Number Strings

A number sequence in the PostScript language can be represented either as an ordinary PostScript array object whose elements are to be used successively or as an encoded number string. Encoded number strings are described in section 3.12.5 of the *PostScript Language Reference Manual, Second Edition.*

The encoded number string format efficiently passes sequences of numbers, such as coordinates, to PostScript operators that take arrays of operands (**xyshow** and **rectfill**, among others). In this form, the arrays take up less space in PostScript VM. In addition, the operator that consumes them executes faster because the data in an encoded number string, unlike a PostScript array object, does not have to be scanned by the PostScript scanner.

To simplify passing encoded number strings in a wrap, pswrap syntax provides the *numstring* data type, which lets you pass PostScript operands as numeric elements in a normal C array. The pswrap translator generates code that produces the encoded number string corresponding to this C array.

Note   *numstring is used only for input. It is invalid as an output parameter in a wrap definition.*

The syntax of the *numstring* data type is as follows; optional items are in curly brackets:

```
(modifier) numstring variablename[arraysize]
(:scale; sizetype arraysize; scaletype scale);
```

Table B.1 *Modifiers with C array encoded number string equivalent*

Modifier	C array encoded number string equivalent
int	intfixed (native integer size)–the default
long	long intfixed (32-bit fixed-point number)
short	short intfixed (16-bit fixed-point number)
float	floatreal (32-bit floating-point number)

Example B.14 shows examples of wrap definitions that pass an encoded number string. In these wraps, *c* is a constant and *n* and *s* are integer variables representing the number of elements and the scale, respectively. Scale refers to the number of digits to the right of the decimal point. Scale applies only to fixed-point numbers; if not specified, it defaults to zero.

Example B.14 *Examples of wrap definitions*

```
defineps PSWNums1(numstring a[5];)
%Array of 5 elements of default format
% (native integer size, zero scale).

defineps PSWNums2(float numstring a[c];)
%Array size is constant.

defineps PSWNums3(float numstring a[n]; int n;)
%Array size is variable.

defineps PSWNums4(int numstring a[n]:s; int n, s;)
%Native integer size, non-zero scale.

defineps PSWNums5(long numstring a[n]:s; int n, s;)
%32-bit fixed point, non-zero scale.

defineps PSWNums6(short numstring a[n]:c; int n;)
%16-bit fixed point, non-zero scale.
```

PSWXShowChars( ), as shown in Example B.15, is a wrap that uses the *numstring* data type to pass an array of user-defined widths to the **xshow** operator.

Example B.15 *PSWXShowChars( )*

Wrap definition

```
defineps PSWXShowChars(char str[4]; long numstring widths[4]:0)
    /Times-Roman 30 selectfont
    100 100 moveto
    str widths xshow
endps
```

Procedure call

```
char str[4] = "test";
long widths[4] = {7,10, 9, 7};
    ...
PSWXShowChars(str, widths);
```

PostScript language code equivalent

```
/Times-Roman 30 selectfont
/str (test) def
/widths <95800400070000000A0000000900000007000000> def
        % encoded number string, hex format,
        % preceded by 4-byte generated header
100 100 moveto
str widths xshow
```

B.3.7   Specifying the Context

Every wrap communicates with a PostScript execution context. The current context is normally used as the default. The Client Library provides operations for setting and getting the current context for each application. To override the default, declare the first argument as type *DPSContext* and pass the appropriate context as the first parameter whenever the application calls the wrap. Example B.16 shows a wrap definition that explicitly declares a context.

Example B.16 *Wrap definition–declares a context*

Wrap definition

```
defineps PSWGetGray(DPSContext c | float *level)
    currentgray level
endps
```

Procedure call

```
DPSContext myContext;
float aLevel;
    ...
PSWGetGray(myContext, &aLevel);
```

```
currentgray
%Pop current gray level off operand stack
% and store in aLevel
```

Warning   *Do not refer to the name of the context in the wrap body.*

B.4   Declaring Output Arguments

To receive information back from the PostScript interpreter, the output arguments of a wrap must refer to locations where the information can be stored. One of the following can be declared as an output argument:

- A pointer to one of the pswrap data types listed previously except *userobject*

- An array of one of these types

- A character string (*char** or *unsigned char**)

- A character array (*char [ ]* or *unsigned char [ ]*)

If an output argument is declared as a pointer or character string, the procedure writes the returned value at the location pointed to.

For an output argument declared as a pointer, previous return values are overwritten if the output argument is encountered more than once in executing the wrap body. For an output argument declared as a character string (*char**), the value is stored only the first time it is encountered.

If an output argument is declared as an array of one of the pswrap data types or as a character array, the wrap fills the slots in the array.

Note   *Whenever an array output argument is encountered in the wrap body, the values on the PostScript operand stack are placed in the array in the order in which they would be popped off the stack. When no empty array elements remain, no further storing of output in the array is done. No error is reported if elements are returned to an array that is full.*

You can specify output arguments in the defineps statement in any order that is convenient. The order of the output arguments has no effect on the execution of the PostScript language code in the wrap body.

pswrap does not check whether the wrap definition provides return values for all output arguments, nor does it perform type checking for declared output arguments.

B.4.1   Receiving Numbers

PostScript integer objects and real objects are 32 bits long. When returned, these values are assigned to the variable provided by the output argument. On a system where the size of an *int* or *float* is 32 bits, pass a pointer to an *int* as the output argument for a PostScript integer object; pass a pointer to a *float* as the output argument for a PostScript real object:

```
defineps PSWMyWrap ( | float *f; int *i)
```

A PostScript integer object or real object can be returned as a *float* or *double*. Other type mismatches cause a **typecheck** error (for example, attempting to return a PostScript real object as an *int*).

B.4.2   Receiving Boolean Values

A procedure can declare a pointer to a *boolean* as an output argument.

Example B.17 *Pointer to a boolean as an output argument*

Wrap definition

```
defineps PSWKnown(char *Dict, *x | boolean *ans)
    Dict /x known ans
endps
```

Procedure call

```
int found;
    ...
PSWKnown("statusdict", "duplex", &found);
```

PostScript language code equivalent

```
statusdict /duplex known found
```

This wrap expects to be passed the address of a variable of type *int* as its output argument. If the PostScript interpreter returns the value *true*, the wrap places a value of 1 in the variable referenced by the output argument. If the interpreter returns the value *false*, the wrap places a value of zero in the variable.

B.4.3 Receiving a Series of Output Values

To receive a series of output values as an array, declare an array output argument; then write a wrap body in the PostScript language to compute and return its elements, one or more elements at a time. Example B.18 declares a wrap that returns the 256 font widths for a given font name at a given font size.

Example B.18 *PSWGetWidths( ) wrap definition*

Wrap definition

```
defineps PSWGetWidths(char *fn; int size | float wide[256])
  /fn size selectfont
  0 1 255 {
    (X)dup 0 4 -1 roll put
    stringwidth pop wide
  }for
endps
```

Procedure call

```
float widths[256];
PSWGetWidths("Serifa", 12, widths);
```

PostScript language code equivalent

```
/Serifa 12 selectfont
0 1 255 {
  (X)dup 0 4 -1 roll put
  stringwidth pop
  % Pop width for this character and insert width
  % into widths array at current element;
  % point to next element.
} for
```

In Example B.18, the loop counter is used to assign successive ASCII values to the scratch string (X). The **stringwidth** operator then places both the width and height of the string on the PostScript operand stack. (Here it operates on a string one character long.)

The **pop** operator removes the height from the stack, leaving the width at the top. The occurrence of the output argument *wide* in this position triggers the width to be popped from the stack, returned to the application, and inserted into the output array at the current element. The next element then becomes the current element.

The **for** loop (the procedure enclosed in braces followed by **for**) repeats these operations for each character in the font, beginning with the first, 0, and ending with 255th element of the font array.

Receiving a Series of Array Elements

A PostScript array object can contain a series of elements to be stored in an output array. The output array is filled in, one element at a time, until it's full. Therefore, the **PSWTest( )** wrap defined below returns (1, 2, 3, 4, 5, 6):

```
defineps PSWTest(| int Array[6])
    [1 2 3] Array
    [4 5 6] Array
endps
```

The **PSWTestMore( )** wrap defined below returns (1, 2, 3, 4):

```
defineps PSWTestMore(| int Array[4])
    [1 2 3] Array
    [4 5 6] Array
endps
```

Specifying the Size of an Output Array

The size of an output array is specified in the same manner as the size of an input array. Use a constant in the wrap definition or an input argument that evaluates to an integer at run time. If more elements are returned than fit in the output array, the additional elements are discarded.

B.4.4 Receiving Characters

To receive characters back from the PostScript interpreter, declare the output argument as either a character string or as a character array.

If the argument is declared as a character string, the wrap copies the returned string to the location indicated. Provide enough space for the maximum number of characters that might be returned, including the null character (\0) that terminates the string. Only the first string encountered will be returned. For example, in the following **PSWStrings( )** procedure, the string 123 is returned:

```
defineps PSWStrings(| char *str)
  (123) str
  (456) str
endps
```

Character arrays, on the other hand, are treated just like arrays of
numbers. In the **PSWStrings2( )** procedure, the value returned for *str*
will be *123456*.

```
defineps PSWStrings2(| char str[6])
  (123) str
  (456) str
endps
```

If the argument is declared as a character array (for example,
char s[num]), the procedure copies up to *num* characters of the returned
string into the array. Additional characters are discarded. The string
is not null terminated.

B.4.5   Communication and Synchronization

The PostScript interpreter can run as a separate process from the application; it can also run on a separate machine. When the application
and interpreter processes are separated, the application programmer
must take communication into account. This section alerts you to communication and synchronization issues.

A wrap that has no output arguments returns as soon as the wrap body
is transferred to the client-server communications channel. In this case,
the communications channel is not necessarily flushed. Since the wrap
body is not executed by the PostScript interpreter until the communications channel is flushed, errors arising from the execution of the wrap
body can be reported long after the wrap returns.

In the case of a wrap that returns a value, the entire wrap body is
transferred to the client-server communications channel, which is
then flushed. The client-side code awaits the return of output values
followed by a special termination value. Only then does the wrap
return.

See Appendix A, "Client Library," for information concerning synchronization, run-time errors, and error handling.

B.5 Syntax

Square brackets, *[ ]*, mean that the enclosed form is optional. Curly brackets, *{ }*, mean that the enclosed form is repeated, possibly zero times. A vertical bar, |, separates choices in a list.

Unit =
    ArbitraryText {Definition ArbitraryText}

Definition =
    NLdefineps ["static"] Ident "(" [Args] ["|" Args]")"
    Body
    NLendps

Body =
    {Token}

Token =
    Number | PSIdent | SlashPSIdent
    | "("StringLiteral")"
    | "<"StringLiteral">"
    | "{" Body "}"
    | "{" Body "}"
    | Input Element

Args =
    ArgList {";" ArgList) [";"]

ArgList =
    Type ItemList

Type =
    "DPSContext" | "boolean" | "float" | "double"
    | ["unsigned"] "char" | ["unsigned"] ["short" | "long"] "int"
    | ["int" | "long" | "short" | "float"] "numstring"

ItemList =
    Item {"," Item}

Item =
    "*" Ident | Ident ["["Subscript"]"]
    | Ident "["Subscript"]" [Scale]

Subscript =
    Integer | Ident

Scale =
    ":"Integer | ":"Ident

B.5.1   Syntactic Restrictions

- *DPSContext* must be the first input argument if it appears.

- A simple char argument (*char Ident*) is never allowed; it must be
  * or *[ ]*.

- A simple *Ident* item is not allowed in an output item list; it must be
  * or *[ ]*.

B.5.2   Clarifications

- *NLdefineps* matches the terminal *defineps* at the beginning of a new
  line.

- *NLendps* matches the terminal *endps* at the beginning of a new line.

- *Ident* follows the rules for C names; *PSIdent* follows the rules for
  PostScript language names.

- *SlashPSIdent* is a PostScript language name preceded by a slash.

- *StringLiteral* tokens follow the PostScript language conventions for
  string literals.

- *Number* tokens follow the PostScript language conventions for
  numbers.

- Integer subscripts follow the C conventions for integer constants.

- *Input Element* is \n[i] where *n* is the name of an input array argument,
  i is a nonnegative integer literal, and no white space is allowed
  between \ and].

Summary of Client Library Functions for NeXTstep

This appendix contains the following two sections:

- List of the Client Library functions in NeXTstep

- List of single operator function calls *specific* to NeXTstep

Descriptions of the functions specific to the NeXTstep implementation of the Display PostScript system can be found in the NeXT documentation. Descriptions of the standard Client Library functions in Section A.1 can be found in Appendix A.

C.1 Summary of Client Library Functions in NeXTstep

The following is a list of Client Library functions in Release 2.0 of the NeXTstep implementation of the Display PostScript system. The functions labeled with a /* NeXT */ comment are specific to this implementation. The others are standard functions in the Client Library and are defined in Appendix A.

Add or remove timed entry

DPSAddTimedEntry   DPSAddTimedEntry(double period, DPSTimedEntryProc handler,
                 void *userData, int priority)   /* NeXT */

DPSRemoveTimedEntry   void DPSRemoveTimedEntry(DPSTimedEntry teNumber)   /* NeXT */

Turn event coalescing on or off

DPSSetTracking   int DPSSetTracking(int flag)   /* NeXT */

Add or remove Mach port

DPSAddPort void DPSAddPort(port_t newPort, DPSPortProc handler, int maxSize,
void *userData, int priority)   /* NeXT */

DPSRemovePort void DPSRemovePort(port_t port)   /* NeXT */

Add or remove file descriptor

DPSAddFD void DPSAddFD(int fd, DPSFDProc handler, void *userData, int priority)   /* NeXT */

DPSRemoveFD void DPSRemoveFD(int fd)   /* NeXT */

Create or destroy a context

DPSCreateContext DPSCreateContext(const char *hostName, const char *serverName,
DPSTextProc textProc, DPSErrorProc errorProc)   /* NeXT */

DPSCreateContextWithTimeoutFromZone
DPSCreateContextWithTimeoutFromZone(const char *hostName,
const char *serverName, DPSTextProc textProc, DPSErrorProc errorProc,
int timeout, NXZone *zone)   /* NeXT */

DPSCreateStreamContext DPSCreateStreamContext(NXStream *stream, int debugging,
DPSProgramEncoding progEnc, DPSNameEncoding nameEnc,
DPSErrorProc errorProc)   /* NeXT */

DPSDestroyContext void DPSDestroyContext(DPSContext context)

Set or return current context

DPSSetContext void DPSSetContext(DPSContext context)

DPSGetCurrentContext DPSGetCurrentContext(void)

Control execution of a context

DPSInterruptContext void DPSInterruptContext(DPSContext context)

DPSResetContext void DPSResetContext(DPSContext context)

DPSWaitContext void DPSWaitContext(DPSContext context)

Change context's text function

DPSSetTextProc DPSSetTextProc(DPSContext context, DPSTextProc tp)

Change context's error function

DPSSetErrorProc DPSSetErrorProc(DPSContext context, DPSErrorProc ep)

Set function that filters context's events

DPSSetEventFunc DPSSetEventFunc(DPSContext context, DPSEventFilterFunc func) /* NeXT */

Add or remove child context

DPSChainContext int DPSChainContext(DPSContext parent, DPSContext child)

DPSUnChainContext void DPSUnchainContext(DPSContext context)

Extract space from specified context

DPSSpaceFromContext DPSSpaceFromContext(DPSContext context)

Destroy space and all contexts in it

DPSDestroySpace void DPSDestroySpace(DPSSpace spc)

Send PostScript code to Window Server

DPSWritePostScript void DPSWritePostScript(DPSContext context, const void *buf,
unsigned int count)

DPSWriteData void DPSWriteData(DPSContext context, const void *buf,
unsigned int count)

DPSPrintf void DPSPrintf(DPSContext context, const char *fmt, ...)

DPSFlushContext void DPSFlushContext(DPSContext context)

DPSFlush void DPSFlush(void) /* NeXT */

Access data from Window Server

DPSGetEvent
int DPSGetEvent(DPSContext context, NXEvent *anEvent, int mask, double timeout, int threshold) /* NeXT */

DPSPeekEvent
int DPSPeekEvent(DPSContext context, NXEvent *anEvent, int mask, double timeout, int threshold) /* NeXT */

DPSDiscardEvent
void DPSDiscardEvent(DPSContext context, int mask) /* NeXT */

Post event without involving Window Server

DPSPostEvent
int DPSPostEvent(NXEvent *anEvent, int atStart) /* NeXT */

Return index for top object of operand stack

DPSDefineUserObject
int DPSDefineUserObject(int index) /* NeXT */

DPSUndefineUserObject
void DPSUndefineUserObject(int index) /* NeXT */

Provide support for user names

DPSMapName
void DPSMapName(DPSContext context, unsigned int numNames, const char *const *nameArray, long int *const *numPtrArray)

DPSNameFromIndex
const char* DPSNameFromIndex(int index)

DPSNameFromTypeAndIndex
const char* DPSNameFromTypeAndIndex(short type, int index) /* NeXT */

Send PostScript path to Window Server

DPSDoUserPath
void DPSDoUserPath(void *coords, int numCoords, DPSNumberFormat numType, char *ops, int numOps, void *bbox, int action) /* NeXT */

DPSDoUserPathWithMatrix
void DPSDoUserPathWithMatrix(void *coords, int numCoords, DPSNumberFormat numType, char *ops, int numOps, void *bbox, int action, float matrix[6]) /* NeXT */

Initiate countdown for wait cursor

DPSStartWaitCursorTimer
void DPSStartWaitCursorTimer(void) /* NeXT */

Enable or disable dead key processing for a context's events

DPSSetDeadKeysEnabled void DPSSetDeadKeysEnabled(DPSContext ctxt, int flag) /* NeXT */

Control debugging tracing

DPSTraceContext int DPSTraceContext(DPSContext context, int flag) /* NeXT */

DPSTraceEvents void DPSTraceEvents(DPSContext context, int flag) /* NeXT */

Handle errors

DPSDefaultErrorProc void DPSDefaultErrorProc(DPSContext context, DPSErrorCode errorCode, long unsigned int arg1, long unsigned int arg2)

DPSSetTextBackstop DPSSetTextBackstop(DPSTextProc textProc)

DPSGetCurrentTextBackstop DPSGetCurrentTextBackstop(void)

DPSSetErrorBackstop void DPSSetErrorBackstop(DPSErrorProc errorProc)

DPSGetCurrentErrorBackstop
DPSGetCurrentErrorBackstop(void)

DPSPrintError void DPSPrintError(FILE *fp, const DPSBinObjSeq error) /* NeXT */

DPSPrintErrorToStream void DPSPrintErrorToStream(NXStream *stream, const DPSBinObjSeq error)
/* NeXT */

C.2 Summary of Single Operator Calls Specific to NeXTstep

The following is a list of single operator calls specific to Release 2.0 of the NeXTstep implementation of the Display PostScript system. Refer to the NeXT documentation for descriptions and recommended uses.

Warning *Functions marked /* Internal */ are reserved for use by the Application Kit. Only call them in applications that don't make use of the Kit.*

```
void PSadjustcursor(float dx, float dy)
void PSalphaimage(void)
void PSbasetocurrent(float x, float y, float *px, float *py)
void PSbasetoscreen(float x, float y, float *px, float *py)
void PSbuttondown(boolean *pflag)
void PScleartrackingrect(int trectNum, userobject gstate)
```

void PScomposite(float x, float y, float width, float height, userobject srcGstate,
    float destx, float desty, int op)
    op values:
    NX_CLEAR
    NX_COPY
    NX_SOVER
    NX_DOVER
    NX_SIN
    NX_DIN
    NX_SOUT
    NX_DOUT
    NX_SATOP
    NX_DATOP
    NX_XOR
    NX_PLUSD
    NX_PLUSL

void PScompositerect(float destx, float desty, float width, float height, int op)
    op values: PScompositerect( ) supports NX_HIGHLIGHT in addition to the
    values listed under PScomposite( ).

void PScountframebuffers(int *pcount)

void PScountscreenlist(int context, int *pcount)

void PScountwindowlist(int context, int *pcount)

void PScurrentactiveapp(int *pcontext)   /* Internal */

void PScurrentalpha(float *pcoverage)

void PScurrentdefaultdepthlimit(int *plimit)

void PScurrentdeviceinfo(userobject window, int *pminbps, int *pmaxbps,
    int *pcolor)

void PScurrenteventmask(userobject window, int *pmask)   /* Internal */

void PScurrentmouse(userobject window, float *px, float *py)   /* Internal */

void PScurrentowner(userobject window, int *pcontext)

void PScurrentrusage(float *pnow, float *puTime, float *psTime, int *pmsgSend,
    int *pmsgRcv, int *pnSignals, int *pnVCSw, int *pnIvCSw)

void PScurrenttobase(float x, float y, float *px, float *py)

void PScurrenttoscreen(float x, float y, float *px, float *py)

void PScurrentuser(int *puid, int *pgid)

void PScurrentwaitcursorenabled(boolean *pflag)

void PScurrentwindow(int *pnum)

void PScurrentwindowalpha(userobject window, int *palpha)

void PScurrentwindowbounds(userobject window, float *px, float *py, float
    *pwidth, float *pheight)

void PScurrentwindowdepth(userobject window, int *pdepth)

void PScurrentwindowdepthlimit(userobject window, int *plimit)

void PScurrentwindowdict(userobject window)   /* Internal */

void PScurrentwindowlevel(userobject window, int *plevel)

void PScurrentwriteblock(int *pflag)

void PSdissolve(float srcx, float srcy, float width, float height, userobject srcGstate,
    float destx, float desty, float delta)

void PSdumpwindow(int level, userobject window)   /* Internal */

void PSdumpwindows(int level, userobject context)   /* Internal */

void PSfindwindow(float x, float y, int place, userobject otherWin, float *px, float
    *py, int *pwinFound, boolean *pdidFind)
    place values:
    NX_ABOVE
    NX_BELOW
void PSflushgraphics(void)
void PSframebuffer(int index, int nameLen, char name[ ], int *pslot, int *punit,
    int *pROMid, int *px, int *py, int *pw, int *ph, int *pdepth)
void PSfrontwindow(int *pnum)   /* Internal */
void PShidecursor(void)
void PShideinstance(float x, float y, float width, float height)
void PSmachportdevice(int w, int h, int bbox[ ], int bboxSize, float matrix[ ],
    char *phost, char *pport, char *ppixelDict)
void PSmovewindow(float x, float y, userobject window)   /* Internal */
void PSnewinstance(void)
void PSnextrelease(int size, char string[ ])
    /* size is the maximum number of characters copied into string */
void PSobscurecursor(void)
void PSorderwindow(int place, userobject otherWindow, userobject window)
    /* Internal */
    place values:
    NX_ABOVE
    NX_BELOW
    NX_OUT
void PSosname(int size, char string[ ])
    /* size is the maximum number of characters copied into string */
void PSostype(int *ptype)
void PSplacewindow(float x, float y, float width, float height, userobject window)
    /* Internal */
void PSplaysound(char *name, int priority)
void PSposteventbycontext(int type, float x, float y, int time, int flags, int window,
    int subtype, int data1, int data2, int context, boolean *psuccess)
void PSreadimage(void)
void PSrevealcursor(void)
void PSrightbuttondown(boolean *pflag)
void PSrightstilldown(int eventnum, boolean *pflag)
void PSscreenlist(int context, int count, int windows[ ])
void PSscreentobase(float x, float y, float *px, float *py)
void PSscreentocurrent(float x, float y, float *px, float *py)
void PSsetactiveapp(int context)   /* Internal */
void PSsetalpha(float coverage)
void PSsetautofill(boolean flag, userobject window)
void PSsetcursor(float x, float y, float mx, float my)
void PSsetdefaultdepthlimit(int limit)
void PSseteventmask(int mask, userobject window)   /* Internal */
    mask values:
    NX_LMOUSEDOWNMASK
    NX_LMOUSEUPMASK
    NX_RMOUSEDOWNMASK

NX_RMOUSEUPMASK

NX_MOUSEMOVEDMASK

NX_LMOUSEDRAGGEDMASK

NX_RMOUSEDRAGGEDMASK

NX_MOUSEENTEREDMASK

NX_MOUSEEXITEDMASK

NX_KEYDOWNMASK

NX_KEYUPMASK

NX_FLAGSCHANGEDMASK

NX_KITDEFINEDMASK

NX_APPDEFINEDMASK

NX_SYSDEFINEDMASK

void PSsetexposurecolor(void)

void PSsetflushexposures(boolean flag)

void PSsetinstance(boolean flag)

void PSsetmouse(float x, float y)

void PSsetowner(userobject context, userobject window)

void PSsetpattern(userobject patternDict)

void PSsetsendexposed(boolean flag, userobject window)   /* Internal */

void PSsettrackingrect(float x, float y, float width, float height, boolean leftFlag, boolean rightFlag, boolean inside, int userData, int trectNum, userobject gstate)

void PSsetwaitcursorenabled(boolean flag)

void PSsetwindowdepthlimit(int limit, userobject window)

void PSsetwindowdict(userobject window)   /* Internal */

void PSsetwindowlevel(int level, userobject window)

void PSsetwindowtype(int type, userobject window)

void PSsetwriteblock(int flag)

void PSshowcursor(void)

void PSsizeimage(float x, float y, float width, float height, int *pwidth, int *pheight, int *pbitsPerComponent, float matrix[ ], boolean *pmultiproc, int *pnColors)

void PSstilldown(int eventnum, boolean *pflag)

void PStermwindow(userobject window)   /* Internal */

void PSwindow(float x, float y, float width, float height, int type, int *pwindow) /* Internal */

void PSwindowdevice(userobject window)

void PSwindowdeviceround(userobject window)

void PSwindowlist(int context, int count, int windows[ ])

Index

Symbols

#define 338
#include 339
#line directives
    debugging 340
%!PS-Adobe-a.a EPSF-b.b comment 228
%%BeginPageSetup 261
%%BoundingBox 218, 229
%%DocumentFonts 215
%%EndPageSetup 261
%%Page 261
%%PageTrailer 261
%stdin 290
%stdout 333
( ) 342
< > 342
= 303
== 282, 303
@end, Objective-C directive 5
@interface, Objective-C directive 5
[ ] 342
{ } 342

A

-a, pswrap command line option 47, **339**
Adobe Developer Association xxv
Adobe Developer Support
    public access file server xxvi
Adobe Font Metric (AFM) files 190, 194
aload 256
alpha 121
Apple LaserWriter II NTX 32
Application class 10
Application Kit xviii, xxiii, 1, 3, 10–11,
    87, 161, 172, 185, 189, 213
    Application class 10
    ButtonCell 3

Cell class 11
Control class 11
creating a class 4
definition of class 2
Object class 10
Responder class 10
View class 11
Window class 11
arct 66
arcto 66
arguments in Objective-C 8
arguments in pswrap
    declaring 343
    input 344
    output 345
array
    Booleans 351
    encoded number strings 353
    numbers 351
    output 359
    receiving a series of elements 359
ASCII encoding 64, 244, 278, 286
ASCII user path description 64
ashow 199, 203, 254
aspect ratio 239
awidthshow 199, 203, 254

B

backstop error handler 284, 297
backstop handlers
    automatically installed 284
backstop text handler 284, 327, 333
Bézier curves xxii, 137–139
binary object sequence 241, 273, 275,
    286, 311, **314**
    definition 243
    extended 317
    header 315

Colophon

This book was produced on NeXT, Sun-3™, and Macintosh computers using FrameMaker®, Adobe Illustrator, and other application software packages that support the PostScript language and Type 1 fonts. Proof copies were printed on PostScript laser and color printers. Working film was produced on a high-resolution PostScript imagesetter.

The type used is from the ITC Stone family. Heads are set in ITC Stone Sans Semibold and the body text is set in 9 on 12 point ITC Stone Serif, ITC Stone Serif Italic, and ITC Stone Sans Semibold.

Chapters 1-14
  Author—Ken Fromm

Appendix A
  Authors—Perry Caro, Amy Davidson

Appendix B
  Authors—Bill Bilodeau, Perry Caro, Amy Davidson, Andy Shore

Appendix C
  Reprinted with permission of NeXT Computer, Inc.

Key Contributors—Ken Anderson, Ramin Behtash, Richard Cohn, Robin Cowan, David Gelphman, Rebecca Hauser, Deborah MacKay, Carl Orthlieb, Paul Rovner, Jim Sandman, Bob Welles

Editor—Louise Galindo

Index—Michael de Leon, Heather Hermstad, Jeff Walden

Illustrations—Heather Hermstad, Dayna Porterfield

Cover Design—Nancy Winters

Book Production—Michael de Leon, Heather Hermstad

Book Production Management—Eve Lynes

Reviewers—Paul Asente, Rebecca Hauser, Deborah MacKay, Carl Orthlieb, and numerous others at Adobe Systems and elsewhere.

Publication Management—Joan Delfino

Project Management—Dano Ybarra

Special thanks to Trey Matteson, Mary McNabb, and Ali Ozer of NeXT Computer, Inc. for their critical review of this material. Also thanks to Paul Hegarty for his work with the Draw application example.

BUSINESS REPLY MAIL

FIRST CLASS MAIL   PERMIT NO. 582   MOUNTAIN VIEW, CA

POSTAGE WILL BE PAID BY ADDRESSEE

POSTSCRIPT® DEVELOPERS ASSOCIATION
ADOBE SYSTEMS INCORPORATED

1585 CHARLESTON RD
P.O. BOX 7900
MOUNTAIN VIEW   CA   94039-9923